INTO THE WHIRLWIND

JOHN SHELBY SPONG

INTO THE WHIRLWIND

The Future of the Church

THE SEABURY PRESS

Library of Congress Catalog Card Number: 82-19647

ISBN: 0-86683-899-6

Printed in the United States of America

E D C B A

The Seabury Press
430 Oak Grove
Minneapolis, Minnesota 55403

Contents

To
John Elbridge Hines
    1909 -
Presiding Bishop of The Episcopal Church
    1964 - 1973

He was for my church a moment of grace
He is for me an admired colleague,
    a heroic role model,
    a treasured advisor,
but most of all
    a cherished friend.

Preface

WHEN I moved to the Diocese of Newark in 1976, I discovered a clergy family that was deeply committed to continuing study and theological inquiry. A number of them had been significantly involved as teachers in an enterprise called the School of Religion, now called the Lay School of Christian Studies. Two of our clergy had earned Ph.D. degrees, and several others had achieved the Doctor of Ministry degree.

In our first clergy conference that September, I was not surprised that a major request that emerged was for a diocesan lecture series to be offered annually. After some experimentation, we settled on a format of four one-day programs a year, one of which I, as the Bishop, would fill. We also settled on a name for this series, "New Dimensions," suggested by the Rev. David Hamilton of Morris Plains, New Jersey.

Since that beginning we have presented to our clergy, through New Dimensions, such respected scholars as Professor Hans Küng, Professor Raymond E. Brown, Dr. Krister Stendahl, Dr. Buckminster Fuller, Dr. Mortimer Adler, Bishop John Hines, Dr. Charles Price, Dr. Reginald Fuller, Dr. Elaine Pagels, Dr. Marianne Micks, Dr. John Yungblut, Dr. James Forbes, Bishop Desmond Tutu, Dr. Peter Berger, Dean Frederick Borsch, and Dr. Peggy Shriver. It has been an exciting and enriching intellectual diet for us all.

The lecture day that I have been privileged to present each year has been for me the organizing intellectual aspect of my life. This series has provided me with the external discipline needed to undergird my commitment to a life of scholarship and regular study. I choose my topic a year in advance and organize my reading and research for the year around that topic. One month each summer and the equivalent of one day each week I commit to this study. Then I write the first draft and begin the grueling, time-consuming activity of editing and rewriting. Before the lecture day my work is in at least its fourth draft, sometimes its fifth. The day of my lectures is for me the emotional high spot of the year. The clergy and laity who attend are enormously supportive. That does not imply that they always agree with me, for this series is designed to offer a forum where Christianity can be explored on its edges, where ideas can be pursued to their conclusions, and where no question is considered illegitimate to ask.

My lectures in this series have been previously published in my earlier books, *The Living Commandments* and *The Easter Moment*. In this book once again my New Dimensions lectures have been the catalyst, pulling together my scholarship and thought to be combined with other material and edited to produce a cohesive volume. The chapters here were originally independent essays, and yet they are organized around a common theme. They reflect an attempt to rethink many parts of the Christian heritage in the light of new realities. My attempt has been to turn the church and its theological enterprise from the past and toward the future.

It has been my intention to raise the very questions that our world is asking but which so much of the religious enterprise seems eager and determined to avoid. Many of these questions threaten the very core of the church's power and authority and are not, therefore, comfortable to face. Yet hiding from reality can never be the path to life, integrity, and authenticity. I yearn to combine honesty with theological scholarship and to confront openly the difficulties, the contradictions, and the complexities present in Christianity. I do not believe that I must seek to protect what I believe from the insights of scholarship and new learnings. In these essays I have dared to do my thinking in public; I have shared the results of my study outside the walls of the church.

I offer these insights to the Christian community at large in the same spirit that I have offered them to the clergy and lay people of the Diocese of Newark. They carry with them no imprimatur. They are ideas to be discussed, insights to be debated. This book will be successful if it enables dialogue and discussion on these issues to become part of the church's life. If every idea presented here is finally abandoned, I will not weep so long as the discussion that led to their abandonment was scholarly, open, and honest.

I salute the clergy and laity of the Diocese of Newark for allowing me to develop the scholar/teacher model of the episcopacy. I have not been permitted to let my drive toward creative scholarship get buried beneath the time-consuming demands of administrative expectations. It takes a mutual interest and a mutual commitment between a bishop and a diocese to enable this pattern of ministry to work. The bishop and the diocese must both appreciate its values, or the time demands that this model requires will be resented. I rejoice that this facet of our life today is anticipated, appreciated, and emulated. The response of the diocese is best seen, I believe, in that the attendance at the New Dimensions lectures, the teaching missions, and the Lay School of Christian Studies classes together exceeds 5,000 people a year—a remarkable statistic.

My gratitude for assistance with this book must be expressed to many.

First, to Sally Kemp, the Bishop's Executive Officer: She has participated in these essays at every stage. She has discussed with me the development of the ideas involved. She has done research in libraries. She has chased down papers and articles. She has seen each chapter through numerous drafts. She has exercised her outstanding editing talents to clarify my thought. She has opened and softened with her gift of sensitivity passages where I was aware that "too much sin" existed. In many ways Sally Kemp is herself very much present in this book, and I am deeply grateful to her.

To James H. Gambrill, Vicar General of the diocese; Beverly Anderson, Diocesan Administrator; Mabel Allen, former Editor of THE VOICE, the newspaper of the diocese; and Stephen C. Galleher, Archdeacon for Program and Communication, who with Sally Kemp have constituted the core staff of our diocese: These people have undergirded me and have contributed their enormous talents to our corporate life. They also have taken over many responsibilities that usually devolve on the bishop's office and have enabled me to do the study necessary to lecture and to write. There are few executives, I suspect, whose closest business associates are also his closest friends, but this is true of the Bishop of Newark. Others on our staff include Herbert Lee Brown, Joseph Gillard Halleck, Dorothy Masterson Lynch, Margaret Ann

Allenspach, Barbara Marie Lescota, Derek Patrick Leahy, Gail Hamilton Deckenbach, Darla La Deane Brown, Melves Grace Mitchell, Olga Hayes, Frank David Stickle, Doris Nealis Grece, and Jean Louise Stufflebeem, all of whom add immeasurably to the quality of our life and to the life of our diocese.

To the Rev. Dr. Phillip C. Cato, the Rev. Dr. L. Jerome Taylor, the Rev. Joseph D. Herring, the Rev. Dr. Peter H. Igarashi, and the Rev. Walter Sobol, who have offered their assistance frequently in setting up the New Dimensions lecture series: Each of these men is in his own right a keen scholar with exciting teaching gifts, and some of them are among the most popular teachers in our Lay School.

To the churches and host rectors where these essays were first delivered as lectures—Grace Church, Madison, New Jersey, the Rev. Hayward L. Levy, rector, and the Rev. R. Martin Caldwell, assistant; Christ Church, Ridgewood, New Jersey, the Rev. Richard L. Shimpfky, rector, and the Rev. James O. Cravens, assistant; Christ Church, Short Hills, New Jersey, the Rev. David B. Earnest, rector, and the Rev. Paul E. Gilbert, assistant; St. Luke's Church, Montclair, New Jersey, the Rev. Walter Sobol, rector, the Rev. Patrick A. Pierce, assistant: In every instance they were gracious, sensitive hosts who filled those lecture days for me with very special and happy memories.

To the Rev. Elizabeth Canham, our "priest in exile" from the Church of England: Elizabeth's ordination to the priesthood took place just three days before the lectures on "The Church and Sexual Stereotypes" were delivered. The sexist oppression that Elizabeth experienced in the church provided a vivid and existential historic example of the truth explored in these essays. The contingent who came from England to be present to support Elizabeth attended those lectures, and their presence gave a note of authenticity to them.

To that special core of readers and critics who have made valuable suggestions that have been incorporated into this text: In Richmond, Virginia, Dr. Eleanor Freed Evans, Jean Leonard LeRoy, Carter Donnan McDowell, and Lucy Boswell Negus, all of whom have worked with me on every book I have written; also Rabbi Jack Daniel Spiro of Temple Beth Ahabah in Richmond, who aided me materially on the Christology chapter and who is my treasured friend; in Lynchburg, Virginia, Betty McManus Giles and Evelyn Owens Stickley; in other parts of the country, Ellen Downing in Santa Barbara, California, and Wesley and Dee Frensdorff in Reno, Nevada.

I have also received major professional help and much encouragement from Dr. Anthony Padovano, Professor of Theology at Ramapo College in Mahwah, New Jersey, though it should be clear that he did not share all of my conclusions; Dr. Elaine Pagels, head of the Department of Religion at Barnard College in New York; Dr. Suzanne Fonay Wemple of the Department of History at Barnard College; Dr. Eric Marcus, Director of Undergraduate Training in Psychiatry, and Dr. Anka Ehrhardt, both of the College of Physicians and Surgeons of Columbia University; Dr. James E. Baxter, a psychiatrist in private practice in New York City; Dr. Leonard Kravitz, Professor at Hebrew Union College-Jewish Institute of Religion in New York.

For special assistance I wish to thank Dr. Eli Pilchik, Rabbi Emeritus of Temple B'nai Jeshurun in South Orange, New Jersey, whose library I raided and whose advice I sought; Rabbi Barry Greene of Temple B'nai Jeshurun, who opened many doors for me; and Katherine and Nicholas Patton, librarians at the Maplewood and Newark, New Jersey, Public Libraries, who aided me time after time in searching for obscure references.

I would also like to acknowledge my gratitude to my two gifted editors at Seabury Press, John Ratti and Donald Kraus, whose abilities with words are rare and whose encouragement and assistance in many areas have been substantial.

I would also like to express my appreciation to the Kanuga Conference Center in Hendersonville, North Carolina, and especially to the Program Director, the Rev. LaRue Downing, for inviting me to that lovely and loving spot where a major part of this book's writing and editing was done. Three members of the adult conference of 1982, Betty Horton Martin of Anderson, South Carolina, and Nancy Connor Smyth and Florrie Stevens Fair of Charleston, South Carolina, were especially helpful in their reading and comments on the sections on sexual stereotypes and on prayer.

Cashiers, North Carolina, was another mountain retreat where major editorial work was done, thanks to an invitation to serve as summer chaplain at the Church of the Good Shepherd from the warden, Mr. B. Turner Schley, and the vicar, the Rev. Stephen Hines.

Chautauqua Conference Center in western New York and Point o' Woods on the southern shore of Fire Island were the final two marvelous resorts where I was privileged both to escape the heat of the summer and to write and edit this manuscript in a community of good friends and strong support. To the Rev. Dr. Ralph Loew at Chautauqua, and to Dr. Gary Shilling and John McCain at Point o' Woods go my sincere appreciation.

The man to whom this book is dedicated also had a major role in its creation, though he is never quoted. His influence came through his example. At the center of the Episcopal Church for almost a decade stood the figure of John Elbridge Hines. His strength, his dedication, and his power inspired a whole generation of Christians to take risks for the sake of Christ and the truth. I am one of his spiritual children. From his example I have found the courage needed to explore and to proclaim my Christian faith while daring to keep my feet firmly planted in the soil of my revolutionary twentieth century. That was his special gift to this volume.

Finally to my family—Joan, my cherished wife of thirty years; Ellen, Katharine, and Jaquelin, our now full-grown daughters; and Hermann, our now ancient cat who completes the family circle: There is a tremendous joy in seeing daughters you adore become women you admire. Each of our daughters read and offered helpful comments on sections of this book. This primary family group has been all to me that any family could be. Through joy and sorrow, sickness and health, pain and pleasure we have held each other up and helped each other grow. Now we enjoy that wonderful experience of developing interdependent adult relationships of deep and rich meaning. When a parent-child relationship grows and changes into mutual respect and real friendship, life has bestowed, I believe, its richest blessing.

John Shelby Spong
Newark, New Jersey
October 1982

Introduction

A PERSONAL WORD: SETTING THE STAGE

WHEN I was in grade school, my life was enriched by a publication entitled *My Weekly Reader*. It was a child's newspaper that related me to the vast adult world in an understandable way. A regular feature, "The World of 1955," was a pictorial page designed to help my childish mind embrace the visionary dreams of an almost incomprehensible future. 1955 seemed a dim and distant year to me at that time, so I read with fascination predictions of cloverleaf highways, jet travel, television, automobiles that ran on something besides gasoline, and instantaneous worldwide communication.

1955 came and went long ago, and today we are but a few short years away from the twenty-first century. Between my childhood and that fantasy world of 1955, change occurred rapidly; but from 1955 until today the change has accelerated at an even more phenomenal rate. Before our normal life expectancy is concluded, the rate and rapidity of change will make our day look as if it had been captured by a slow-motion camera. Within this whirlwind, the church must live and worship and witness. How can we Christians be faithful to our Lord and still embrace the emerging future?

In many ways the future has already arrived, and its manifestations are rending the life of the church at this moment. When the changes of an inbreaking future come faster than they can be absorbed emotionally, two diametrically opposite responses are inevitable. Both are discernible in the body of the church today.

1

The first is overt and clear. When the pain of modernity and future shock is too great, there is always withdrawal into familiar security systems. A shift to the right with its focus on yesterday is evident in every branch of Christianity the world over, and the rise of an anti-modern spirit, complete with a neofundamentalism emotionally akin to Christian fundamentalism among the Moslem people in Iran and the Middle East, causes one to suspect that the movement transcends any religious tradition.

In Roman Catholicism there has been a distinct retreat from the liberal spirit of the great ecumenical Pope John XXIII, first to Paul VI and then to the present Bishop of Rome, John Paul II. One symptom of Rome's increasing conservatism is reflected in the renewed emphasis on doctrinal orthodoxy. In recent years the Roman Catholic hierarchy has disowned such frontier theologians as Teilhard de Chardin and Hans Küng. It has harassed such scholars as Edward Schillebeeckx and David Tracy. When these actions are combined with a refusal to rethink an all-male celibate priesthood in the face of the sexual revolution or to rethink the position on birth control in the face of a world population explosion, a commitment to the past is clearly indicated. These are the signs of a church in retreat from today, a church reluctant to confront tomorrow.

As if not to be outdone, the popular voices of Protestantism are also in a headlong flight into the past. The social activism of the sixties has faded into the spiritual piety of the seventies and the inertia of the eighties in every major Protestant tradition. We have witnessed the spectacle of state legislatures responding to the religious right wing and enacting laws designed to fight evolution in the name of biblical inerrancy. We see biblical literalism being proclaimed with renewed power through the electronic media. We observe conservative evangelical movements in Protestantism taking specific stands on such issues as women's rights, Israel, the Panama Canal, and homosexuality on the basis of their understanding of the literal truth found in an ancient biblical text. We see new seminaries being formed in mainline Protestant traditions because their founders assert the existing seminaries are hopelessly infected by a disease called "secular humanism" and no longer hold the "true faith." Responding to this renewed evangelical fervor, we have seen the born-again Christian stance exploited politically as an asset to gain election on national, state, and local levels.

One can sense a tremendous level of fear and frustration in each of these issues. It is clear to many that the future has proved too dynamic for some parts of the church to embrace. The church is frequently not at home in the fast lanes of today's increasingly impersonal, transient world. Hence in a rapidly changing revolutionary age, many church people seek to return to that simpler era of the past when choices were clear and when certainty, not relativity, was in the very air we breathed.

The second response to the inbreaking future is quiet and subtle. While the swing to the right goes on publicly, at the same time a stream, indeed perhaps a flood, of people are abandoning organized religion to take up citizenship in the secular city. The most rapidly growing organization in the church today might be called the Church Alumni Association, and people drop out of the church daily to enroll. Basically these people are not angry or alienated; they simply are not interested. The church no longer seems to touch them with any meaning. The God worshiped in the church appears to them to be too small to encompass the arenas in which they live or too impotent to be the center of their existence. They view the church as a kind of crutch on which weaker people lean when they lack the courage to live in the brave new world. The church increasingly seems to them to be neither necessary nor eternal.

Every time the church wastes its limited energy in debating a part of its security system, such as whether to change its prayer book or hymnal or its scheduled hour of worship, another segment of people becomes convinced that the church is an inept and limited institution, neither vital nor important in our life today. These turned-off people do not show up statistically in the latest Gallup poll. Their names in many instances are still on church rolls, but their involvement is best symbolized by the increasing number of empty pews on Sunday morning or in how little of themselves they are willing to invest in any church activity. Today their name is Legion.

Contemporary Christianity is caught between these two poles. Future shock is upon us Christians. The dual response to the tumultuous tide of change is present at this moment in the life of the church. This is not a comfortable era for those of us who share in the leadership of the Christian church today. If we have integrity, if we are informed by any semblance of scholarship, we can neither join the march into yesterday nor sit idly by and watch the quiet exodus of former Christians into secularity. Our faith must be real enough to enable us to enter into our new world with its vast knowledge, its revolutionary and competing truths, even though in the process our understanding of Christianity and religion will change dramatically. If Christian leaders cannot walk into this whirlwind, we cannot hope to survive as an effective church in the coming decades.

Standing before the Christian church today, I see three major frontiers. They stand like barriers, blocking our path into tomorrow unless they can be entered and crossed. But entering any one of these frontiers is fearful indeed, for each has the potential to separate traditional Christianity from its past in a radical way. These frontiers are calling Christians to new definitions that will question our very continuity, our deepest self-identity. Whether we Christians have the courage to risk what entering these frontiers will require is to me an open question. If we do not risk all that we are in this moment, then I am convinced that Christianity will cease to be a force in this world. But even if we do risk all that we are, there is no guarantee that Christian survival will be achieved. The stakes are high; the fear is great. But in my mind our only choice is to step boldly into the storm, to walk forward into the future. To take a tentative step in this direction is my purpose in this volume.

The three frontiers that I identify are the relativity of all human truth, the revolution in sexual understanding, and the emerging human consciousness that transcends tribal identity.

Christianity has been identified with a specific and unchanging content for which in some form we have claimed infallibility or at least a standard by which all ideas must be judged for orthodoxy. That understanding of Christianity must be abandoned as we walk across the frontier created for us by a knowledge revolution, for that revolution has reduced every human endeavor to a sea of relativity. Can Christianity give up its claim to certainty and survive?

Christianity has played a primary role in Western civilization as the definer of sexual roles, sexual understanding, and sexual behavior. Sexual symbols are at the heart of our understanding of God. God is a Father who had a Son by the Virgin Mary. This story is at the heart of the Christian tradition, yet it is now obvious that particular sexual definitions are hidden in that simple phrase. A revolution in sexual mores and understanding has engulfed the Western world. Stereotypes are being challenged, and they are proving to be something less than self-evident, less than eternal. Can Christianity escape its commitment to a premodern sexual consciousness and redefine itself in terms of new understandings of human sexuality? If so, a dramatically different understanding of Christianity will emerge. Can Christianity surrender its traditional sexual definitions for both God and human life and still survive?

Christianity has been tied to a particular cultural consciousness since it was born out of the womb of Judaism. Yahweh was, in fact, a tribal desert God of Israel. Through Christ Yahweh became the Trinity, the tribal God of Western Europe. Following the flag of Western imperialism and colonialism, Christianity has swept into Asia, Africa, North and South America, Australia, and the islands of the Pacific. Local tribal deities have influenced Christianity in these parts of the globe, and in the emerging nations of the Third World there is a rush to decolonialize Christianity in the name of a more local tribal religion in order for it to survive the rising tide of nationalism.

No religion has ever escaped fully its tribal origin. Islam is intensely nationalistic. Judaism is intensely nationalistic. The Oriental traditions of Hinduism, Buddhism, Shintoism, and Taoism all shape to varying degrees the nationalistic yearnings of Japan, China, India, Vietnam, Korea, Burma, and the other nation states of the Orient. Can Christianity be separated from our tribal mentalities? If so, what will that Christianity look like, how will it shape our life, determine our values, or preserve our identity?

These are the frontiers that separate us Christians, I believe, from tomorrow. Can Christianity transgress these frontiers? Should we? Surely death awaits any human movement that hides from new truth, no matter how sacred its past or how holy its tradition. But death may well await us if we do make so radical a departure from our self-understanding. Christianity has never been defined outside these three fortresses: the presumption of certainty, the universal acceptance of sexual definitions, the limited tribal mentality that enables us to cope with the world.

Some people are clearly not ready for these questions to be raised, and they will react with varying levels of negativity. Some will never understand and will be deeply critical, even scandalized, that these issues are being forced into their conscious minds. Some people will comprehend the questions but will disagree with the solutions or the directions I and others are proposing. Some people will walk with me step by step into the future, finding in these pages roadmaps for a territory that is as yet largely unexplored. I understand all of those responses and consider them each to be legitimate, for all are present in every moment of historic change.

Before entering the formal content of this book, I want to take my reader very briefly inside my own life and share something of the personal faith out of which these probing words arise. Long ago I ceased to be impressed with any claim by any writer to objectivity, so let the obvious be stated. This is a subjective, a personal, and, in some ways even for its author, a disturbing book. Objectivity for me can be approached not by a single person but by the interaction of many persons, the challenge and response, the dialogue and confrontation, as we grapple with the truth behind every tentative and partial articulation of that truth. My fond hope is that this volume will create such a dialogue and debate, and in that process both the church and this author may well be changed. So listen for a moment to the one who is writing and to the context of faith out of which he writes.

I believe there is an ultimate reality that can only be called God. This God is experienced as holy. I am not always comfortable with the limited, personal words we use to describe that ultimate reality, yet God's manifestations within me and within my world are always intensely personal. I feel that the drive to achieve life, to share love, to enhance being is nothing less than the call of God meeting response in and through me. God for me is never foreign to the experience of living, and this, I believe, is the deepest meaning of incarnation.

I also find evidence for the reality of God in the natural world's regenerative power, its incredible balance, and its inevitable movement toward wholeness. The healing powers of the human body and the regenerative power within the natural order to adapt and to overcome enormous abuse for me point to the mystery and undeniable presence of the creating God. Creation itself demonstrates an unquestioned ability to adjust to new circumstances while continuing its own inner destiny to achieve a purpose and a fullness that I can only glimpse. To me, these are the natural footprints of God.

I am a Christian. I live my life deliberately and self-consciously inside the Christian revelation. I am fascinated by and drawn to many insights from the other great religious traditions; but in the last analysis they compromise only my theological security, while in fact they expand and enrich my own Christian thinking. My Christian life focuses uniquely on the historic life of a man from Nazareth who is for me more than just a man. He is, in the words of Professor Donald Winslow of the Boston Theological Consortium, "the embodiment and articulation of God's self-giving reality and sacrificial love for all people."

Jesus the Christ is a vital center of my understanding of this Holy God. I perceive, in and through Jesus, glimpses of what surely must be the meaning, the revelation, the inbreaking of that presence and power that I call God. Clearly to me Jesus is what God is. I am not prepared, however, to limit, nor do I think the import of the Bible requires that I limit, God's incarnating presence to Jesus of Nazareth; but, for me, that Christ-figure is the determinative figure of burning divine intensity by which I must evaluate every other incarnation.

If I believe that God is one, then the God that I meet in Jesus cannot be different from the God I meet in anyone else. I claim for Jesus the perfect revelation of God, though I would never claim for anyone's understanding of Jesus a perfect articulation of that revelation. Jesus shares in the ultimacy of God, but the church's understanding of Jesus can do nothing more than point to that ultimacy. The church cannot claim that ultimacy for its understanding. God has been revealed in many ways, at many times, under many symbols, and through many traditions. Only those arrogant enough to think that they have captured God—and are therefore empowered to speak for God—could claim otherwise.

The Christian understanding of God the Holy Spirit "who will lead us into all truth" (John 16:13) seems to me to undergird this position, for the Holy Spirit cannot be limited to any human institution. That Holy Spirit was clearly active in history before Jesus and has been active since Jesus. God's all-pervasive spirit works in and through many traditions and symbols, some quite foreign to my own experience. Therefore the test of the spirit for me must be the manifestation of enhanced life, heightened love, and expanded being. A freedom from the debilitating pain of human insecurity and the destruction of human prejudice must be obvious if that which I would identify with the Holy God is at work.

Jesus of Nazareth meets this test not by claims of a miraculous birth or by tales of supernatural power but by his amazing ability to live, his unending capacity to love, and his phenomenal courage to be all that he was created to be in every set of circumstances that the broken world thrust upon him. His life seems to have hurdled barrier after human barrier. For this reason I am not surprised that this Jesus was believed to have transcended the seemingly ultimate barrier of death and finitude and that the transcendence of this barrier apparently loosed upon his disciples the life-giving, love-creating, being-enhancing power of his spirit. For me the moment we Christians call Easter is both real and vitally significant.[1] It is the heart of the Christian revelation.

But since Jesus is a time-limited figure of history, there must be a community where the infinite power of this Jesus can be experienced as eternally present and ever-available in time, where one can meet the life-giving power of God. The existence of a church is imperative, but there is no compelling need for any particular ecclesiastical or institutional expression of that church.

I even claim for the church the content of that medieval slogan, "no salvation outside the church." Obviously, however, I do not identify church solely with a particular structure or tradition. To me, rather, the church is any life that brings to another the freeing, enhancing presence of God. In every personal history there must be personal lives that act as conduits for the experience of God. Those lives in my definition are "the church" to the recipient of the experience. Those lives are therefore the Body of Christ to me. Inevitably the church had to be organized in order to be sustained in history. Almost as inevitably, when it was organized, its own institutional needs for power, dominance, and survival emerged. The claim to be the dispenser and source of salvation was identified not with the experience of the meaning of God in Christ mediated through a human life but rather with the legitimate authority of the institution. If people are convinced that they need forgiveness, grace, and salvation, and if an institution can make good its claim to be the exclusive dispenser of forgiveness, grace, and salvation, that institution has achieved enormous political power. So an effective control system was built around the dispensing of forgiveness, the means of grace, and the promise of salvation.

An extension of this control system was seen in the power to excommunicate and the ability to assign one to the ultimate destiny of heaven or hell, to say nothing of the ability to define infallibly "the faith of the church" for all times. This authority certainly gave order to the institutional church, and through it order was imposed on the world. But no matter how corrupt that institution becomes or how critically one might deal with the behavior and power needs of the church in history, I could never reach the point where the reality of the church ceased to be of the very essence of the experience of the Gospel. The gathered people cannot finally cease to be a meeting place with the Holy God.

There has to be a church, a community, a structure, an order into which lives can be grafted anew in every generation. There have to be channels of grace, sacraments, rites of initiation, the waters of baptism, the bread and wine of the Eucharistic observance.

The ultimate need of the church was and is to keep ongoing tradition in tension with the reforming spirit that constantly opens the symbols of worship to the ever-inbreaking presence of God. No matter how critical I might become of the shape of the institutional church in history, I still must have a church. I must be part of a life-giving community where faith can be explored and the presence of grace and love can be experienced anew in every moment of life and in every generation.

One of the primary functions of that community is to encourage me and all others to develop in the most personal and unique way our own intense relationship with the Holy God. This is what prayer means to me, at least in its private and personal manifestation. No day goes by that I do not take time specifically and self-consciously to engage in the practice of prayer and to probe the power that I am convinced lies yet to be discovered inside that activity. Beyond the phoniness and superficiality that so often accompanies prayer, beyond the superstitious claims for prayer issued by well-meaning but painfully shallow and frequently self-serving people, there is in prayer, I am convinced, a power to be tapped, a meaning to be shared, a reality to be touched. So I pray and I wait and I hope. When I try to put my thoughts on prayer into words, I shudder. As soon as the ink is dry on the page, the words will be frozen; but the author of the words will be moving on. That is the way it must be if journey is the mode of the Christian life, as I believe it is.

As is now obvious, I have what is surely a deeply ambivalent relationship with the organized church, with the traditions, with Christian theology. I could not possibly live without the church, and yet the church is the source of my deepest and most agonizing frustration. I am moved by the traditions that worship celebrates, but I am repelled when these traditions are hardened into sacred and unchanging practices which no longer point beyond themselves. I am willing to commit my lifetime to an exploration into the truth of God that is for me the meaning and hope of theology, but I despair when theology degenerates into a series of petty limitations that are so often placed upon God or when the quest for truth degenerates into dogmatic statements that claim infallibility. I am willing to explore daily the incredible power that the Bible expresses or that the creeds seek to define, but I cannot abide the ultimate claims made by those who would literalize the words of either into a final authority. I do not believe the Christian faith is a closed system. I do not believe that God has enjoyed an eternal sabbath of rest since the birth of Christianity. I cherish the responsibility and the trust that are mine as a bishop of the church, but I am offended by the pomposity and ego-needs that so often mark the church's hierarchy and in which I have participated, much to my shame.

I want to be a part of a new reformation in the history of Christianity. I want to call the church to frontiers that need to be crossed, to new truth that needs to be embraced, to changed realities that need to be faced. I shall offer pointers far more often than I offer solutions. My hope is to create public debate on the issues. My desire and wish is that the debate will center not on whether my ideas fit the narrow orthodoxy of the past but on whether they are true. Truth cannot be dismissed because it does not fit easily into yesterday's categories. To be right is not my goal; to find and enjoy the truth is. In the words of Professor William Sparrow of the Virginia Theological Seminary, let us together "seek the truth of God, come whence it may, cost what it will."

---

1. This issue is explored in depth in my book *The Easter Moment*, New York, Seabury, 1980.

Section I

MOVING
BEYOND
THE
FACADE
OF
CERTAINTY

Chapter 1

THE FIRST FRONTIER:
ALL TRUTH IS RELATIVE

T HE twentieth century has given birth to forces which have had a dramatic impact on all of those truths that we regarded yesterday as self-evident certainties. Many of the unquestioned assumptions of the past are in our generation casually dismissed as no longer adequate for our time. New insights are born daily in almost every sphere of knowledge. With increasing rapidity those insights are tested, refined, established; and then they create a ripple effect that extends to every branch of human learning. In no time at all, others building on these new insights spring out in still newer directions in the ever-increasing search for the fullness of truth.

In such a world the Christian church more and more seems to be alien and even anachronistic. Long ago theology surrendered its position as the "Queen of Sciences." Despite some well-known exceptions, the vocation of the priesthood and the study of religion are not today attracting the most brilliant scholars. The system of thought that the secular world historically identifies with the church seems to deny free inquiry lest it disturb essential doctrines. Such an intellectual stance is not likely to challenge today's most incisive minds.

When one studies the history of ideas in the Western world, the Christian church is often not the hero of the drama. Most of the creative insights or knowledge breakthroughs in postmedieval Western history were achieved in spite of the active opposition of the organized church speaking through the members of the hierarchy.

Time after time the standard Christian response to new insights has been to condemn the scholar. Galileo and Copernicus were excommunicated. A wide variety of things from vaccinations to birth control have been condemned by the church. As late as 1950, in a papal encyclical entitled "Humani Generis," Pope Pius XII in the name of the church was still attacking Charles Darwin. Every new scientific discovery seemed to shrink the legitimate area of the church's authority. For hundreds of years now the church has at best been engaged in an intellectual rearguard action.

In our own day the claims of the church are generally ignored in secular circles, and the church seems to me to respond in kind by trying to ignore the secular knowledge explosion. On one side we are presented with the incredible vistas of the space-exploring astronomers which seem to point not to God so much as to an infinite void. On the other side we face the startling discoveries from the microscopic world of the molecular biochemists and biophysicists that explain so many of the mysteries of life for which God was heretofore the primary explanation. Too often when the church ventures out of its narrow religious domain to confront this modern reality, it seems fragile and inept indeed; so it ventures seldom, while frantically trying within its own shrinking orbit of influence to protect and to buttress its claims to authority.

Slowly but surely it is dawning on the leaders of Christianity that the church today faces a tradition-rending frontier. We are being forced to make a decision. We can withdraw from life and chant our liturgies in splendid isolation, or we can step outside the certainties of the past into the churning relativities of the present to grapple with the increasing uncertainties of the future. This is a critical moment in Christian history. If we can risk stepping over this line, we will have to lay aside forever the cherished claims of the past that the church possesses the ultimate and unchanging truth of God. A legitimate fear grips us in such a moment. It is never easy to surrender that in which one has trusted for centuries, especially when nothing gives evidence that the security produced by the certainty claims of yesterday will ever be replaced.

Many wonder if the Christian church can give up the claim to possess certainty or unchanging truth and still be the church. Certainty has been the hallmark of every historic missionary religion. Few religious systems in the long human pilgrimage have survived without such a claim. The establishment of that claim compels people to conversion, fuels the expansionary endeavors, and binds a discipline on the lives of believers. It is the traditional base of authority for the Christian church. If that base is eroded or if it has to be sacrificed, then every ecclesiastical claim to infallibility will be destroyed, whether it be the infallibility of the pope or of the scriptures or of the creeds or of the tradition. Every assertion that Christianity in any form possesses by divine revelation the ultimate and unchanging truth will have to be abandoned. Every identification of the truth of God with any human group's understanding of the truth of God will have to be surrendered.

If we Christians, willingly or unwillingly, are engulfed by this tide of modern life, it is quite clear that the church as we know it will be in jeopardy. Yet anyone who breathes deeply of the intellectual revolution or the knowledge explosion of our day must surely be aware that no other alternative is possible.

Is it credible to suggest that the Christian church can confront this world armed with the claim that in our holy book, which was completed before A.D. 150, the unchanging, eternal truth of God has been captured for all time, or that in our ancient creeds, which achieved their final form before the fifth century, the parameters around the truth of God were forever set? Surely such claims would be ludicrous in any other branch of human knowledge. Is it less ludicrous because they speak of holy things or carry with them the stained-glass accents of the ages?

The contrasts and distance between these ancient claims of the church and of change in every other human pursuit is today so vast that the word polarity, which reflects a relationship of tension but nonetheless a relatedness, may no longer be appropriate. In this century the cyclonic force of new thought and new possibilities has engulfed us. We have moved from horse-and-buggy locomotion to space travel in one lifetime. We have moved from communications based on the Pony Express to communications bounced off a Telstar space satellite in one century. Many of us feel as if the dikes protecting our personal security systems have been broken or flooded or both. There are few fields of human knowledge where a textbook written as recently as ten years ago would not at this moment be hopelessly dated and hopelessly irrelevant. That relentless tide of change will sooner or later tear the church free from its moorings to float without anchor on the sea of relativity.

To be cut loose from the anchor of theological certainty seems to me to be the inevitable fate that awaits us Christians in our day. Can we survive as a pilgrim people without an ultimate authority, a pilgrim people always on a journey? Can we endure the anxiety of a journey that has no discernible doctrinal fixed points? Can the church be a body of people who are restless, uncertain, living by hope and faith more than by unchanging conviction? In my mind we must, because the only alternative to embarking on this path is to drop out of the world and to cultivate the narcotic of religion for those decreasing few who cannot embrace the vision or the reality of exploding knowledge and the subsequent relativity of all truth.

So this is one of our beckoning frontiers. This is the first gale-force edge of the whirlwind that we Christians must embrace. What will Christianity look like if we step ahead? The time has come to move forward.

Chapter 2

THE DEATH OF AUTHORITY, THE JOY OF UNCERTAINTY

To equip Christian people to enter the insecure world of relative truth and to sacrifice willingly the traditional Christian claim to be the possessors of unchanging certainty, it is essential to have a broad historic viewpoint. We need to examine the ways in which the claim we are being asked to surrender came into being in the first place. Was it legitimate at its inception? Was it a universally held conviction? Was there no minority tradition that embraced freedom with its inevitable anxiety of uncertainty, or did everyone become seduced by the need for security which created both the assertion of certainty and ecclesiastical control?

If we discover that in the broad stream of Christian history a minor tributary has constantly been flowing, sometimes openly, sometimes underground, frequently forging new territory, constantly disturbing the peace of the authorities, then perhaps we can discover continuity with that part of our past that will help us define ourselves as a pilgrim people in this brave new world. Perhaps the only change that we are facing today is that a minority movement is becoming the majority—in spite of opposition from most ecclesiastical authorities—because the knowledge explosion of our day has destroyed the claims and the power of those who heretofore constituted the majority point of view.

Christian history, despite our common image, has not been static. Every movement of history is born like new wine breaking the old wineskins. The dramatic birth of Christianity into the history of the world was no exception. When any historic movement is victorious, however, it becomes established and joins the social order. Inevitably, then, it becomes one more old wineskin, holding, containing, and protecting its understanding of truth and its special revelation. Those well served by that system obviously have a special need to defend it. Invariably they surround their defense of "the Faith," which is essentially nothing but their institutional guard duty, with holy and lofty rhetoric. They see themselves as divinely commissioned vigilantes, protecting their saving truth from erosion from within or attack from without. That was and is the traditional pattern in the history of the Christian church.

In lofty theological phrases Christians have given lip service to our belief in the ever-present power of the Holy Spirit. In practice, however, it is frequently apparent that we believe the Holy Spirit was new power only in the past and is today allowed to work only within the religious structures of another era which we identify and which we must authenticate. At that moment the dynamic, inbreaking God of history became domesticated, tamed, and forced to abide by human ecclesiastical rules. The fact that this same kind of religious system led to the crucifixion of the church's Lord seems not to be noticed.

The religious leadership of first-century Judaism was quite sure that the only proper channel through which God could or would operate was the one the Jewish religious hierarchy controlled. Since Jesus was clearly outside that channel, he could not be of God, they asserted. Since Jesus claimed to speak and act for God, he was either guilty of blasphemy or he was demon-possessed. No other possibility was allowable. In either case the religious decision-makers were quite justified in their moves to destroy him. After all, they were protecting God and God's truth from the distortions of this imposter. On historic and sociological levels, this pattern has been repeated time after time.

William James, in the Gifford Lectures, spoke to this reality when he said

> A genuine, firsthand religious experience is bound to be a heterodoxy to its witnesses, the prophet appearing as a mere lonely madman. If his doctrine proves contagious enough to spread to any others, it becomes a definite and labeled heresy. But if it then proves still contagious enough to triumph over persecution, it becomes itself an orthodoxy; and when a religion has become an orthodoxy, its day of inwardness is over. The spring is dry. The faithful live at second hand

exclusively and stone the prophets in their turn. The new church, in spite of whatever human goodness it may foster, can be henceforth counted on as a staunch ally in every attempt to stifle the spontaneous religious spirit and to stop all later bubblings of the fountains from which in purer days it drew its own supply of inspiration.[1]

When one analyzes the primary beneficiaries of a closed religious system, it becomes easy to understand the need for control that such a system engenders. Once the church is identified with "the Truth," then the power of the church is in direct proportion to the maintenance of the credibility of this claim. If this claim can be established in the popular mind, then those who direct the institution have enormous status, power, and prestige. If this claim is ever relativized, however, that status, power, and prestige are immediately eroded. So in Christian history there was a drive toward authority and control which enabled the institutional leaders of the church legitimately to claim that they were the ones who articulated the faith in a final form and who defended it against all comers. They and their descendents became those who opposed the emerging ideas they could not incorporate into their system.

All of us must recognize that this structure was not evil either by intention or design. The church clearly could not have endured without it. Every ongoing institution needs the contribution of those who are the tradition bearers. There is a tremendous dedication in those whose deepest commitment is to transmit intact the faith and heritage they have received. When the church is viewed through the eyes of this perspective, the internal institutional needs of the church with its budgets, conventions, canons, and constitutions are seen as worthy of devotion, care, and involvement. The proper methods of worship will be defended, and the historic depth of worship will be preserved. The tradition bearers seek to be conduits through which the past enters the future. The only adjustment that is legitimate in their minds is to enable the tradition to meet unexpected or unforeseen circumstances.

If there is no ongoing tradition that can receive a challenge, then there will be no continuity, no cohesion, and no roots to the institution's life. Tragedy comes, however, when the tradition bearers make idols out of the tradition and view every new idea as a threat to the very life of the tradition, thereby forcing the creative thinkers outside a dialogue with the faith of their fathers and mothers. That tragedy can prove a disaster in a world, like our own, that is in the turmoil of rapid change. But that does not mean that tradition is evil or should be destroyed. Actually, the church at its best has always been traditional and open, Catholic and Protestant, ancient and reformed, conservative and liberal. The lines that denote who is Christian and who is not need to be enormously wide, embracing those the traditionalists would call wild radical heretics as well as those that people who walk on the theological frontiers would call dull, inert, and irrelevant.

I am convinced that life as well as truth will only be found in tension. Today the dialogue between Christianity and its world must be broader and more provocatively dangerous to the church's vested interest than ever before. If the frontier voice cannot be heard and affirmed in the life of the church, if theological and biblical relativity cannot be embraced, if the rigid control systems of the past cannot be opened, then I see little future hope for the church. This is not a mere game our generation of Christians is playing. This is, I am convinced, a battle for the survival of Christianity as a force with integrity. It will prove, I believe, to be a battle more intense than that which the church fought and won in the first centuries of its life.

The natural response of the tradition-bearing person living in the storms of new learning is to batten down the hatches and seek safety. My conviction is that if such a pattern becomes dominant in the church, it will lead not to safety but to death, inevitable and inescapable death. The church today needs the ability to bear the pain of anxiety and to live in the fear of uncertainty, while we embrace the storm and face the howling winds of change in the confidence that ultimate truth, while not possessed by any of our words or doctrines, can nonetheless never be destroyed, and our security systems, no matter how comfortable, that are based on the illusion that we possess the unchanging truth can never be sustained. When in the life of the church our need for order and security becomes sanctified and identified with God, idolatry is born. The inevitable fate of idolatry is destruction. That, I submit, is what is occurring in our day. The church is not dying, but the church's idols are; and those who have confused the two are in despair.

The presence of this idolatry in the life of the church is always obvious and easy to identify. It is boldly announced whenever a claim of infallibility is made for any part of the tradition. No words articulated in and related to time can capture eternity or finally achieve infallibility. To claim that they can is to become idolatrous. Inevitably, in the passage of time, either the idol will be broken open or that for which the idol stands will be destroyed. There is historically no other alternative.

In Christian history two major candidates for the position of infallible and ultimate authority have been offered by the church. The first and most powerful was the hierarchical claim to be the definitive articulator of orthodoxy that finally evolved into the Roman Catholic assertion of the infallibility of the papal office. Papal infallibility is an ultimate claim made for the views of the hierarchy as that hierarchy came to be crowned and symbolized by the Bishop of Rome. Not surprisingly it was officially declared dogma of the church in 1870. A majority of the council fathers who ratified this proclamation had grown up in the antienlightenment, antirational romanticism of the first half of the nineteenth century. It was a time of political restoration in which the people of Europe, after confusion and the excesses of both the revolutionary forces and the Napoleonic threat, had an irresistible longing for peace, order, and the good old days. By and large, Catholic churchmen in this period were supporters of political reaction.[2] The claim of infallibility was deliberately employed to counter liberalism, advancing industrialization, belief in the inevitability of progress, the scientific revolution, and socialism, all of which, to church leaders, seemed intent on abolishing religious authority and tradition.[3] This authority had been claimed in differing forms prior to the proclamation of the dogma of papal infallibility. This claim had not, however, always been associated with the See of Rome.

Infallibility was and is an effective authority system because it is controllable. If one disagreed with the authoritative pronouncements of the church, one had to be wrong. It was even simpler when the primacy of the Bishop of Rome was fully established. If there was disagreement over the interpretation of the *ex cathedra* utterances of the pope, the pope himself could settle the dispute at once, so there would be no doubt as to who was right and who was wrong. For one pope to clarify the pronouncements of a previous pope was satisfactory because the authority rested in the office, not in the person. Cardinals, archbishops, bishops, and priests derived all their authority from the authority of the pope. For a lesser figure in the hierarchy to challenge the infallible pronouncements of the papacy was not only to stand in opposition to the truth but also to erode one's own basis of power. No more effective system of control has ever been devised, as evidenced by the enduring presence of the Catholic tradition and its continuing power.

To oppose the authority of the hierarchy in any form and still to claim to be within Christianity demanded the substitution of a different ultimate authority. Attempts to achieve such a substitution struggled for life somewhat unsuccessfully until very late in Christian history. From the beginning Christianity confronted the task of embracing in a cohesive unity a seemingly infinite variety of human experience. This made the maintenance of a definition of certainty and the claim to possess a final authoritative position a complex task indeed. From the earliest conflicts between the Gentile Christians and the Jewish Christians a sub rosa pluralism has been a fact within Christianity. The creeds of the church were not born in a moment. They traveled a tortuous road of debate, conflict, insight, and compromise until they were transformed into the long theological phrases of the Athanasian formula in the sixth century. The Lucan story of Pentecost affirmed pluralism with its assertion that the unity of the church was in the spirit which enabled the varieties of human beings to hear the Gospel in their own language (Acts 2:1ff).

As the centuries began to fade into history, the task of defining and redefining the Gospel was the ever-present vocation of the church, but always officially within rather narrow limits. Pluralism was considered a significant liability in the church, so ideas that could not compel a majority opinion were read out of the church, and those who adhered to these nonmajority ideas endured persecution and even death at the hands of the church's dominant majority. The major losers of the theological debates are remembered in history as the classical heresies.

When orthodoxy's victory was complete, the writings of those thought to be heretics were repressed and are therefore generally lost to us forever. All that tends to remain are the orthodox polemics against the heretical position. They are not free of exaggeration or distortion. The discovery of some original gnostic texts in the archeological excavations at Nag Hammadi in our own generation has helped to alter our understanding of what gnosticism was, for example, because now for the first time in these documents the gnostics can speak for themselves.[4] We can only wonder what other misunderstandings might be cleared away if Arius, Marcion, Nestorius, or Appolonarius could speak for themselves. But these movements were routed, and the deviant ideas were driven underground. Thus the authority of the church, ultimately symbolized by the papacy, was successful and has been sustained for many centuries.

The Protestant Reformation did finally succeed in tempering this ultimate authority, and that reformation and its pluralism have thus far endured. Protestantism's success was, however, in direct proportion to its ability to find a powerful counterauthority with which to displace or at least to stand first alongside and ultimately against the authority of the hierarchical church. Scripture thus emerged as the basis for authority and was installed as the "paper pope" of Protestantism.

Nothing was to be taught in Protestant churches as generally necessary for salvation that could not be documented by an appeal to scripture. Using that standard as a norm, the reforming spirit of Protestantism did away with relics, indulgences, rituals, many forms of Mariolatry, and numerous other practices determined to be "Romish" rather than biblical in origin. The hierarchical claim to ultimate authority in defining faith and order was matched by the Protestant claim of ultimate authority and inerrancy for Holy Scripture. In many ways scripture was not a very cohesive authority, and pluralism in Protestantism was almost inevitable. Even the infallible Bible had to be interpreted, and the interpretations differed widely with all sides of every conflict appealing to the authority of the "Word." The exasperation experienced in Christian history by Protestants seeking to establish the ultimate authority of scripture is best seen in the quotation "Even the devil can quote the scripture for his purposes." To find only one consistent authority in a volume that contains sixty-six books written over a period of more than a thousand years has proved to be quite impossible.

Historically, institutions without a powerful central authority inevitably splinter into many parts and never seem to be as long-lasting as the more centralized systems. The many denominations of Protestantism are examples of this historic truth. The fact that the Southern Kingdom of Judah, with its royal House of David and its symbolic unifying holy city of Jerusalem, outlived by more than a century the Northern Kingdom of Israel, which never produced a lasting royal family or built enduring legends into its capital city of Samaria, is a political example of the same phenomenon.

Protestantism, sensing, I suspect, the weakness of the inerrancy claim for its central authority of scripture, tried to build buttresses around it. Appeals to reason and to sacred tradition were the most frequently used of the ancillary authority props. They were not helpful in preventing the splintering of traditions in Protestantism, but they did aid immeasurably in allowing scholarship to find a fertile field for a full expression, especially in Anglican, Lutheran, and Presbyterian churches. When the critical study of Holy Scripture developed with the Graf Welhausen school in Germany in the nineteenth century, at least a part of Christendom was open to receive and incorporate that new learning into an ongoing body. As such, some relatively small branches of Protestantism exercised an influence on Christendom far beyond their numbers. I have gratefully been nurtured by these scholars.

The major fact which all Christians must sooner or later face today is that all authority claims, whether of the hierarchy or of scripture, have become so badly eroded that neither can carry the load that the Catholic or Protestant traditions still try to place upon them. The buttresses of reason and tradition cannot sustain them either.

There is a crisis in authority in every branch of Christendom today and for good reason, for all truth is being relativized, and with it the security systems of the Christian church are visibly shaking. Vigorous attempts at artificial respiration will not revive the corpse of yesterday's authority base. Neither the authority of the papacy nor the authority of scripture is taken very seriously today except among a very limited group of internal dogmatic adherents. The infallibility claims for either cannot stand a very close scrutiny.

Turning first to examine the Roman Catholic authority system, students of history, both ecclesiastical and secular, dismiss with little argument the claims of papal infallibility. This is true even when the focus is narrowed to include only the most limited understanding of those specifically *ex cathedra* utterances of the Bishop of Rome. Just a glance at such utterances would reveal that claim to be indefensible. On the surface, infallibility claims assert that the historically and culturally conditioned understandings or utterances of a particular person who lives in a particular time—infected as we all are by the particular prejudices and the world view of the age in which we live—and who possesses a particular consciousness, can within the limited human vocabulary of even the dead and therefore supposed universal language of Latin state for all time eternal truth. No other field of human endeavor would make such a claim. Sanctified ignorance, though seldom confronted by people unconcerned with sacred tradition, is ignorance nonetheless. If the church expects to be a force in the emerging world, its claims cannot be exempt from the same searching scrutiny to which every other institution competing for power and influence is subjected.

A critical study of the history of the papacy raises doubts that no authority system can ease, and it will make radically anxious those who find security in that path to certainty. First, papal infallibility presupposes papal primacy. A study of the early centuries of Christian history reveals something less than the primacy of the Bishop of Rome. When, in the second century, Victor, the Bishop of Rome, excommunicated all of Asia Minor over the new Roman date of Easter, he was vigorously opposed by bishops of both the East and West, including Irenaeus. Victor was not able in this instance to establish the claim of primacy.[5]

The great schism in the eleventh century between the Eastern Orthodox tradition and the Western Catholic tradition, which occurred when the Bishop of Rome excommunicated the Patriarch of Constantinople and all his followers, came about because Rome's claim of primacy could not be substantiated in the East. J. Largen, a nineteenth-century historian, gathered all the facts and texts he could find to prove in four volumes that from the seventh to the twelfth centuries the pope was not regarded as infallible.[6] His work has not been refuted.

Secondly, the errors in the pronouncements of the Vatican are not difficult to identify. The excommunication of the Patriarch of Constantinople, Photius, was withdrawn by Paul VI 900 years later in a public admission of mistake. The papal prohibition of interest at the beginning of the modern period was modified time after time until it was abandoned. The papal condemnation of Galileo that set the church against the natural sciences is a present-day embarrassment. The relatively recent Vatican condemnation of the modern critical approach to the Bible or the attempt to maintain the traditional authorship claims for the books of the Bible in the face of contemporary biblical scholarship casts grave doubts on this source of authority.[7]

Of course, the claim is made that in these incidents the papacy was not defining faith or morals *ex cathedra*. But it was the same papacy that made these grievous errors that was declared infallible in 1870.[8] Since that time errors have continued to come forth from that same source. Pius XII in 1950 declared Mary to be bodily assumed into heaven. Despite all theological arguments to the contrary, the naive literalism that surrounds this dogma cannot be dismissed. The words of the dogma of the assumption are based on a concept of a three-tiered universe and a literal "up" heaven. This dogma, incredibly enough, was proclaimed at the dawn of the space age that rendered those concepts meaningless.

When Vatican I declared papal infallibility to be dogma, which meant to Roman Catholics that it was to be believed under pain of excommunication, it leaned heavily upon the writings of Thomas Aquinas. The sources on which Thomas relied, however, have since been revealed to be forgeries, placing serious doubts on the entire process.[9]

Despite the historic evidence to the contrary, when the assumption of papal infallibility is questioned, as Professor Hans Küng has questioned it, the official ecclesiastical response is not to engage the issue in discussion or to demonstrate where Küng might be wrong; it is rather to condemn and remove the one who raised the question. The assumption made by the ecclesiastical leadership is that one who questions their closed system has to be wrong by definition. That is idolatry. A closed system must remain closed, and its defenders recognize that better than anyone else. If that system were ever opened to scholarship and reason, it would quickly evaporate into an ancient idea having historic interest but no present power.

On the Protestant side of the authority claims, the "inerrant scriptures" are equally without the capacity to be sustained in our day. Biblical scholarship in the last one hundred years has absolutely destroyed biblical fundamentalism as a living option for the Protestant world. This clearly does not mean that there are no more fundamentalists; but it does mean that this particular attitude can simply not be sustained in serious scholarly circles, nor is it even entertained as worthy of debate. The fundamentalist claim is something like the smile of the Cheshire cat which lingers long after the cat has departed. Or it is like a cut flower that still has appeal but no root and no future hope of regeneration. It would be hard to imagine the secular press today treating William Jennings Bryan's defense of the Bible in the Scopes trial in Tennessee in 1925 as anything more than an embarrassing aberration. The most cursory understanding of the formation of the Bible, the most shallow reading of many parts of the biblical text, the barest knowledge of biblical scholarship, the simple recognition of many of the internal biblical conflicts and contradictions—any one of these would immediately render a view of an inerrant Holy Scripture impossible to defend.

The emotional dimension of the commitment to the infallibility of the paper pope of Protestantism is revealed in the anger and fear biblical fundamentalists express when their assumptions are questioned publicly. Here too there is only the facade, the self-hypnosis of security. This too is idolatry. Ultimate authority can never reside in the assumption of an inerrant Bible.

The one fact that is certain in our world is that no ultimate authority exists that can define truth in any area for all time. The obvious corollary is that any system built on the assumption that there is such an authority is doomed, for it is built on an unsupportable foundation.

All claims to possess infallibility that have been historically employed in Christianity, even within the community of believers, are simply losing their power. In the secular circles of contemporary scholarship, these claims have had no power for years. We are thus entering a brand new world where certainty more and more will be seen as a vice rising out of an emotional need, and uncertainty will be seen as a virtue possessing integrity and a willingness to risk security in the quest for truth. Increasingly appeals to authority will fall on deaf ears as we enter the radical insecurity of an honest examination of the roots and the viability of our deepest commitments and our holiest beliefs. The institutional church will have to learn to live without its traditional sources of authority if it is going to live at all.

I harbor a hope based on no historic evidence whatsoever that the institutional church in some manifestation will be able to respond to this challenge creatively. As I look at the formal structures of the church, I see little willingness yet to face this reality. There is rather a continuous scurrying to shore up defense lines, to sustain the institution's status and power, even if that means that the purpose for which the church was created is inevitably distorted. To read the Anglican-Roman Catholic agreed statement on authority is to enter an ecclesiastical world of "let's pretend."[10] Because the document assumes that some form of infallibility must be maintained, it does not reflect the issues and realities of the twentieth century. To attempt to replace infallibility with indefectibility, as this document does, is merely to engage in a verbal gymnastic performance.

Yet there are some saving precedents in Christian history which, if unearthed, give us hope and promise that we can live in a new way in our new world. When Jesus our Lord broke upon human history, no authority system could contain him. He offered freedom, not control—the "glorious liberty of the children of God," St. Paul called it in the Epistle to the Romans (Romans 8:21). It was truth, the Bible said, that would make us free (John 8:32). That same freedom to find the truth that is in Christ apart from the authority systems of the past is, I believe, the only legitimate Christian goal for our day. This is what Dietrich Bonhoeffer meant, I believe, when he called us to find Christ apart from religion or to explore religionless Christianity.[11]

It is quite obvious that not every Christian will have the courage to join this search. It is also certain to me if some Christians do not take up this search with a consuming commitment, there will be little future for this church of ours as we now understand it. Once more, I believe, history is calling the Christian church to produce a faithful remnant that will be the means through which the renewal of the church can begin on a basis different from any that has yet existed historically.

I am encouraged in this hope by a study of Christian history, which reveals that there has always been a creative remnant within the body of the church that refuses to consume itself in "defending the Faith." That tiny minority position understands Paul's exclamation regarding "the depth and riches and wisdom and knowledge of God, the unsearchable judgments, the inscrutable ways" (Romans 11:33). They seem to know intuitively that this vision makes relative every authority claim for ultimate or infallible truth, every creed, every Bible. That minority tradition finds an ally in the author of Ephesians who wrote that "the love of Christ surpasses human knowledge" and presumably surpasses every supposedly infallible formulation of that institution, which to its own discredit acted as if the Holy God could be captured in any human form.

Paul and the author of Ephesians seem to believe that Christianity can never be a closed system that can be mastered, and once mastered needs only to be defended. Christianity, rather, must be a journey marked by the courage to enter the unknown. For those persons who cannot believe in human certainty, Christianity will always be an incomprehensible mystery that beckons the willing pilgrim to search out its unlimited terrain with a lifetime of great expectations. To such a person Christianity will never offer the mirage of security. It will only offer the joy of exploration beyond all knowledge into the fullness of God. This understanding of Christianity will never affirm as final the institution that, historically, instead of leading that pilgrimage, organized itself to claim that it already possessed the power that the pilgrimage was designed only to explore. Those who are called to be pilgrim people will never legitimize the claims of any who assert that they alone have the right to articulate or to define with authority the truth of God for all time or "the Faith" for all Christians.

The vision that both Paul and the author of Ephesians offer us relativizes all claims to ultimate authority and dismisses all claims to infallibility. Those of us who have historically been the minority within the church who are constant pilgrims in the quest for truth claim with delight the legitimacy of this endeavor and of this position within Christianity. It is with joy that we recognize that our legitimization is found in the canon of scripture itself, which includes both Romans and Ephesians but which has been used to ban uncertainty from the family of believers. At this moment the church desperately needs this minority to come out into the open and to assume leadership.

Those who have lived within this minority throughout Christian history have inevitably been the expansive, creative, enriching spirits in every age. Most of these great spirits have lived uncomfortably within the Christian system. Many have fought losing battles against the church establishment; but when the smoke of battle cleared, their radical ideas, born out of freedom to search apart from authority, began to wind their way into the structures of the church until they appeared to be normal and were defended as orthodox in another generation against the new wave of questioning, uncomfortable voices.

In many ways those within this critical minority of Christian thinkers have always been my heroes. In the formative years of Christian history, I think of Origen, Valentinus, and some of the early gnostic writers. From the Middle Ages on, there was the young Aquinas who had his original writings indexed by the Vatican; there were the pre-Reformation voices of John Hus, John Wycliffe, and Meister Eckhart. In the nineteenth and twentieth centuries there were the liberal giants who struggled to keep Christianity alive in the face of incredible new intellectual breakthroughs: men like Friedrich Schleiermacher, Albrecht Ritschl, and Rudolf Otto. Finally, in our own day, there have been people in the Anglican Communion like James A. Pike in America and John A. T. Robinson in England, and, in the Roman Catholic Communion, like Teilhard de Chardin and Hans Küng who have bent the barriers of a narrow orthodoxy and in the process suffered the abuse of their ecclesiastical superiors. The defenders of the faith who seek to discredit these prophetic voices tend to be quickly forgotten, while the insights and memory of these gadflies enrich the church's life and continue to live for centuries.

I mention these few names not in any sense as an exhaustive list of those who have resisted the setting of petty boundaries around the infinite truth of God but only in order to call to mind the existence of this challenging, constant stream that has always been a part of Christianity, and to suggest that this is the source to which Christians today more and more will have to look for a way into tomorrow's world. Many who have populated this minority movement in history have loved the church with all their being, even the church that has a history of silencing its critics, killing its prophets, and condemning, at least in their lifetime, its most creative and original thinkers.

The exhilarating truth before the church as the twenty-first century dawns is that in this heretofore minority tradition seems to me to lie the only hope that Christianity has to live with integrity in the future. So, to the valiant who can live in the radical uncertainty of constant relativity, comes the call of Christ to lead this church into the future, to risk all our security and our faith in a daring venture to baptize our dynamic world.

1. William James, *The Varieties of Religious Experience* (The Gifford Lectures, 1901–1902), New York, a Mentor Book, 1958, p. 263.

2. Hans Küng, *Infallible? An Inquiry*, New York, Doubleday, 1971, p. 89.

3. Ibid., p. 90.

4. Elaine Pagels, *The Gnostic Gospels*, New York, Random House, 1979, pp. XIII-XXXVI.

5. Küng, pp. 112–113.

6. J. Langen, *Das Vatikanische Dogma von dem Universal-Episcopat*, Bonn, Germany, 1871–76, 4 vols. Vol. II, p. 123ff.

7. Küng, pp. 21–33.

8. Clearly there was not unanimity in the church in 1870, and the Old Catholic schism in Germany, Austria, Switzerland, and the Netherlands resulted.

9. Küng, p. 119.

10. Anglican-Roman Catholic International Commission, *The Final Report*, ed. H. R. McAdoo and Alan C. Clark, Cincinnati, Forward Movement Publications, 1982.

11. Dietrich Bonhoeffer, *Letters and Papers from Prison*, ed. Eberhard Bethge, trans. Reginald Fuller, New York, Macmillan, letter of April 30, 1944, p. 161.

Chapter 3

RUACH-DABAR: A NEW WAY
TO VIEW THE CHRIST

IF no ultimate and unchanging authority exists in Christianity today, then all theology is relativized and fluid. That conclusion means quite simply that the formulations of the major tenets of the Christian faith may have to be rethought and reframed, not so much because they are wrong but rather because their words are limited in their ability to convey ultimate truth for all time. On one level this should certainly not come as a surprise, for theology and doctrine are not ultimate: they only point to that which is ultimate. On the level of maintaining the power of the institutional church, however, it is an almost inadmissible threat. Orthodoxy is orthodoxy, and to deviate from orthodoxy is to be wrong, say the institutional defenders. The tacit assumption seems to be that orthodoxy is set in concrete and can never be altered. This has never been the historic reality, but it is the historic claim. Despite the claim, however, the fact remains that if the authority on which orthodoxy rests is in flux, then orthodoxy itself will be in flux and no fearful institutional defender will finally be able to steady the ship.

Time after time, on position after position, new study, new scholarship, and new insight have raised theological possibilities that the traditional position never contemplated. For example, traditional orthodoxy once proclaimed that belief in the "physical bodily resurrection" of Jesus was an essential part of the Christian faith. Yet recent

New Testament studies by such renowned scholars as Reginald Fuller[1] and Raymond E. Brown[2] have opened up almost breathtaking possibilities that make the old argument designed to define the "physical" resurrection both irrelevant and unimportant. Both of these New Testament professors take their stands deeply inside the Christian revelation, and few would want to banish their learning from the life of the church.

Contemporary studies in Pauline thought make it at least a viable possibility that Paul's understanding of Jesus' resurrection *not only* does *not* require a "physical" resurrection but actually finds the idea of a resuscitated corpse repugnant. Paul listed his experience of conversion as a resurrection appearance distinguished from the appearance to Cephas, James, and the apostles in no way except that it was last, "to one untimely born" (I Corinthians 15:5–8). There is a legitimate school of Pauline thought that maintains that for Paul only when Jesus shed the physical body could he assume the spiritual body. That spiritual body was clearly of a new order. Corruption and mortality had put on incorruption and immortality (I Corinthians 15:53). The old orthodoxy with its emphasis on "physical resurrection" has been seriously compromised by no less a person than Paul, yet few orthodox spokespersons are likely to pronounce Paul a heretic.

The choice before modern Christians is to ignore new scholarship in favor of sustaining traditional dogmatic understandings or to walk boldly into the insecurity of theological and doctrinal relativity. To do the former is to perpetuate ecclesiastical security for a few years longer at the price of losing intellectual integrity and guaranteeing the long-term demise of credibility. To do the latter is to accept the radical insecurity of this moment of enormous flux in the confidence that the living God who cannot ever be captured by creeds will finally lead us into truth.

I choose to follow that latter path and go forward in this chapter to the very central understanding of our faith. I do not pretend that I will write the new theology of Jesus. I only hope to offer a new angle of vision. It is not my desire to diminish in any way the saving truth of our Lord Christ. Rather I hope to point to that truth in a way that is both in touch with the experience of Christians through the ages and open to the realities of our day and our journey into the future.

At the heart of Christianity stands Jesus of Nazareth. From his life, his presence, and his power the whole Christian enterprise has sprung. We Christians call him a list of majestic titles: Christ, Lord, Savior, Redeemer, Son of God, Son of Man, Master. For hundreds of years in the early Christian era the major debate that shook the Christian world concerned the nature of this Jesus. Was he human? Was he divine? Was he both? Was he God? How could God be compromised by humanity? How could humanity be lifted into God? All theological debates have political consequences, and so did this battle over Christology. The side that won the right to define the precise nature of the Savior also won the right to speak authoritatively for him in all matters as the representative of Christ on earth. This ultimate prize and powerful goal shaped the debate as surely as did the theological issues at stake. The orthodox solution, known as the Chalcedonian formula, did not really end the debate; it only set some parameters and defined some concepts. Read these words written in A.D. 451:

> Therefore, following the holy fathers, we all with one accord teach men to acknowledge one and the same Son, our Lord Jesus Christ, at once complete in Godhead and complete in manhood, truly God and truly man, consisting also of a reasonable soul and body; of one substance (homoousios) with the Father as regards his Godhead, and at the same time of one substance with us as regards his manhood; like us in all respects, apart from sin; as regards his Godhead, begotten of the Father before the ages, but yet as regards his manhood begotten, for us men and for our salvation, of Mary the Virgin, the God-bearer (Theotokos); one and the same Christ, Son, Lord, Only-begotten, recognized in two natures, without confusion, without change, without division, without separation; the distinction of natures being in no way annulled by the union, but rather the characteristics of each nature being preserved and coming together to form one person and subsistence, not as parted or separated into two persons, but one and the same Son and Only-begotten God the Word, Lord Jesus Christ; even as the prophets from earliest times spoke of him, and our Lord Jesus Christ himself taught us, and the creed of the Fathers has handed down to us.[3]

Clearly the Chalcedonian authors utilized the categories of their day to proclaim their understanding; but those categories have proved to be less than eternal, as all human categories finally do. John Yungblut argues that at Chalcedon the "Christ myth" was frozen in time. Unless the "Christ myth" can be freed from this prison to continue to evolve and expand, it is doomed to pass away in time, he asserts.*

Contemporary New Testament scholarship has focused new insights here also. In the early years of the Christian era, when the nature of Christ was being debated, Matthew was assumed to be the first Gospel written. For this reason alone Matthew won the place of the opening book of the New Testament. At that time Mark was generally thought to be a shortened version of Matthew. That concept has been dismissed in contemporary New Testament circles, and Mark is now universally acknowledged to be the oldest Gospel. The implication of this simple fact is that for at least twenty years Mark was the only Gospel that the Christian church had. Mark alone would hardly undergird the traditional Chalcedonian formula on which the doctrine of the incarnation was based. Mark seemed rather to support what later came to be called adoptionism. He appeared to say that God elected Jesus to be the Messiah at his baptism and filled him with the Holy Spirit (Mark 1:1ff).

If that was a legitimate theological position for Mark, does it become heresy by virtue of the passage of time and the continuing political/ theological debate? Was Mark included in the New Testament only because there was a corrective for his inadequate Christology in some of the other writing? Have we yet embraced the fact that no book in what we now call the New Testament achieved the status and authority of holy scripture until well into the second century? If Mark's view was outside the boundaries of orthodox Christianity, what then happened to the salvation of those Christians who died before any other Gospel was written and who knew no other Christological understanding? The only creed abroad at this time among Christians appears to have been the ecstatic proclamation, "Jesus is Lord." How Jesus was Lord had not yet been addressed. In an age when ancient formulas are being opened in the light of new insights, producing inevitably a time of doctrinal relativity, these at least are interesting questions.

Building on this same idea, contemporary studies into the theological meanings reveal that the apostle Paul had a far closer connection with his Jewish roots and even with some forms of Jewish mysticism that were popular in the first century than has yet been recognized.[4] Paul quite obviously had a predisposition toward mysticism and set himself, as he says, to advance in Judaism "beyond many of my own

*From New Dimensions Lectures given by Dr. Yungblut in the Diocese of Newark in October 1982.

age among my people, so extremely zealous was I for the traditions of my fathers" (Galatians 1:14). He makes references to the knowledge of mysteries and secret lore (I Corinthians 13:2) and tells the Corinthians about his experience of being caught up to the third heaven and of hearing ineffable words which no human being is permitted to utter (II Corinthians 12:2–4). The rabbis distinguished seven heavens or degrees of initiation. When, according to the system popular among first-century Jews called Merkabah mysticism, one reached the fourth heaven, one was "with the Lord."[5] Paul, by entering the third heaven, was in ecstasy but not in total communion. In Philippians (1:23) he expressed a yearning to be "with Christ," which he said is far better. But his task was not yet complete, he concluded, for "to remain in the flesh is more necessary on your account" (Philippians 1:24).

Merkabah mysticism also was involved with certain religious practices that its critics thought were magic. "Putting on the name" of one's God or "clothing of the name of God" were among these practices. Echoes of this may be heard in Romans 13:14 where Paul exhorted his readers to "put on the Lord Jesus Christ" or his suggestion in Philippians 2, "at the name of Jesus every knee shall bow."

The issue here is not to prove this case, for my study has not been sufficient to create certainty for this possibility in my own mind; but it is to focus attention on what seems to be Paul's possible involvement in the movement of Jewish mysticism. This dimension of Paul's life would have been missed or ignored or completely misunderstood by early church fathers, who were both so separated from and so negative toward Judaism that they simply could not see or hear this aspect of Pauline thought. No one disputes today that Gentile mystery religions and especially Mithraism shaped the vocabulary of the Christological battles in the second, third, and fourth centuries. Paul tended to be interpreted retrospectively in the light of these Gentile mystery traditions. Now, however, we are discovering that it could have been Jewish mysticism, Jewish occultism, that was a primary force in shaping Paul's thought about Jesus. When one reads Paul illumined by new studies in Jewish mysticism, his Christology takes on a very different nuance that may well stretch the heretofore orthodox concepts beyond anything yet imagined.

From the perspective of these Jewish roots, Paul's Christ appears to be God's first creation, a theory that would place Paul in opposition to the trinitarian formula of the Athanasian creed. This creed proclaims what came to be called the orthodox Catholic position.

Whosoever will be saved, before all things it is necessary that he
hold the Catholic Faith,

Which Faith except everyone do keep whole and undefiled, without
doubt he shall perish everlastingly.

And the Catholic Faith is this: That we worship one God in Trinity,
and Trinity in Unity, neither confounding the Persons, nor
dividing the Substance.

For there is one Person of the Father, another of the Son, and
another of the Holy Ghost.

But the Godhead of the Father, of the Son, and of the Holy
Ghost, is all one, the Glory equal, the Majesty co-eternal.

Such as the Father is, such is the Son, and such is the Holy Ghost.

The Father uncreate, the Son uncreate, and the Holy Ghost
uncreate.

The Father incomprehensible, the Son incomprehensible, and the
Holy Ghost incomprehensible.

The Father eternal, the Son eternal, and the Holy Ghost eternal.

And yet they are not three eternals, but one eternal.

As also there are not three incomprehensibles, nor three uncreated,
but one uncreated, and one incomprehensible.

So likewise the Father is Almighty, the Son Almighty, and the Holy
Ghost Almighty.

And yet they are not three Almighties, but one Almighty.

So the Father is God, the Son is God, and the Holy Ghost is God.

And yet they are not three Gods, but one God.

So likewise the Father is Lord, the Son Lord, and the Holy Ghost
Lord.

And yet not three Lords, but one Lord.

For like as we are compelled by the Christian verity to
acknowledge every Person by himself to be both God and Lord,

So are we forbidden by the Catholic Religion, to say, There be
three Gods, or three Lords.

The Father is made of none, neither created, nor begotten.

The Son is of the Father alone, not made, nor created, but begotten.

The Holy Ghost is of the Father and of the Son, neither made, nor
created, nor begotten, but proceeding.

So there is one Father, not three Fathers; one Son, not three Sons;
one Holy Ghost, not three Holy Ghosts.

And in this Trinity none is afore, or after other; none is greater, or
less than another.

But the whole three Persons are co-eternal together and co-equal.

So that in all things, as is aforesaid, the Unity in Trinity and the
Trinity in Unity is to be worshipped.

He therefore that will be saved must thus think of the Trinity.

Furthermore, it is necessary to everlasting salvation that he also
believe rightly the Incarnation of our Lord Jesus Christ.

For the right Faith is, that we believe and confess, that our Lord
Jesus Christ, the Son of God, is God and Man.

God, of the Substance of the Father, begotten before the worlds;
and Man, of the Substance of his Mother, born in the world;

Perfect God and perfect Man, of a reasonable soul and human flesh
subsisting;

Equal to the Father, as touching his Godhead; and inferior to the
Father, as touching his Manhood.

Who although he be God and Man, yet he is not two, but one
Christ;

One, not by conversion of the Godhead into flesh, but by taking of
the Manhood into God;

One altogether; not by confusion of Substance, but by unity of
Person.

For as the reasonable soul and flesh is one man, so God and Man is
one Christ;

Who suffered for our salvation, descended into hell, rose again the
third day from the dead.

He ascended into heaven, he sitteth on the right hand of the
Father, God Almighty, from whence he shall come to judge the
quick and the dead.

At whose coming all men shall rise again with their bodies and
shall give account for their own words.

And they that have done good shall go into life everlasting; and
they that have done evil into everlasting fire.

This is the Catholic Faith, which except a man believe faithfully, he
cannot be saved.[6]

If the scholars who now see Paul's Christology from the perspective
of Jewish mysticism are correct, Paul's position would be vastly different
from the assertion of this creed. Paul would hold Christ to be both
heavenly and divine, but his Christ would nonetheless finally be a
creature who was distinguished from other creatures primarily in that
he did not grasp after equality with God, nor did he rebel against God.
Clearly it is not a virtue if one is God to refrain from grasping after an
equality one already possesses, yet Paul cites this as a virtue (Philippians 2:1–11). This perspective would interpret Paul to be asserting that
the archetypal being, God's first creation, God's first self-expression
who possessed, these proponents believe, a Godlike form, left the
spiritual realm and in Jesus became wholly human, only to return to
the realm of God in the resurrection/ascension.

Samuel Sandmel, the Jewish New Testament scholar, sketched this
possibility in a very sensitive way in his book *The Genius of Paul.* He

argued that incarnation means "to change into a body."[7] The Christ was the divine being, the heavenly messiah, the primal man, the figure Ezekiel may have been referring to in his vision (Ezekiel 1:26), who entered the world in the person of Jesus. But in the Jewish thought patterns, according to this viewpoint, that would mean that the divine spirit who became the Christ was the creation of God—divine, but nonetheless a creature; made, not begotten, but still sharing the very essence of God.

If Paul was, in fact, of this persuasion and in this tradition, then Christology, which he proclaimed rather than discussed, was not so much the perfect union of God and human life as it was the complete identification of the archetypal heavenly messiah with the earthly man Jesus. If that possibility can be proved to be the Pauline Christological position, was Paul orthodox? Was his view a true incarnation? Was it trinitarian? In an age of transition when all truth is perceived as relative, not absolute, can the church allow debate in this central citadel of its power and faith? I believe we must and inevitably we will. The author of I Timothy was certainly Pauline when he asserted, "There is one God and one intermediary between God and man" (I Timothy 2:5). Can such words finally be squared with the Chalcedonian formula? Do the ontological categories of the Greek mind lend themselves to the theological task of defining Christ in either biblical or in modern times? Was it possible in Hebrew thought forms to use the phrase "the God and Father of our Lord Jesus Christ" and still to mean that God the Father was somehow not primary or that God's indivisible unity could ever be compromised even by one perceived to be God's Son?

At stake here, Christians believe, is not just a creed or a doctrine but rather the trustworthiness of the Christian hope of salvation. Hence it is more than an academic discussion. God alone, Christians assert, can be the author of salvation, so if salvation is accomplished in Jesus of Nazareth, clearly God was, is, and must be present in him. To safeguard that truth was the compelling reason to formulate the doctrine of the Trinity. If salvation is not accomplished in Jesus of Nazareth, then the Christian enterprise will not long endure. Behind the words of the creed and the formulations of the theological doctrines of the church was a primary experience that cried out for the proper words to give it articulate and rational form.

When people met the Jesus of history, they were engaged by a power they believed to be beyond the human. The kingdom of God, they believed, was clearly breaking into human history through Jesus. Through him the brokenness of human life was healed, the guilt and sin of human life were forgiven, the anxiety of human life was embraced, the peace that passes all understanding was experienced, and the inevitability of human death was transcended. Through the life, death, resurrection, and glorification of Jesus a new hope was born. God and human life were brought together. Atonement was achieved. The function of Christ was all important; the being or nature of Christ was a later concern.

Dr. Sandmel asserted that in Paul's thought Christ is kept distinct from God.[8] For Paul, Christ was a preexistent divine being who became incarnate and in Jesus had a human career. Sandmel argued that in Paul's mind Christ was not interchangeable with God; he was subordinate to God. God acted in Christ for Paul. Christ did not act for God. Christ was not the mediator but the medium. He was the vessel of salvation. "God was in Christ reconciling the world to himself" (II Corinthians 5:19). For Sandmel, Paul did not deify Jesus so much as he humanized the divine Christ. He even seemed to dismiss a concern with the earthly Jesus. "We regard no one from a human point of view; even though we once regarded Christ from a human point of view, we regard him thus no longer. Therefore, if any one is in Christ, he is a new creation" (II Corinthians 5:16ff).

After the crucifixion, Sandmel argued, Jesus reverted to his spiritual status at the side of God. Ascension for Paul was thus more important than resurrection. Resurrection appearances for Paul seem to be more revelatory encounters with the ascended, glorified, divine, spiritual Christ than they were physical resuscitations of the human Jesus.

I share these insights from my study of Judaism, not to endorse them but to raise the possibility that continuing scholarship might find new angles of vision, new treasures that have escaped us for centuries in our own scriptures that will open up new possibilities for new truth even at the heart of what we tend to treat as the closed system of orthodoxy. My burden is not to adopt these insights but to allow them to rise, be discussed and debated, be corrected or dismissed, or integrated and embraced in a dynamic and ever-changing Christianity. Theology is not eternal. Only God is eternal, and no human mind or concept will ever capture that eternal reality.

Behind orthodoxy and behind theology is the experience of Christian people with the living God which cries out to be defined. The great minds of Christian history have sought to do just that. Inevitably they did it in the words, concepts, and thought forms available to their time. Whether these theologians succeeded for all time is relatively unimportant. What matters is that theology gave outer form to the inner meaning of the experience that enabled what they believed to be the essence of the Gospel to be communicated from one life to another for centuries. If those forms are no longer adequate, as many are discovering, our need is not to abandon the substance now hidden under the inadequate forms. It is rather to go back to the original experience of the Christian to seek to let that power create new forms, new words, that will carry more adequately the originating truth of the Gospel.

The faith crisis of so many modern people is, I believe, directly related to the inability of the classical Christian formulations of creeds and doctrines to carry the power and message they were originally created to carry. Ontological categories of humanity and divinity, heaven and earth, being and supreme being, nature and supernature are not the self-evident descriptions of reality that they were once thought to be.

The primary Christian theological tradition is built on Greek philosophical understandings. Augustine leaned on Plato, Aquinas leaned on Aristotle, and the two together shaped the language and content of most theological doctrine and debate in the Western church. For us today to call theological formulations based on Greek thought infallible or eternally true is to ask theology to be something it was never designed to be. This becomes particularly apparent if we discover that some traditional theological formulations are not even biblical. Yet to dismiss the experimental essence that these formulations are struggling to express, no matter how inadequately, is to be arrogant at best and to step outside the Christian experience at worst. Creeds and traditional doctrine must be taken seriously, not literally, and every generation has the task of searching beneath and behind the forms of faith for the essence of faith.

I believe that my salvation comes from Jesus who is the Christ through the Holy Spirit. Since for me God alone can be the author of salvation, Jesus has to be in some sense God for me. His life is the means through which God is experienced in history, and God cannot be diminished or compromised by the mediator. Hence the Christian's experience is that God and Jesus must in some sense be one: Jesus does for me what only God can do. I believe that the words of the creeds are a human attempt to capture this truth, and as such I give to the creeds both my assent and my loyalty. But I am open to new revelations that may cause the creeds to seem not nearly so precise or authoritative as they have seemed in the past; and I would encourage committed, inquisitive Christians to explore steadfastly the truth behind the creeds with every scholarly tool available to our generation. Because this search was a possibility for me, my life has been infinitely richer.

In one of my earlier books, *This Hebrew Lord*,[9] I acknowledged my debt to Judaism in the shaping of my own Christian faith. In seeking the roots out of which the one I call Lord has sprung, I have found a fresh perspective from which to confront Jesus and Christian theology. That exploration and study of Judaism has been for me a lifetime pilgrimage, and time and time again I find therein an insight that illumines my Christianity dramatically.

I have been fed by the likes of Martin Buber, Will Herberg, Joshua Heschel, and Maimonides. I have treasured my friendship with Jewish theologians like the late Samuel Sandmel and Jack Daniel Spiro, not because we have reached agreement on a common denominator but rather because each of us has stood with integrity inside his own system of belief and listened deeply to the insights of the other. I now wish to move another step further into the Jewish perspective, to look again at Jesus, my Jewish Savior and Christ, who is for me both Lord and in classical religious language "Son of God."

Biblical and rabbinic Judaism seem to me to escape much of the dualism that underlies the supernatural language of Western Christianity. Because that supernatural framework has been systematically dismantled by the continuing march of modern science so that it is today an increasingly inadequate vehicle to carry Christian truth, I find this Jewish perspective even more appealing. It is apparent that thought about Jesus needs a new starting point, not because the traditional approaches are wrong but because they no longer communicate adequately to this generation. My studies in Judaism have provided me with exactly that—not a new conclusion but a new point of departure. Enter the Hebrew mind for a moment without the theological presuppositions of the ages and explore briefly the Hebrew view of God and of life.

My doorway into this reality lies in two Hebrew words—*ruach* and *dabar*—words that seem to lose their power in translation. *Ruach* passed first into Greek as *pneuma* and *psyche* and then into English, where it became *spirit* or *soul*. *Dabar* was probably the Hebrew word lying behind the Greek word *logos* in the Fourth Gospel before it was rendered *word* in English.[10] At least *dabar* is the word used in Hebrew when "the word of God" becomes the medium of revelation or communication with human life.[11] To penetrate to the inner meaning of these words is for me to discover a new angle of vision, a new understanding of God that has not been eroded by the skepticism of our century.

Ruach in Hebrew is an incalculable, almost violent word. It means literally the sudden, scorching wind of the desert, always present but not always perceived. It means something closer to us than our breath, without which we could not live but of which we are not always aware. The Hebrews drew upon these associations to convey their understanding of Spirit—Holy Spirit, *ruach*, God. In primitive Hebrew history the *ruach* came on men and women like possession, creating a fullness of life that enabled them to escape their brokenness and to experience an ecstatic wholeness that literally overflowed their limits.[12] This *ruach* was the inspiration of the artisan, the superhuman strength of the hero, the extraordinary insight of the prophet. In no case did *ruach* miraculously create something that was not already there in creation; but in every case *ruach* heightened sensitivity, released potential, and enhanced being. *Ruach* was the force that set free the knowledge and power latent in creation and in every creature, enabling life to well up from the very depths of the unconscious in new and wondrous ways.

God to the Hebrew was primarily power—almighty, unrestricted power—calling creation into being. God was perceived as *ruach*, the all-pervading wind, blowing where God willed. Jesus said, "You hear the sound of it, but you do not know whence it comes or whither it goes" (John 3:8). *Ruach* for the Hebrew was like breath; it was intimate, deep, the sign of life itself. *Ruach* was unfathomable mystery and yet always in touch with something real that lay at the heart of creation and in the depth of human life. When a life responded to this Spirit, that life revealed its deepest identity, and the biblical affirmation that human life was created in the image of God received substance in human experience. This was the Hebrew view of *ruach*-spirit-God.

However, such a nonspecific, elusive sense of the presence of God was not enough for the Hebrews, and so they had another word that was sometimes coupled with *ruach*. That is the word *dabar*. *Ruach* was the all-pervasive presence of God; but wherever *ruach* erupted in a specific form or in a specific place, it became *dabar*, the Word of God. *Dabar* was a revelation of *ruach* in a unique, particular set of circumstances and for a specific purpose.

The *ruach* of God moved the prophets to speak, but the message they spoke was the *dabar*, the specific and unique Word of God to a specific, unique situation. When the Hebrews became sensitive to the nuances of *ruach*-Spirit, they immediately were confronted by a specific *dabar*-Word to which they had to respond. When the Hebrews encountered God, they met not only presence and power, but also form and direction. When they discerned the hand of God in all of creation, that was *ruach*; but when that hand pointed in a particular direction or wrote in a particular language, it was *dabar*. The *dabar* revealed that the eternal and universal *ruach* was in that moment creating and recreating life, expressing a new sensitivity, an expanded awareness, and a heightened potential.

From this Hebrew perspective, new dimensions of Jesus of Nazareth emerge for me. His Hebraic roots become specific. He is a complete human life in focus at a particular moment; yet the vision, depth, and fullness of God that men and women saw in him and experienced through him is also perceived. Human life—completely open, loving, and alive—becomes a transcendent channel through which ultimate being, life, and love can be known. Perfect humanity is not compromised. Divine presence incarnate, if you will, is not diminished.

In Jesus the universal and all-pervading *ruach* broke forth in a specific way, at a specific time, and in a specific place. So John the evangelist could say of him, "The Word became flesh and dwelt among us" (John 1:14). Jesus was the Word, the *dabar* of God.

But the God revealed by Jesus was not an alien, supernatural power who somehow invaded Jesus as if the supernatural realm of the divine was distinct from the natural realm of the human. The God met in Jesus was rather the creator-Spirit who universally pervaded and permeated the world as the life-giving *ruach* that spoke a specific word of salvation to the world through Jesus of Nazareth. Jesus was the complete *dabar* of God, God's saving word being specifically lived out. Hence the Gospels of Matthew and Luke could say Jesus was conceived, fathered if you will, by the Holy Spirit, the *ruach* (Matthew 1:18–25, Luke 1:26–38). And John could assert that when the *logos*, the *dabar* of God, took human form, Jesus was his name (John 1:14).

Jesus' life, Jesus' meaning originated in the mysterious breath and wind of God that is the animating vitality at the very heart of the universe. In Jesus the power of God touched and ignited the complete potential of this human life so that he could become a full, whole, complete expression of humanity and, as such, the perfect conduit through which the Holy God could act, be seen, and be experienced in saving fullness. Jesus' life was so open he could discern God's truth and God's meaning even in the broken, distorted lives that he confronted, and he could call them out of their brokenness into a new being, into the meaning and the power of his revelation. As a whole person, a perfect channel, a complete *dabar*, the *ruach* of God was made personal and available. When the powerful, mysterious, impersonal wind, the *ruach*, finds a complete manifestation in human life, God is perceived as intensely personal. As has often been noted, "It is not so much that Christ is Godlike that matters; it is rather that God is Christlike."[13]

When men and women experience Jesus of Nazareth, they discover that he can elicit from them the ecstatic cry, "My Lord and my God" (John 20:28). They are not speaking metaphysically; they are speaking existentially. When Jesus is no longer physically among them, they still find that the Christpower is present, the all-pervading *ruach* that erupts in many specific expressions of *dabar*. Standing within that experience, the whole creation looks different. "The Kingdom of God has come," we say. Miraculous language is adopted, supernatural concepts are employed, for nothing else seems big enough. But to the Hebrew mind, it is only the *ruach* erupting in a *dabar*, the Spirit finding a specific manifestation. The original Christian claim was not that something different happened in Jesus; rather, it was that the power which has been seen partially in countless lives, in thousands of moments, in endless events was now seen complete in wonder so startling that it seemed to be of another order of creation and could properly be understood only as God coming to earth in human form. "Jesus, you are THE Christ" is the confession at Caesarea Philippi (Mark 8:29).

I think traditional orthodoxy, when freed of its tendency toward literalization, has erred substantially at only one point: the suggestion that Jesus was different from other human lives "in kind." I think Jesus was different from other human lives only in degree, but it was such a great degree that men and women assumed it was a difference in kind and developed a mythology of a literalized virgin birth and supernatural manifestations to account for what they perceived in Jesus because their normal earthbound language seemed so inadequate to capture their experience.[14]

God is one, not many. The God who was in Jesus cannot be a different God from the God who is in me. Jesus was human. There is only one humanity; so if Jesus is human and I am human, that is a reality shared in common. He is the source of salvation, and I am a recipient of that gift. His humanity had to be a perfect channel for God, while mine remains a broken channel. His life was so full that his human needs did not distort his message. My life is so incomplete that only a tiny, twisted beam of God's presence manages occasionally to escape me and to bring life to another. That is a difference in degree, not kind. Orthodoxy's attempt to portray Jesus as different in kind, I believe, destroys the basic truth behind the doctrine of the incarnation, for it compromises Jesus' essential humanity. If my contention is correct, then the neat divisions in the doctrine of the Trinity become blurred the closer they come to God. These divisions in the Trinitarian definition have value only on the human side as they provide us with ways and means for sorting out our experience inside the Christian revelation. It is after all not the doctrine of the Trinity but the truth to which the doctrine points that is inviolable.

The Christpower, the *ruach* of God, clearly has moved throughout history and upon the face of the waters since the dawn of creation, so I affirm the concept of preexistence. The Christpower, the *ruach* of God, has clearly moved in the life of the church since the experience of Pentecost; so in the power of the Spirit I worship a living Christ. But the specific *dabar* who is the perfect channel by which all other manifestations of God's *ruach* must be judged was a single, time-rending human life named Jesus of Nazareth through whom a timeless salvation became available in human history.

When I look through Hebrew eyes at my Lord, I find new ways to understand this central affirmation of the Christian faith. God is the author of our salvation. Jesus was the historic means through which this salvation was and is accomplished. Clearly God was present uniquely and decisively in Jesus. But the power of God experienced in Jesus is timeless; and when lives meet this essence of Jesus, they still meet God. Jesus is experienced as eternally available, and so he is. Yet the heavy theological burden of the explanation of the ages is escaped, not because it is wrong but because it no longer bears the essence of the

Gospel to many. A look through Hebrew eyes gives me a new vantage point that I believe enables me to understand Jesus freshly and experience the God I worship through him directly.

Through Hebrew eyes God has become for me power that is deep within this world but always more than this world, a holy "other" who is known only when God ignites and illumines an answering spirit that is deep within us all. God is a light that lightens every man and woman, a Spirit that leads us into the truth of our own being, a Spirit who bears witness with our spirit to teach us who we are—sons and daughters of God who are free to cry, "Abba, Father!" Here we have our deepest selves awakened by love to perceive the depths of life and to find the springs of wonder and adoration revived within us. God is no longer for me an external supernatural miracle-working deity. I do not believe God was ever that to those Hebrews who understood the depth of their own tradition. God is, rather, that power of life that draws me out of myself, enables me to risk, to meet, to love, and to live in the honesty of human community. God opens me to the incredible and seemingly inexhaustible potential that is in every one of us and that only a brooding spirit, hovering over all creation, can finally call into life and into being.

My journey into the depths of my Christ thus becomes for me a journey beyond religion, beyond creeds, beyond language, even beyond rationality. It is a simultaneous journey into the meaning of life and into the heart of God.

Ruach—the all-pervasive presence of God. *Dabar*—the point where that presence erupts and is seen as specific. These are mere words, but beyond them, for me, there is a new vision of God and a new grasp on life.

1. Reginald Fuller, *The Formation of the Resurrection Narratives*, New York, Macmillan, 1981.

2. Raymond E. Brown, *The Virginal Conception and Bodily Resurrection of Jesus* Ramsey, N.J., Paulist Press, 1973, and *The Gospel According to John* (2 vols.), Garden City, N. Y., Doubleday, 1966-1970.

3. Taken from historical documents of the church, *Book of Common Prayer*, 1979, p. 864.

4. See W. D. Davies, *Paul and Rabbinic Judaism*, London, SPCK, 1948; Gershom G. Scholem, *Major Trends in Jewish Mysticism*, New York, Schocken Books, 1961; Samuel Sandmel, *The Genius of Paul*, New York, Farrar, Strauss & Cudahy, 1958.

5. Scholem, *Major Trends*, p. 78.

6. Taken from historical documents of the church, *Book of Common Prayer*, 1979, pp. 864–65.

7. Sandmel, *The Genius of Paul*, p. 67.

8. Ibid., p. 69ff.

9. John S. Spong, *This Hebrew Lord*, New York, Seabury, 1975.

10. A second Hebrew word, *memra*, could also be a part of this translation, though more frequently it is used as a word of command. (*Dabar* seems more likely in the context of the Fourth Gospel.)

11. G. F. Moore, *Judaism*, Cambridge, Harvard Univ. Press, 1927, pp. 417–18.

12. Ibid., p. 421.

13. I first met this phrase in a booklet entitled *The Bridge of the Cross*, Cincinnati, Forward Movement, 1982, written by James H. Gambrill. Since writing this, I have come to recognize that similar words have been used by William Sloane Coffin and Michael Ramsey.

14. This point of view is powerfully argued by John A. T. Robinson in *The Human Face of God*, Philadelphia, Westminster Press, 1973. It is also maintained by Quaker scholar John Yungblut in his book *Rediscovering Prayer*, New York, Seabury, 1972, p. 19ff.

Chapter 4

PRAYER: ANOTHER POINT
OF DEPARTURE

FOR as long as I can remember, I have filled unspecified speaking assignments by choosing the subject of prayer. This is not because I am an expert in prayer or in the spiritual life, but specifically because I am not satisfied with my life of prayer or my own spiritual pilgrimage. The pressures of these assignments force me to search more vigorously, to probe more deeply, to walk more steadfastly toward the reality of God.

When my turn came as a senior in seminary to deliver my one senior sermon to the assembled students and faculty, I deliberately chose for myself the subject of prayer and put my deepest probings out for debate, for ridicule, for correction. Needless to say, I received all three. When I was asked in Lynchburg, Virginia, to take over a series of Friday lectures during Lent that had become a community tradition, I forced myself once more to lecture on the subject of prayer. When, in Richmond, Virginia, I began to work on my first book, it came as no surprise that prayer was my chosen subject. *Honest Prayer* became the published title.

At every stage of my life prayer has attracted me magnetically. It attracts me still. It drives me to venture beyond my always unsatisfactory levels of spiritual development. I yearn to possess that pearl of great price, that singular sense of God's presence, but honesty compels me to admit that I do not; and so I continue to search, to probe, to explore this vital terrain. I have always had something akin to a love/

hate relationship with prayer. I am drawn to the experience and re-pelled by the content that seeks to interpret the experience.

There is an unquestioned reality to prayer in my life. I have tasted rare moments of transcendence. I have confronted the Eternal in what seemed to me to be the suspension of time. I have known depths of relationship where my being seemed to meet Ultimate Being, or, in the words of Martin Buber, where my "I" met a holy "Thou." I have been the recipient of power from the prayers of others that has called me beyond what surely must have been the limits of my ability. I believe I have been the agent through which power has entered another in healing, in transformation, in energy. I use these holy-sounding words unashamedly, but still I know that they are frail attempts to use a human vehicle called language to convey a meaning and an experience that in my life cannot adequately be captured by such rational sym-bols. The experience of prayer always transcends the description of prayer.

When most people talk to me about prayer, however, I often find it hard to listen. There is an embarrassment to so much of our prayer verbiage. Frequently people shift into a juvenile attitude when prayer is discussed. Both sick persons in hospitals and even chaplains tend to use the word "little" when talking about prayer. "Can we have a little prayer together?" one will ask. I wonder why prayer creates diminu-tive words, childlike phrases.

The more glib a person is about prayer, the less I want to pursue a conversation with that person on this subject. Many people act as if prayer is so tangential to life that they must self-consciously tack it onto other concerns. At the Lambeth Conference of Anglican Bishops in 1978, one bishop moved with monotonous regularity that a call to pray about the issue be added to almost every resolution.

I cannot appreciate those who seem to manifest the confidence of certain knowledge in the face of this ultimate mystery called prayer. Nor am I drawn to those who want to be folksy or intimate when they discuss or address the Holy. When I listen to the rational content of the words employed in prayer, what I frequently hear comes dangerously close to being manipulative, mechanical, imperialistic, or downright superstitious. Also, under the guise of prayer, frequently we lecture God and our audience with information that surely is not appropriate to the divine-human encounter.

Prayer groups in my experience have been far less than that for which they were billed. National conferences on prayer have always left me singularly unimpressed. Books on prayer are plentiful. I have read many of them in my constant search, but most of them assume and even advocate the lifestyle of a monastic community or a medieval social structure, neither of which has much appeal for me.

People who are known as specialists or experts in prayer appear to me to idealize a retreat from life as the starting place for the activity of prayer. I cannot start there and still be a child of the twentieth century. The subject of prayer is, in my experience, too profound to talk about with those who are the so-called "experts in prayer." So the first major problem for me in the life of prayer is the enormous gap between the experience of prayer and the explanation or rational understanding of that experience. Love/hate still operates. I love the experience; I hate the various explanations. They seem, at least to me, to be so shallow, so limited, so inept.

The more deeply I enter this subject, the more the problem of prayer fades for me into being the problem of God. I suspect that most modern people who no longer pray have ceased that activity because the God to whom they were praying became unbelievable. Most theologians expend enormous energy on the doctrine of God, but few relate that thought to the activity of prayer. Paul Tillich wrote almost nothing at all about prayer. In Hans Küng's recent volume, *Does God Exist?*, there are only six one-word references to prayer in 702 pages.

There are also numbers of books on prayer written by people who show little evidence of having done either serious or adequate theological study. The language of worship and prayer frequently lapses into the language of mythology and precritical concepts. Bad theology may sound good set to music, but in the cool light of rational thought, it poses huge problems of credibility.

God thought of as a divine king on a heavenly throne who must be praised by his subjects or supplicated by the penitent and powerless is frequently the object of our prayers. How often prayer portrays us as begging for mercy, asking a boon, being rewarded or punished according to the faithfulness of our prayers or the deeds of our lives. This activity forces me to confront a God I cannot worship, a God in whom I cannot believe. I suspect most educated citizens of the twentieth century cannot either. People argue that this is a caricature of God that no one takes seriously in theological circles. I agree, but I submit that the language of prayer has not escaped these images even if more sophisticated theology has. The church's corporate prayer carried by the momentum of the ages continues to use them, while private prayer among the Christian rank and file is in a state of advanced decay. When we open the subject to serious inquiry, the problems seem to multiply.

The ancient philosophical debate between the God who is "almighty" and the God who is "all loving" stumbles anew on the reality of the problem of evil, which has been raised with particular poignancy in Western civilization by the Holocaust. But to this ancient and still unanswered concern must be added at least three new obstacles to belief in God and in the experience of prayer.

First, there is the impact of the thought of Charles Darwin in the nineteenth century on our understanding of God. It is far more profound than the debate between the evolutionists and the creationists and the tension of Scopes-like trials. A post-Darwinian world no longer sees human life as different or apart from the biological process. We see and experience a continuing creation, not a finished one. The deity we perceive at work in this continuing creation is not the traditional deity. Evolution, for example, reveals extravagant waste in the rise and fall of species after species in seemingly endless biological experimentation. Extinction is the known fate of those species such as the dinosaur that cannot adjust to environmental reality.

Perhaps the species *Homo sapiens* may turn out to be no more eternal in the vast evolutionary process. No one could argue that the species *Homo sapiens* is necessary to the world, for clearly the world was here long before human life. We can thus envision a world continuing after the species *Homo sapiens* has become extinct. The splitting of the atom and the loosing of poisonous substances into our air and water make that possibility no longer just theoretical. These facts raise real questions about the God who is supposed to number the hairs of our head and has not let a single sparrow fall without God's knowledge. If, as biologists now contend, overspecialization spells doom for various species and if survival for some means extinction for others, then how can the author and sustainer of such a process be addressed in prayer? If the whole species can be destroyed, what value do we suppose resides in the individual member of that species? If we continue to pray, must we pretend that we can still be pre-Darwinians? These are real questions that are seldom faced by prayer manuals.

Secondly, we modern men and women are also post-Freudians, and

Freudian thought challenges traditional religious thinking at its very core. A God called Father, understood as the superparent who dispenses reward and punishment, who comforts us in pain, who encourages us when we are in despair, who watches over and protects us when we are in danger, and who can be implored to intervene to save us when in distress, is clearly a God who is suspect in a post-Freudian world. Yet much of the organized life of the church, including the activity of prayer and specifically the continued use of parental words for God and the clergy, seems designed to encourage continued pre-Freudian childlike dependency. It is as little children that we yearn for "a closer walk with God." How far removed is the proud child who says, "My Daddy can lick your Daddy," from the adult who sings to God, "How great Thou art"? How similar is the powerful childhood need to be loved and embraced by an accepting parent to that of the adult who sings to God, "Just as I am without one plea" and "O Lamb of God, I come"?

Beyond these illustrations, a post-Freudian world cannot pretend that our conscience is the voice of God as once we assumed. We see conscience rather as the social implantation of taboos and sanctions, of culturally-related values and guilt, none of which can finally be absolute. Our moral certainty sinks (perhaps has sunk) into a sea of relativity. Even our noble aspirations may, we suspect, rise out of our need for parental approval. All of these feelings and these ideas erode the fabric of the life of prayer. A post-Freudian world will not forever continue to pray using pre-Freudian understandings.

Thirdly, we are the sons and daughters of a scientific age. The world view that is assumed in our secular society seems to have in it no place for God, no way of understanding transcendence or divinity. It is a world in which mystery seems no longer to be ultimate. Life may not yet be controllable, but it is understandable. We may be the victims of what once was called "an act of God," but few of us today would attribute such things to the realm of the holy. Rather we chart hurricanes for weeks with high levels of predictability. We are able to give tornado advisories, to anticipate the crest level of a flood, to predict the probable progress of a disease, to anticipate the exact impact of a drug as well as the possible side effects, to portray in intimate detail on a television screen what used to be called "the heavens," to predict tides, eclipses, earthquakes, and volcanoes with remarkable accuracy. Not many years ago God was the working hypothesis in these and many other aspects of life. Today the modern world seems to have no further need for that hypothesis.

Johnny Carson, on his television show, once offered explanations for the strange winter weather patterns in Europe and for the drought-stricken parts of the southwestern United States in the summer. Atomic bomb testing in the atmosphere was suggested as a possible cause. The volcanic explosion of Mount St. Helens was also mentioned. Then Carson said that some theologians have warned that in these deviations from the normal weather patterns "God was trying to tell us something." The audience laughed. The God who once was believed to be the intimate cause of all natural phenomena has now become a humorous line in the repertoire of a late-night comedian. Clearly, the traditional patterns of prayer are affected by the secular scientific consciousness.

Gone from the modern consciousness are so many traditional religious ideas that once were dominant. Gone is the God up there or out there. Gone is the sense of human depravity, the literal fall from grace. Gone is the impossible command to be righteous even though fallen. Gone is the doctrine of man (as we used to call it) which produced the concept of the substitutionary atonement of Christ, that strange vision of a God whose justice had to be served by punishing his son with crucifixion instead of giving us our due in hell or purgatory. Gone is the God who plays favorites, answering some prayers and denying others. Gone is the God who predestines, who sits on a throne to judge, the capricious authority who withholds healing unless we ask for it, who desires to be exalted. All of these images are in a state of rigor mortis. They are largely dead in theological circles, if not yet among the rank and file of the church's life. Yet many of these images still adorn the language of prayer, making it easy to see why prayer is becoming a forgotten language in our day.

Many religious people sense these and numerous other modern pressures eating at the very soul of religious belief. Once again, the dual responses to a threatening, inbreaking, new religious consciousness are seen. Those who cannot rethink their religious symbols respond in rage against the people they call "secular humanists" who they feel must be responsible for the demise of religious certainty and conviction while they themselves, with fervent vigor, try to recapture the simple faith of yesterday. Others who seem aware of more than the church leadership recognizes simply drift away from church life, from prayer, from religious symbols. This latter group is the ever-ascending majority in our modern world. For us to pretend that a return to the religious nostalgia of the past is somehow the wave of the future is naive. Yesterday's religious security, I am convinced, will not last into very many tomorrows. For us to assume that the drift away from the church into secularity is temporary, or that this generation will return to God when they get older, hopelessly underestimates, I believe, the thought revolution that has engulfed our world.

In the modern world shaped by Darwin, Freud, and modern science, the traditional language of prayer and concepts of worship seem increasingly archaic. If prayer becomes, as some suspect it already has become, an activity with little meaning that is rooted in a tradition we no longer take seriously except in our nostalgic emotions, then surely it will not survive, no matter how desperately we seek artificially to respirate it.

When Christians, including many pastors and priests, find that they can no longer pray in private in any traditional sense, a credibility gap is created that tears at our meager supplies of internal integrity. In response to this threat we alternately leap anew into an imposed rigorous prayer discipline or we sink into the despair of spiritual emptiness. We learn time and again that the will cannot carry forward a disciplined practice that the reason cannot accept. Many members of the priestly and pastoral professions live here, including myself more often than I like to admit.

In the arena of prayer I do not need others to judge me as inadequate. I do that for myself quite well enough. The forms of prayer and the traditional religious definitions of God are increasingly empty for me. Yet the experience of God and the power of prayer remain realities I do not want ever to abandon.

When one reaches a point where he or she clings to God yet abandons much of the God content of the past, where he or she cannot give up prayer and yet cannot utilize the ancient traditions or formulas of prayer, there is only one open alternative. That person must walk forward into unknown and uncharted territory, boldly moving beyond the boundaries even of the religious institution in which he or she stands, abandoning the security of the patterns of the past in the dangerous quest for new meaning. I believe that there are many people who stand here but who are afraid to admit it. For their sake, to give them courage and the sense of not being alone, let me be candid and say this is where I am.

To walk into this great unknown is what, I am convinced, the Christian church must be willing to do if it expects to survive as a viable force in the twenty-first century. To leave the familiar for the unfamiliar is an act of courage. To admit that the problem is deeper than apostasy or inadequate understanding is to walk the razor's edge of faith. To rebuild worship and prayer on the basis of contemporary experience, to rethink ancient formulas so radically as to separate meaning from form—this is our task. It threatens our security, makes vulnerable our deepest integrity and our faith. It runs the terrifying risk of our having to admit that God is not real, that prayer is a hoax, that the church is founded on a lie. Yet unless that risk is taken, no approach will be radical enough to survive the certain death that seems to await organized religion and the experience of prayer. So into that abyss I invite you.

The first task in this quest, for me, is to move beyond the personal images of God. This is an extremely delicate step, for so deeply are these images attached to the way we think about God that, for many, God and the personal images are identical. Most people also seem to think that the only thing beyond a personal image for God is an impersonal image, and they are loath to replace the concept "Father" with "Fate," "Force," "Energy," or other impersonal concepts.

If personal becomes an adjective that attempts to describe or define the Holy God, then there is a clear danger of limiting God with our definition, as well as sinking into inadequate anthropomorphic and literalized thinking. If, however, personal is an adjective that is limited to describing the way we experience the Holy, then it is appropriate; for it is impossible for human life to escape its humanity when it describes anything, even that which is nonhuman.

So it is inaccurate to say that God is personal, but it is accurate to say that personal terms are the most effective way we can describe the way God has been and is experienced in our lives. Personal means God is capable of relating to me and I am capable of relating to God. But when I seek to understand God, I must move beyond the concepts of the personal. This does not mean moving toward the impersonal so much as toward the nonpersonal, moving beyond the limitations of the personal into the realms we might describe as transpersonal or metapersonal. When I found the courage to take this step, new doors began to open. Many in our world need to sense this new possibility, for the personal images traditionally applied to God by the church have become for them, as they have for me, increasingly offensive and unbelievable, creating more problems than they solve.

God as loving father collides with a world in which pain and inhumanity are rampant. A God perceived as sparing one suffering victim of disease in answer to prayer but not sparing another appears capricious at best, demonic at worst. A God who allows the death of a Dietrich Bonhoeffer or a John Fitzgerald Kennedy while failing to bring merciful release to lonely, depressed, semiconscious and all but forgotten dwellers in a nursing home seems difficult to comprehend. A God to whom southern Christians and northern Christians both prayed for victory in the American Civil War in sure and certain confidence of the righteousness of their cause is quickly dismissed by the cynic who suggests that God is on the side of the army with the biggest guns. The God who withholds rain in time of drought or who sends too much in time of flood is increasingly not a God in which modern people can believe.

These and many others are the personal images which force modern men and women to wonder if they can with integrity any longer believe in a personal God. The Christian church must hear this anguish and address it as a legitimate but fearful question which thinking Christians will inevitably ask.

There is a very real sense in which this personal God died as long ago as the time of Copernicus. In the pre-Copernican three-tier universe, God was an intimate, personal overlord of the universe who kept the world in his constant vision from above the sky. The concepts of nature/supernature fitted this world view. Theology defined God in these terms. Revelation was from the realm of the supernatural being made manifest in the natural order. The great Christological debates of early Christian history turned on the way in which the supernatural entered the natural without destroying the essence of either. The biblical accounts of miracles, from the plagues of Egypt to the Resurrection of Jesus, were interpreted in this framework. They were supernatural occurrences experienced in the natural order. When this framework became no longer believable, there was an attempt to give natural explanations for apparently supernatural phenomena. The concept of miracle was kept in the timing of the event. God was perceived as using the natural order as a vehicle for the revelation of God's power.

Prayer in its traditional form assumes this nature/supernature structure of reality. The human being who lives in the natural world prays to the God in the supernatural world to intervene to heal, protect, bless, watch over, or save. Many religious people would feel bereft if this framework were not part of their thinking process. They will say quite frankly that unless we believe that the supernatural God, in answer to their prayers, can and does intervene in the natural order to do what otherwise God might not do, then prayer has no meaning for them.

But we modern people look to the sky and no longer see a God ready to hear our prayers. We see the vast expanse of space. We see our tiny solar system that we have now explored as far as Saturn to be minuscule in the heavenly constellations. Our solar system is one of millions in our galaxy; but our galaxy is one of millions of galaxies. There appears to be no intimate Father or Mother God hovering above us, ready to hear our prayers and to intervene. There is rather a terrifying loneliness, a terrifying emptiness. It is easy to understand the frantic attempt to resurrect the religious comfort and security of a simpler world by those who do not want to comprehend this world. It is also easy to understand the departure from the church into an unbelieving skepticism by those who do seem to comprehend this world. This unbelieving skepticism lies behind the "pleasure principle" way of living that fuels the morality revolution. It lies behind the drug culture that seeks a way to escape this vision. It lies behind the noble stoicism that many believe to be the best alternative in a post-Christian age.

For years theology has allowed the supernatural view of God to fill in the gaps of human knowledge. With the rise of science and technology, this God has beat a slow but steady retreat from the center of life to the very periphery of our understanding of reality, until this traditional image of God has been rendered obsolete.

Today molecular biology, biochemistry, and biophysics no longer need the God hypothesis in those determinative turning points in the evolutionary process. Not even the emergence or beginning of life seems to require divine intervention. The ancient distinction between animate and inanimate things is considerably blurred by contemporary physics. God is admissible in scientific circles only at what might be called the alpha point, best framed by the question, "Why is there something and not nothing?" That is not a question to which a personal concept of God can provide a ready or simple answer.

Contemporary theology seems to recognize that the nature/supernature starting point for thinking about God is no longer credible. So in theological circles there has been a struggle to devise a way to make the experience of God that is the force behind theology find another rational expression which will be able to compete in the world of ideas and truth. There has been a loss of the sense of transcendence in theology which has corresponded to the loss of the category of the supernatural. When God could no longer be found up there or out there, theologians began to look for God within. In some ways theology was collapsed into anthropology. Transcendence was collapsed into immanence. When Tillich defined God as the Ground of All Being, he was being responsive to this thought. Process theology, liberation theology, the theology of hope, and certainly the critical rethinking of classical theology by such people as Hans Küng and Edward Schillebeeckx were and are attempts to think about God in a new way.

By almost common consent, the God who is discussed in these theological developments must be a God who is perceived not as spirit over against matter, supernature against nature, above, beyond, up there, out there, or in any other words that separate God from the world. God must be the source and ground of all that is being experienced and perceived in and through life, as the final depth of matter, as the source of all meaning, as the holy, mysterious, ultimate power never separated from life but never wholly contained in life, transcendent only in immanence, the infinite perceived in and through the finite, the absolute met in and through the relative. Professor Küng describes this God in these words: "God does not operate on the world from above or from outside but from within. God acts in the world process. God acts in, with, and among human beings and things. God is the source, the center, and the goal of the world process."[1]

Küng asserts that there is neither a world without God, which is the classical atheistic position, nor a God totally within the world, which is the pantheistic position. There is God and there is the world, inseparable but not identical. The personal images that could be used to address the God beyond the world fade in such a view into meaninglessness, and we wonder if and how we can think of God and be aware of God in our time with our understanding of reality.

When I step beyond personal images, I find that nonpersonal words are not as limiting as I once thought. Perhaps nonpersonal words properly understood can ultimately preserve the values we seek to locate in personal words better than the personal words can. Perhaps it has been the inability of human beings to think abstractly enough that has produced for us a God who is so human, so anthropomorphic as to be rendered by our age as unbelievable, a God who must be defended, or revived, or imposed, but who cannot finally be sustained. Perhaps the limitation in the human vocabulary between personal and nonpersonal needs to be obliterated and the idea expanded by such new constructs as metapersonal or transpersonal. At least I would like to explore this path for a moment to see where it leads.

There is something unique and rare about personhood and personality. Human beings have the capacity to transcend themselves, view themselves, objectify themselves, judge themselves. Human beings can scan the infinite spaces of the universe and raise questions about it. Human beings can be destroyed by natural phenomena and yet transcend those phenomena by knowing that they are being destroyed by them. Human beings can isolate a virus as infinitesimally small as the universe is vast. We can name it, seek to control it, be victimized by it, and even understand the victimization. Human personhood is a new frontier that must be explored.

John Yungblut, in his book *Rediscovering Prayer,* asserts that nothing like human personality exists outside of human life. Personality is a uniquely human experience, an indescribable mystery.[2] Teilhard de Chardin suggests that the way to God is found in the evolution of a higher and higher human consciousness, so that enhanced personhood for Teilhard must be akin to the reality of God.[3] If immanence has replaced transcendence and humanity has replaced divinity, then our task must be to explore the immanent and human more deeply than ever before to see if it is possible that immanence will finally break open into a new understanding of transcendence and humanity at its deepest heart and core will finally touch the divine.

Is it really possible that the experience of God, which is so universal in human life, and the reality of prayer, which is attested in every religious tradition, are manifestations of nothing? Can wish fulfillment or mindless superstition alone account for this powerful force? I doubt it. But I am also convinced that our traditional concepts for understanding the experience of God and the reality of prayer have been destroyed. To move beyond this destruction of our concepts and into the new reality of our experience is our task. To accomplish this is to move to the very edges of rationality and into what many believe to be the next frontier in human understanding, for it is to explore the human mind and delve into the human unconscious.

Psychic phenomena are not unknown to any of us, but our understanding of them is certainly incomplete. We are aware of many human transactions that seem to have no moral explanation but whose reality cannot be doubted. So we postulate a level of communication called extrasensory perception. Accounts of people who were restored to life after experiencing physical death read with remarkable similarity and cause many to probe more and more deeply into that mystery.[4] We have from time immemorial had some people who appeared to possess the gift of clairvoyance, who could communicate across the chasms of distance and space, sometimes the chasm of time, occasionally the chasm of death. Gene Bylinsky, in his book *Mood Control*, documents cases in which drugs created clairvoyance and broke through the blood/brain barrier to open new vistas of consciousness that mystics and occult enthusiasts have frequently talked about.[5] Obviously many of these moments cannot be verified or are not fully understood, and fraud is certainly a possibility. As the data pile up, however, we begin to wonder if we are not on the edge of discovering a new world that will revolutionize all our assumptions about human life.

Hypnotism seems to offer a doorway into that world. Hypnotism is an ancient art that continues to produce noncalculable results that appear to fit none of our existing categories. People under hypnosis have described in astonishing detail places they have never seen. They have spoken in languages they have never learned; they have talked of people they have never met. When the barrier between the conscious and the unconscious is transgressed, the mystery of human life deepens.

The practitioners of yoga give us new insight into this arena of human depth. The art of learning to breathe properly and of using relaxation to gain control over one's body has produced remarkable experiences. Under the direction of a well-trained guru, the experience of human transcendence has been achieved in so total a way as to cause people to believe they have in fact left their bodies, and they have seen things in dimensions for which there are no human words to provide description.

The great mystics of the past tell us of similar transcendent human moments of union with the source of life that produce a transformation of life, a heightened consciousness that allows barrier-free communication. Some psychiatrists, taking a clue from Carl Gustav Jung, talk today about the collective unconscious that seems to be a part of every human life.

On a far more mundane level, the experience of dreams has taught each of us that our unconscious is constantly active, that nothing we experience is ever lost. We are startled in our dreams to dredge up memories we have long since forgotten, people we have not seen or thought of in years. People have testified to receiving messages in their dreams that were verified the next day in their waking. I do not want to place my thesis on so fragile a basis, but I suspect that Freud has not written the last word on dreams.

I know that human consciousness can be expanded, that personhood can be enhanced. I know that one's being can grow, one's life can be opened, and that all barriers can be broken. I believe that all of these bits of data point to an interconnectedness of human life and of human consciousness. I perceive that the mystery of the human consciousness transcends the limitations of time, space, individuality, and finitude. Most of the great Eastern religions are trying to make sense of this reality.

Wandering out on this frontier necessitates saying an immediate cautionary word to possible misinterpretations. By examining dreams and hypnosis, I do not mean to suggest a view of God that is weird or arcane. I am not impressed by seances, fortune tellers, or mediums. I am drawn not to the occult as a place of revelation but to the expanded human consciousness as the place where, at least for me, the Holy is seen. God transcends our understanding and is wholly different, not because God acts in bizarre ways but because God perfects the virtues we admire and expands the human realization that we know to be so partial. We experience God as that infinite power who calls our humanity into ever-increasing expansiveness. God has an ultimate ability to lift us out of our limitations, to enable us to soar beyond compassion, to break the boundaries of what we mean by love. God is incapable of being defined in human categories because the experience of God breaks open and transcends all of those categories.

Once again personal words point to our experience of God. They distort when we leap from describing our experience to describing God. With this word of warning I feel an increasing need to explore these realms that the rational content of the West has tended to downgrade.

Daily I am more convinced that there is a way into that interconnectedness of life and consciousness that will allow us to commune both with the collective consciousness and with other persons who are part of the collective whole. I believe that someday we will be able to measure personal energy that travels on thought waves across vast distances to be experienced as love and as power by the recipient for whom they are intended. I find that only words like God are big enough for me to apply to the collective consciousness and that only words like Holy Spirit become the appropriate title to apply to the Divine Energy that links us both to the collective consciousness and to each other. Since this God is perceived when consciousness is expanded and personhood is enhanced, then God must participate in but cannot be limited by the concept of the ultimately personal. The moment that concept is defined, it limits rather than expands God. Nonpersonal, metapersonal, or transpersonal images seem to me more adequate, not less, when we reach the edges of our minds.

Consciousness and divine energy are nonpersonal words, but they are less limiting for me than personal words. Personal words become legitimate, I discover, when they describe the effect of God on me; they become illegitimate and distorting when we think they describe God. Expanded consciousness opens me to the Source of Life. The immanent God I meet deep within life finally calls me beyond the limits of life, and transcendence becomes real once more. Humanity driven deep enough touches power that is not human and can only be called divine.

So prayer drives me into life, into myself, into the connectedness of all human experience. I do not implore God to intervene, but I do open myself and others to the Divine Energy that is a force for wholeness and healing. I do commune with the Source of Life, which is called adoration. I am filled with a gratitude for life that demands thanksgiving. I do face myself openly as alienated from the person I can be, and that requires confession. I do feel embraced anew, and I interpret this as absolution and forgiveness. I do stay open to all that I can be, and in this all petition is subsumed. Finally, I do believe that all life is interconnected, that time and space are only categories of our limited consciousness, so intercession can and does transcend any barrier and releases energy, opens lives, changes reality. Thus the traditional kinds of prayer find new expression for me when I move beyond the limiting personalistic concepts of another age.

Expanded consciousness does not just happen. If God is to be discovered in the depths of life, then some disciplined way to enter the depths of life must be found. To accomplish this, the traditional rules of life and the various methods of meditation have been devised. They may or may not be helpful to us in our day, but some discipline, I am certain, must be developed. For me it has to involve the body as well as the mind or the spirit. Yoga shows us how vital the body is to the whole of life. A spiritual discipline that ignores the body will fail to move beyond pious words and empty clichés.

As a jogger, I know the experience of hyperventilation, the feelings of ecstasy, and the expansion of consciousness that come in jogging. Breathing exercises to force oxygen into every cell of the body are vital to yoga. St. Paul tells us that our bodies are "the temples of the Holy Spirit" (I Corinthians 6:19). Certainly our bodies must be part of the expansion of our being. If we are serious about the spiritual life, we must be serious about the care and nurture of our bodies. I find it difficult to reconcile concern about the development of one's spirituality with the continued abuse of one's body by improper diet, by the lack of exercise, by smoking, by excessive drinking, by drugs, or by obesity. Let me quickly say, however, that the observance of any of these physical disciplines is in no way a guarantee of heightened consciousness or spiritual development. Obese people who smoke heavily can be more loving than austere ascetics who devote hours to spiritual exercises; yet the development of spiritual wholeness does demand discipline that affects the body.

Let me illustrate this by sharing the direction in which my spiritual quest has carried me in recent years. I offer it not so much as a guide but as one possibility. Spiritual development for me includes regular exercise. My form is jogging. It has also resulted in the curtailment of alcohol save for an occasional glass of wine, the removal from my diet of all beef, pork, and lamb in favor of more vegetables, fruits, grains, fish, and fowl; and my present task is gradually to lower, perhaps even to eliminate, my coffee intake. These physical and dietary activities are coupled with time set aside for prayer, meditation, study of scripture, contemplation, concentrating, and a conscious opening of myself to my own depths and to the collective consciousness through which I believe God works and of which I believe I am a part.

I find that the kind of growth the prayer masters of the past spoke of is not now foreign to me. The scriptures open to new levels. I now see the wisdom in the Jewish practice not to allow God to be symbolized with any human construct, not to allow God's name even to be spoken. I see why a nonpersonal force like the desert wind became a

Jewish symbol for the life-giving Spirit. Yet individually and corporately these Jewish people believed themselves to be addressed, indeed called, by this unfathomable mystery, this nameless reality who seemed to work in them and through them. God to the Jews was so distant, so holy, so other; and yet God was nearer than hands and feet. The biblical concepts are so opposite and yet so true; for the infinite consciousness is participated in by the finite consciousness, and the absolute spirit flows into and is engaged by the human spirit. Body and soul are inseparable. So are worship and life. So are God and God's world.

There is God in me and God beyond me, so prayer is my depth calling to the depth of God. I think Paul understood this when he stated that the Spirit searches all things, even the deep things of God (I Corinthians 2:10). The Trinity opens to me anew, not as a formula to test orthodoxy, but as a human attempt to interpret the experience of the Holy. When we speak of the Creator, we are saying God is more than the world. It is a claim of transcendence. When we speak of the Spirit, we are saying God cannot be separated from the world. It is a claim of immanence. And when we speak of Christ, we are asserting that transcendence and immanence are connected, that there is a point where the two come together perfectly, a channel through which transcendence and immanence flow as one, a determinative moment in which the God within transcends all limitations, breaks all barriers, and is experienced in fullness. There is God in me and God beyond me, and there is one life in which I can perceive the two perfectly at one, so that life becomes for me a perfect picture of God and a perfect picture of humanity. Experience confirms the truth to which the words of the Christological debates were addressed.

I am convinced that all life is bound together in a way none of us has yet imagined. I believe that there is a world of the Spirit that we all share in and in which our prayers for each other do open that other to a deeper experience of energy, power, God; and that that opening does free, expand, and heal.

Increased self-knowledge for me is the ultimate gateway to the knowledge of God. Perhaps sensitivity training, community building, process consciousness, Zen, meditation, transcendentalism, transactional analysis, yoga, and dream analysis are all doorways into a reality which the mystics have always said was there and which most of us, blinded by our shallow busyness, could never imagine. I am certain that there is enormous power that can be tapped and harnessed by some activity like prayer that people have always experienced but never understood. I am even willing to admit that the use of a mantra or the name of Jesus pronounced over and over again does serve to expand the limits of consciousness until other voices than our own can be heard, power can be released and received, and wholeness of both body and mind can be restored.

If these possibilities on the edges of life do begin to come into a clearer focus, then so much of both the Bible and the human activity of prayer and worship can be seen with new eyes. The experience which we cannot deny will be validated, and the explanations by which we sought to speak of that experience, using words shaped by the only language and concepts we had to employ, will be transformed.

I believe we are on the edge of such a breakthrough, and we must walk forward boldly out to this frontier, offering for transformation all of our symbols, our limited understandings, our creeds, our Bibles, our theologies, in the conviction that our symbols point to a truth that we see through a glass darkly but someday will see face to face.

I walk this razor's edge delicately. I pray, I meditate, I claim little; I am unimpressed with the claims of those who claim much. I hope that I am open to what lies before us. Even more I hope this church of ours will be open to the truth of God within us even when that truth calls into question the certainty on which our institutional power in the past has been based.

1. Hans Küng, *On Being a Christian*, Garden City, N. Y., Doubleday, 1976.

2. John Yungblut, *Rediscovering Prayer*, New York, Seabury, 1972. See especially Chapter 2.

3. Teilhard de Chardin, *The Phenomenon of Man*, New York, Harper & Row, 1959. The entire argument of the book makes this point.

4. Dr. Kenneth Ring of the Department of Psychology of the University of Connecticut devotes his complete academic study to this phenomenon.

5. Gene Bylinsky, *Mood Control*, New York, Scribner's Sons, 1978.

Section II

MOVING BEYOND TRADITIONAL SEXUAL STEREOTYPES

Chapter 5

THE SECOND FRONTIER:
SEXUAL STEREOTYPES
ARE NOT ETERNAL

THE change that has occured in Western civilization in the area of sexual understanding and sexual behavior is recognized by everyone. Traditionalists give evidence of this in their condemnation of the sexual behavior of today's generation as simply immoral. Those who claim to be modern and free reveal their knowledge of this tide of change when they refer to the sexual attitudes of the past as dated, oppressive irrelevancies. Those who would identify with neither extreme nonetheless make it clear that they recognize that new standards are emerging which do not fit the definitions of the past.

Among women particularly, the old stereotypes are being set aside, as each generation embraces new possibilities of which the previous generation could not conceive. My mother is today in her seventies. Growing up in a small southern community, it did not occur to her that there was any acceptable role open to her other than becoming a wife and a mother. To keep a house, to give birth and to tend the children was the time-honored and unquestioned female vocation. Indeed, it was a status role, even a success symbol, for the lower-class women who did not marry well might have to seek employment sewing, or taking in someone's washing and ironing, or even finding work in the textile mills and industrial complexes that were emerging and which did employ some women around the turn of the century. Very few women in my mother's generation attended college; and when they did, it was more like a finishing school with the emphasis on music, literature, and social graces.

One generation later, the pattern was changing, but the corner had not been fully turned. My wife is a college graduate, a zoology major; and an increasing percentage of women in her generation expected to and did go to college. Nonetheless, most of them still anticipated the domestic homemaker/mother role to be their ultimate destiny. High levels of frustration were experienced by women in this age group; for their education was in many instances equal to their husbands', but opportunities to use that education were still quite limited. A particularly difficult time came in the mid-years when the children departed for college; the nest became empty, and so did the life of many a woman. Many women thought themselves too old or too untrained to enter the job market. The role of volunteer or auxiliary to an institution seemed increasingly empty. They also discovered that the homemaker/mother role was frequently denigrated in the society at large, and they felt themselves to be denigrated as human beings in the process. This generation did not experience the same affirmation in the traditional role that their mothers had known, and they tended to feel in most instances that it was too late to adopt a new role. They were the generation of transition.

My daughters grew up assuming that college was as natural an expectation for their lives as sleep was for the night. They also thought in terms of a broad spectrum of careers. Marriage was not ruled out, but marriage no longer seemed to mean automatically accepting the homemaker/mother role. They talked of trade-offs between career and family. The prospective husband would have to accept their professional aspirations, or he would not be a prospective husband. They experienced firsthand the pain of breaking barriers, the insensitivity of a male-dominated business world. One of our daughters is moving up the executive ladder in a major bank, one is a lawyer, one is a scientist whose Ph.D. in physics will open the doors to a life of research. Their grandmother looks at their lives with disbelief but with pride.

These new opportunities arise only because the whole social order is in flux. Many assumptions about both males and females that once were considered self-evident and eternal are now clearly in transition. Stereotypes, role expectations, sexual mores, and moral standards all reveal patterns of rapid change. Some are being adjusted to new

realities, while others are simply being abandoned as no longer operative. In practice, if not yet in the stated and publicly accepted moral
principles, marriage is no longer acknowledged as the only relationship in which sex is to be shared. Marriage itself has seen its sacredness
eroded. Other less eternal patterns of living together are increasing.
Divorce in the United States is nearing the one-out-of-every-two-mar-
riages level. Marital fidelity is not the norm it once was proclaimed to
be, and today it is not just the male who has his lover, his mistress, or
his prostitute on the side. A mobile society has freed both the male and
the female to pursue countless opportunities where the once-guarded
forbidden fruit of sexual desire is now clearly accessible.

As the traditional sexual convictions fall, the social superstructures
that were designed to support those convictions will also inevitably
fall. Today they are tottering before our eyes. When they fall, the crash
will carry with it the myths, the assigned sexual roles, and the stereotypes by which men and women have defined and understood each
other for thousands of years. It will not be a comfortable time.

Beyond the changes in heterosexual patterns, there have also been
new insights and new understandings from the various life sciences
regarding homosexually oriented people. These have resulted in a new
acceptance and a new freedom for this frequently oppressed minority.
The homosexual person is today far more capable of pursuing his or
her lifestyle openly; and in many parts of our world homosexuality is
no longer considered either a sickness to be pitied or an evil to be
expunged. It is rather looked upon as a normal minority variation in
the spectrum of human sexuality. Obviously that is not universal, but
a new acceptance is increasing. A subliminal fear still exists in many
which is real and virulent and which can be fanned by demagogues,
but the tide seems to be flowing in a more open direction. With as
many as 10 percent of the population believed to be homosexual in
thought, desire, and action,[1] there is hardly a family that does not
claim, at least in its larger constellation, one member who is gay.

In the midst of this changing world of sexual consciousness, the
Christian church seeks to live. In this sexual revolution Christianity
will have a deep stake. Many of the sexual definitions in Western
civilization have emanated from or been shaped by the Christian church.
Moreover, the church has built into its very structure, its liturgy, and
its theology, a deep commitment to the sexual stereotypes of the past.
As these stereotypes fall or come into serious dispute, much of what
we recognize as Christianity will also fall or come into serious dispute.

For these reasons the sexual revolution that is rampant today will affect the church dramatically. It will pose, I believe, the most serious threat in history to the power of the institutional church. Whenever power is threatened, fear and anxiety are loosed, and the traditional patterns of the past will be defended with an intense emotion. We should expect to witness religious backlash movements that attempt in the name of a masculine God to return women to the home or to the veil. We should not be surprised to find church hierarchies to be the most unyielding, the most resistant, and the most vocal in opposition to change. Anything that removes human sexuality from the masculine control systems of the past or that seems to allow women to assert and to claim power over their own bodies will encounter a volatile emotional religious negativity.

In the sexual debate that has raged inside the institutional church as these issues have risen to consciousness, I am convinced that the church conservatives have understood and appreciated more profoundly the dimensions of this revolution than have the church liberals. The liberals tend to see the women's movement, for example, primarily in terms of justice and human rights. That is too shallow a judgment in my view. The conservatives on the other hand see the women's movement as a fundamental break with history and tradition. It is for them an unacceptable challenge to their understanding of life itself. At its deepest level the women's movement is all of those things; so while liberals glibly welcome the changes as one more opportunity to march to the sounds of freedom songs, conservatives greet this threat with anguish and hardline opposition to the point of schism. They recognize, as the liberals seem not to do, that much of what we Christians think of as crucial to the life of the church will not survive the revolution in sexual consciousness that is upon us. They are correct.

But the women's movement, like all revolutions, is not prone to ask for permission before continuing its inevitable process. That movement is not likely to be weakened or diminished by church opposition. Rather history will reveal, I suspect, that it will be the church that was weakened and diminished by its opposition to the relentless, inbreaking waves of the future.

Indeed I fear that the church itself is in danger of being swept aside if in our understanding of sexuality we Christians are not able to separate fear from fact, tradition from truth, ancient taboo from rational behavior. Many lives escaped the impact of even so great a historic movement as the Reformation in the sixteenth century. Theological disputation, even in a believing age, is not, however, at the core of every person's identity. Sexuality is. Consequently, there will be no hiding place for anyone in this revolution. The trickle-down theory may be a bad economic understanding, but we must recognize that it works in the area of dominant ideas and heightened consciousness. Recall that Sigmund Freud died in 1939, less than five decades ago; yet there is no life in Western civilization today that has not felt the impact of Freudian thought, even though that life may never have read a single word written by this pivotal thinker. The revolution in sexual awareness is having a similar impact.

Because I am convinced that the breaking of the antiquated, outdated stereotypes is inevitable, I believe that the church, by clinging to them, runs the terrifying risk today of becoming a discredited institution. I do not relish the vision of the church of the twenty-first century reduced to a museum piece that could not escape its sexual stereotypical thinking of the past, and therefore sank, with all of its treasures being lost, after breaking apart on the sandbar of a changing sexual consciousness.

The church's hope, I believe, lies in the possibility that a saving remnant within its life can face the new realities and raise a public voice in self-criticism. That remnant will be a radical, an uncomfortable, and an unpopular voice in traditional circles. For the church to be purged of its ancient sexist prejudices ultimately will require that many theological formulas, liturgical practices, and the familiar symbols of our Christian heritage undergo serious questioning and essential changes. There is in my mind no alternative except oblivion. We Christians, both Catholic and Protestant, who are debating birth control, abortion, celibacy, women in the priesthood, divorce, and other issues that emerge from our premodern understanding of human sexuality must soon move into a newer world where fresh breezes will blow where they have never blown before. Definitions will be altered, consciousness will be raised, psychological fears will be probed and loosed. As old orders are threatened, disaffection may be serious, and a new sexual awareness and sensitivity will be achieved.

The Christians who are able to do so must, as the saving remnant, welcome this moment of history, embrace it, and hold it until the larger body can be assimilated into the emerging new synthesis.

My task first is to examine the development of sexual stereotypes

and, most especially, the role of the church in shaping those understandings. I want to inquire into the cultural and evolutionary adaptations that have perhaps too uncritically been assumed to be the will
of God. That will force us to see the church, I believe, as a major guilty
party in the long historical oppression of women.

I am aware that to study or to speak about human sexuality, sexual
stereotypes, or sexual oppression is fraught with peril. This is a subjective, volatile, and emotional topic. Like Erasmus, I recognize that it is
never popular to expose or to challenge the comfortable and ancient
myths of the majority. I approach this task with a normal, anxious fear
because I know many will not understand. However, the task of freeing Christianity from its historic sexual prejudices simply is more compelling than that fear. For me, there is no responsible alternative.

Anyone who attempts to write on this subject may also be aware that
he or she cannot presume to speak with sexual objectivity. I cannot
escape my own sexual identity, so let me state the obvious. I am a male.
I am a male with a heterosexual orientation, though I believe that is
far too limiting a concept to encompass the whole of anyone's sexuality. How secure I am in either my male identity or my heterosexual
nature, I will never be able to assess accurately, but I do know that my
maleness, my heterosexual orientation, and my level of sexual security
will inevitably find expression in my understandings, my insights, and
my conclusions. I am personally convinced that the sexual spectrum
is broad and that no person is fully masculine or feminine. Most aca-
demically recognized assessments of human psychology assert that
there is in each of us a potential emotional bisexuality that opens us
at the very least to the possibility of a vicarious identification with and
understanding of one another.[2] That potentiality has down through the
years been distorted time and again by prejudice, ignorance, superstition, and anxiety. Inevitably we oppress what we do not understand,
and we fear what we cannot control.

When we talk about sexuality, we invoke into the public arena our
most personal selves. Here as in no other human encounter there is no
rightful place for rejection or condemnation. As Christians, we affirm
that persons are of infinite value, whether they be male or female and
regardless of their sexual orientation. We need to explore this terrain
openly; and if we discover that the church, a dominant institution in
shaping values, is possessed of a distorted view of sexuality that en-
slaves both men and women, then in the name of the God of sexual

wholeness that institution must be confronted powerfully and critically. If in doing so with passion and conviction I descend to the presumption of judgment, I will have failed in my intention even if I succeed in my task. I hope to speak tenderly, as the noted Quaker theologian John Yungblut says, as "one solitude calling to another."[3] Yet I want to expose, examine, and open for all to see the sexism in the church that is deeper, I suspect, than any of us have yet supposed. I do this not to undermine or weaken the church but to encourage and enable the church to relinquish its prejudice that has for so long lain beneath the conscious level. I want the church to be healed of that oppressive tradition which has distorted both men and women through our words and our deeds over many centuries.

1. This is the average figure quoted today in medical and psychological circles. Dr. Kinsey suggests a much higher figure.

2. From private correspondence with Dr. James E. Baxter, a practicing psychiatrist in New York City.

3. John Yungblut, *Sex and the Human Psyche*, Pendle Hill Pamphlet #203, p. 7.

Chapter 6

MISOGYNY: A PATTERN
AS ANCIENT AS LIFE

To understand our traditional sexual attitudes, we need to look at data from many sources. First, there are some obvious psychological facts. Second, there are biological and evolutionary considerations that need to be explored. Third, there are attitudes shaped by both history and prehistory that need to be understood. This task will require the help of anthropologists who can lead us into that gray area before recorded history where many of our sexual attitudes and customs had their genesis. Then we need to examine how these attitudes were incorporated into Christianity. To some degree, Christianity transformed sexual prejudices. To some degree, these prejudices badly distorted Christianity.

We begin this search for sexual understanding by acknowledging some basic physiological realities that exist in men and women that are both sex-related and culturally conditioned. Beyond the obvious primary differences of genitalia and breast development, there are also hormonal and structural differences.

Puberty creates in male bodies a hormone, testosterone, which adds bulk to muscles, while puberty brings to the female an increase in body fat that not only shapes her figure but also in some ways actually curtails her physical capacities. The body of the average grown male, for example, contains 40 percent muscle and 15 percent fat, while the body of the average grown female contains 23 percent muscle and 25 percent fat. Men also have larger hearts, larger lungs, and more hemoglobin in their blood, which enables them to pump oxygen to their muscles more efficiently than women. The male's wider shoulders and longer arms increase his leverage, making him able to move more rapidly than the female. To cite the physiological differences is easy. To interpret or explain the origin of these differences is quite complex and speculative. I am not an anthropologist. My knowledge of these subjects is secondhand, not primary. I present here, however, a possible interpretation of this data, not ruled out by experts but also not universally agreed to. From my study, however, I find merit in these possibilities.

As we begin to embrace the Darwinian principles of evolution, the physiological differences between men and women may be less related to the being and definition of a male or a female than they are to the evolutionary quest for survival. Indeed the biological sexual differences may have produced the organized structure of human life which in turn produced the evolutionary changes that we historically have tended to think of as given or natural to the sexes. When we think only in terms of reproduction, a case could be made that the woman is far more valuable than the man in the struggle to survive. In the course of a woman's life she will produce only about four hundred mature egg cells or ova, of which a maximum of about twenty can be converted into human fetuses. The demands on the ancient woman for the maintenance of life from conception through birth and nursing were enormous and caused her to be thought of as indispensable.

The male on the other hand produces approximately 100 million spermatazoa with each ejaculation. One male could theoretically fertilize countless numbers of females in a lifetime and thus father literally thousands of offspring. This would suggest that any single male could be easily replaced, for his relative value in the struggle for human survival was not nearly so important as the female's. It was perhaps for this biological reason that the risky business of hunting and fighting may have fallen to the dispensable male, while the more protected, less venturesome role of gathering, tending, and nurturing fell to the more indispensable female. In time the faster, stronger, larger males would survive in the hunt or in the wars and would therefore be available to change the structure of the human evolutionary process, for the smaller, less well-endowed males would not survive to reproduce their inadequate characteristics. At the same time the developing female characteristics might tend to evolve in favor of those who were the successful childbearers. The wider pelvis is an asset to childbearing. The mother's ability to produce adequate milk was almost the only hope her offspring had for survival. It is obviously dangerous to speculate about the evolutionary adjustments in the prehistory of the human race, but only by such speculations can we probe that unknown realm.

If this specialization along sexual lines did transpire, then perhaps other things that we tend to think of as sexual differences might also have developed. Aggression served the hunter/warrior well but would not have been easily adaptable to the domestic community where the gifts that we have come to think of as intuitive—feeling, touching, speaking, relating, smiling—would help the home front to function smoothly and thus to survive. At the same time the adventuresome or aggressive woman who wandered away from the protective community would not live to reproduce.

These possibilities, advanced by some anthropologists, would tend to put survival premiums on aggression in the male and on passive dependency in the female to the point that these characteristics might in time come to be thought of as sex-related, emotional, given facts of life rooted in the created order and therefore not open to change. The male's supposed superior ability at problem-solving and math and the female's supposed superior ability at sensitivity, intuition, and the arts may well prove to be adaptive survival skills in the evolutionary process, rather than sex-related "givens" as we have heretofore been led to believe. Since evolution is a never-ceasing process, when the need for adaptive changes disappears, in time the adaptations will also fade. Many of the male-female characteristics that we observe and even measure today may not be noticeable in another thousand years.

Still on the level of sexual differences, a male's aggression may also be related in part to his desire to reproduce himself. The number of males and females at birth is essentially equal, but many more women than men may seem to be necessary to keep the human race alive. A pregnant woman is removed from the reproductive process for nine months, but a male is always capable of impregnating. If a male can court and win one woman after another, some males will be big winners and some big losers. So, historically, it would appear that it has paid the male to be aggressive, hasty, fickle, and undiscriminating. The much more valuable female, however, historically would appear to have found it more profitable to be coy, to hold back until she could identify the most successful male with whom she could produce presumably the best offspring. She might also seek to select a mate who would stay with her after insemination and share the child-rearing responsibilities.

Since more women than men survived into adulthood, it is not surprising to learn that the large majority of human societies have allowed multiple wives, while only about one percent have historically allowed multiple husbands. In those few societies that practice monogamy, the prevalence of divorce and extramarital sexual relationships means that the commitment to monogamy has been significantly compromised.[1]

These factors mean that historically men have tended to see women as a prize to be won, so they pursue and acquire. If women were treated as the prize, they had to be protected and bartered. This attitude may have contributed to the creation of what we call the double standard of sexual morality. Sons who are sexually aggressive are said to be "sowing wild oats," but daughters who have been sexually active are said to be "ruined" or "cheapened." Yet there is always present in the easily replaceable male the fear that he will be rejected by the female. This fear feeds and distorts the relationship between the sexes and may have made domination and control by the physically stronger male psychologically necessary as part of his defense system.

There is another universal experience affecting the psychology of male-female relationships that needs to be lifted into our consciousness. Every person, male and female, starts life as a helpless infant; but overwhelmingly, because of both biology and sexual role typecasting, the person who traditionally has been the nurturing adult responsible for the life of that infant has been a woman. Thus every male has a memory, perhaps buried in the unconscious but still a memory, of being helplessly dependent on a woman. For the male, conditioned by biology and trained by the society to be aggressive, the memory of intense, helpless dependence on a woman would appear to be more unacceptable than it is for the female. Dependency would therefore set up for the male problems that the female might not have to face or at least might not have to face with the same intensity.

These factors, however, are not sufficient to account for the sometimes unconscious and sometimes overt hostility that historically has marked the relationship between the sexes. Women seem to exert a strange power over men that makes the battle of the sexes appear to be the most ancient game of *Homo sapiens*. It is my thesis that this battle reveals that the male seems motivated to go to enormous lengths to make his life secure from the female. To accomplish this, he has used his increased physical strength not just to gain food or defeat the enemy but to dominate the woman, sometimes with cruel authority. Rather than accept as of equal value the contribution the woman has made to the social development of the tribe or community, the male has created a derogatory stereotype of weakness and domestic docility that the female has been compelled to accept as the ideal in feminine behavior. He has originated role-enforcing legends in which the hero is always a male, a Prince Charming who rescues the weak, swooning damsel in distress. He has expressed his unconscious fear of the female in the strange image of a witch who is always an evil woman holding firmly to an erect phallic symbol significantly placed between her legs and only thinly disguised as a broom. He has built a civilization based on the dominance of the male and his supposed innate superiority in every area. He has covered his hostility toward women with emotion-controlling female ideals which he has identified with the will of a masculine God, so that to rebel against these ideals was thought to be nothing less than a sin against this father God. Why has the male been so purposefully intent throughout history to control the female?

To begin to form an answer to this question, we must look beneath what has thus far been stated, for these possibilities alone, even if fully documented and agreed to by widely accepted scholarship, still cannot account for the pervasiveness of these feelings. Fortunately, to aid our quest, we are able to turn to that wondrous repository wherein the understandings and insights of our ancient ancestors are kept. I refer to the area of cultural taboos, for here the origins of so many of our attitudes have been carefully but not consciously preserved.

The taboos that surround women in primitive societies are quite revealing. It is fascinating to discover how many of these ancient attitudes continue to inform our sexual thinking today. Anthropologists tell us that taboos were matters of life and death in primitive society; they had enormous power. They represent an "inculcated system of ego defense mechanicms," says C. D. Daly.[2] There were few more serious crimes in the ancient social order than the violation of a life-defining taboo. Such an infringement was frequently punished by either death or banishment from the tribe.

A major taboo regarding women that can be found in the study of countless early human communities originated in and centered around the experience of menstruation. Although the human female is not the only mammal who menstruates,[3] the higher human intelligence makes menstruation in the human female the subject of speculation that is not a part of any other animal's experience. A major sexual difference separating the human female from all other animal life is that she appears to be the only mammal who does not have estrus or a time of sexual receptivity.[4]

What purpose this menstruation served in the evolutionary process of human life is not certain, but one of its effects seems to have been the heightening of "pair bonding" between the male and the female *Homo sapiens*. The female of the other higher mammals is sexually active only when reproduction is possible and is thus sexually available to the male only when she is "in heat." At other times the always sexually active male roamed, looking for other sexual adventures and partners. The human female, however, is sexually available at all times, and pair bonding can provide for human beings a more deeply satisfying mutual sexual commitment. This sexual availability of the human female developed even though her body prepared on a regular cycle to receive the fertilized egg cell and nurture it to full term. When fertilization did not occur, the uterus shed its preparatory lining and began once again to achieve readiness for the next ovulation and hence the next potential conception. But the woman's sexual availability was neither heightened by ovulation nor retarded by its absence. The menstrual process that accompanies this cycle is taken for granted in our day, but we nonetheless reveal a deep negative historic attitude when we refer to menstruation as "the curse."

Long before the connection between sexual intercourse and pregnancy had been established in the minds of our ancient forebears, the regular experience of bleeding from the genital region was recognized as a unique female phenomenon. Anthropological study and many records reveal that the fear of blood is all but universal, lodging deep in the human psyche. Bloodshed was and still is a synonym for war in many languages. To shed another's blood meant quite simply to kill. Blood and life have always been deeply intertwined to the point where the ancients believed that the very life itself was in the blood of the person. In the book of Genesis, Noah, after the flood, received instruction from God when the new covenant was being established. One requirement was that Noah and his family could not eat flesh with "its life, that is its blood" still in it (Genesis 9:4). That conscious and subconscious connection between life and blood can be documented in one ancient society after another.

Yet always present in the midst of these ancient people were women who regularly bled from the most mysterious and provocative openings of their bodies, and still they did not die. Imagine the mystery, the fear, the opportunity for wild interpretations that this phenomenon presented. Since the menstrual blood flowed from the same opening in the woman's body that the male penetrated in sexual intercourse, somehow menstruation was looked upon in many instances as a wound caused by the male; and the fear of female retribution abounded. To others, menstruation was a hostile sign of the female's rejection of the male sperm. To others, it bespoke a foul contamination. Men feared that sexual relations with a menstruating woman might result in castration. To still others, the menstrual process was evidence of the fact that women themselves had been castrated by an angry god for some evil deed, and in this way the female body mourned its inadequate physiology on a regular basis. This divine castration was thought to be the "curse" women had to bear.

Common to all of these ancient explanations was the sense that menstruation gave women power and that their power was ultimately evil and destructive. Clearly this power and this evil were intimately connected with a woman's sexuality and were directed, men clearly felt, primarily against men. Paula Weidiger documents at length the conclusion that the menstrual taboos are the result of male fear of the female.[5] Misogyny, which Webster defines as "hatred of women," is still characteristic of much of the prevailing male attitude. Misogyny finds, I submit, its primary origin in the fears and superstitions surrounding menstruation from which men are not yet free. Negativity toward menstruation feeds negativity toward women to this day.

A study of primitive puberty rites further corroborates this thesis. In many ancient societies, before the onset of menstruation the girl child was protected by rigid taboos against incest and by tribal laws against child molesting and rape. To give authority to these laws and taboos, the premenstrual girl was characterized by images of purity and holiness. Her virtue was undefiled. When the menstrual cycle began, however, anthropological studies indicate that the young girl's image was dramatically changed and she was viewed as both unclean and capable of spreading her pollution.[6] In the premenstrual concept of purity and holiness as the definition of a woman and in the postmenstrual concept of uncleanness and pollution as the definition of a woman, we discover, I believe, the seeds of that later male ambivalence that tends to see women as either sacred or evil, pedestal creatures or guttersnipes, virgins or whores, Virgin Marys or Magdalenes.[7]

Further, there is evidence in many aspects of primitive life of the establishment of a supposed connection between the menstrual cycles of women and the various phases of the moon, the seasons of the year, the movements of the tides, and even the disappearance of the sun at night.[8] These cosmic phenomena were thought to be caused by or related to this mysterious female menstrual cycle which was interrupted only by the birth of a child. Women were thus again invested with frightening power, and this fear gave birth to superstitions and taboos and made the domination of women a psychological necessity for the supposed safety of the male.

There were a few positive ancient traditions connected with the menstrual blood, but they were rare indeed. Some ascribed to it curative power for leprosy, birthmarks, warts, and headaches.[9] Others deemed it able to ward off evil river spirits.[10] Very rarely it was considered a fit offering for a tribal god.[11] But for the most part menstrual blood was looked upon as evil, and efforts were made to isolate and control this evil and to isolate and control the one who brought this dreaded danger upon the community. Most important for the sexual power equation, the menstrual blood was thought to be a threat to the life and the virility of the male.[12]

It was the general assumption that the evil of menstruation would adversely affect only men if they were inadvertently brought into contact with it. Men seemed not to fear for the woman's safety during menstruation. They seemed to believe that men alone would be victimized by this female power. So exclusion of the menstruating females from the tribe was demanded in order to protect the males. It was the first line of male defense. Before the ostracized women could rejoin the tribe, ceremonial cleansing rituals had to be performed. Menstruating women were also forbidden to handle the food that men would eat. They could not bathe in the sea for fear of ruining the fishing. In a 1961 study of forty primitive societies, anthropologist William Stephens found that each society believed menstruation to be a danger only to men.[13]

Woman was thus perceived as man's psychological enemy, and menstruation was in some strange way her weapon. This fear found expression in the Roman myth that attributed the deformity of the male god Vulcan to menstrual intercourse between Juno and Jupiter. Man in contact with a menstruating woman was believed to lose his masculine powers. Certain strongly patriarchal primitive Semitic tribes of the Middle East used puberty in girls as the occasion to remove surgically the female clitoris to reinforce her need for male dependency.[14] This barbaric practice is still known today in some Islamic societies. Sociologist Bruno Bettelheim argues that these practices were signs of the male's aggressive enmity and hostile expressions of his fear of the female's blood and her sexuality.[15]

Sigmund Freud, whose work reflects more than he suspected the patriarchal attitudes of his Austrian and German origin, wrote extensively about what he called the female's penis envy.[16] Alfred Adler countered Freud almost immediately on this issue and suggested that the woman's envy was connected with man's power far more than with his physiology.[17] The combination of the male's physical power and the female's "curse" of menstruation created, argued Adler, female envy of the male that Freud believed was universal in women. If menstruation had been a male phenomenon and could therefore have been combined with the male's dominance and physical power, it might have become not a curse but a source of male bragging, a sign of virility. This suggestion at least is offered in a *New York Times* review of a book entitled *The Curse* which appeared on September 21, 1976, and is quoted with relish in Nancy Friday's book *My Mother, Myself*.[18] Anthropological studies indicate the possibility that the exact opposite of penis envy may actually have been the case in ancient society. Perhaps it was the male envy of young girls in puberty that gave impetus to the development of the male rite of circumcision, for circumcision was originally performed not in infancy, but at puberty.

The supposed health benefits of circumcision have never been adequately documented. Even if it could be proved that the uncircumcised male brought infection to the female, the foreskin would still be the only part of the male anatomy that was surgically removed to prevent it from getting dirty and infected. Surely there are better means than a surgical procedure to achieve cleanliness. I am impressed by the argument that the origin of circumcision was not a health consideration at all, but was designed rather to meet ritualistic and psychological needs. The other explanations, both ancient and modern, appear to come after the fact. I lean toward the suggestion that circumcision was originally a ceremonial rite that served the purpose of allowing young boys at puberty to emulate young girls at puberty.[19] The circumcised male could then also bleed from his genitals and not die. He thus captured some of the female's magic power. I also suspect that circumcision had overtones of a symbolic act of castration and an offering of the male organ to the god of fertility.

It is difficult for us today to overestimate how the fear surrounding menstruation and the various superstitions developed by that fear affected the role of women in history. The Roman historian Pliny calls menstruation "a fatal poison, corrupting and decomposing urine, depriving seeds of their fecundity, destroying insects, blasting garden flowers and grasses, causing fruits to fall from branches, dulling razors."[20] The Koran calls woman "a pollution" and describes menstruation as harmful and urges men "not to go near the menstruating woman until she is clean."[21] Zoroaster, around 1000 B.C., wrote "A menstruous woman is the work of Uhremaum, the devil. A woman during her periodic illness is not to gaze upon the sacred fire, sit in water, behold the sun, or hold conversation with a man."[22] In the code of Manu (Hindu law) it was written "a woman during her menstrual period shall retire for three days to a place apart. During this time she shall not look at anybody, not even her own children, or at the light of the sun. On the fourth day she shall bathe."[23] Many other similar attitudes adorn the great philosophical voices and holy writings of history. This attitude was powerfully effective in the past and is still operative today.

Menstruation has been used by men as the justification for denying women opportunities in every area of life. Some Victorian scientists argued that if women seriously used their brains, they would impair their fertility by draining off blood cells needed to support the menstrual cycle. So, in their minds, the dawning feminist movement threatened the survival of the race and therefore had to be opposed. Dr. Edward Novak, in a Johns Hopkins Hospital bulletin in 1916, reported that no woman was allowed in the Saigon opium industry in the nineteenth century because of the then-accepted supposition that menstruation would cause the opium to turn bitter and therefore kill the economy of the country.[24] As recently as 1976 an American politician spoke against the idea of a woman Vice-President on the grounds that her monthly period would affect her decision-making faculties. The menstruation myths of the ages have ranged from the economic and political spheres to absurd folktales. In the 1920s in this country, for example, it was commonly believed that a permanent wave would not "take" if the recipient were menstruating.

As a man, I have no way of discerning and no right to suggest how many of the physical symptoms that accompany the menstrual cycle are physiologically based and how many are psychologically influenced.[25] In either case the physical distress is equally real and has become in some circles the culturally expected behavioral response. What is clear, however, is that the image of the woman in distress during menstruation has been an ally in the furthering of the male stereotype of women as weak and subservient, and therefore incapable of achieving economic independence.

The sickly attitude and the need to take to one's bed during the menstrual days were also encouraged by the personal sense of embarrassment that women were made to feel during menstruation. Complicating that embarrassment was the woman's inability to be certain that her menstrual status was not revealed. Before sanitary napkins became widely available in the early 1920s, only a bulky, reusable cloth, not unlike a diaper, was worn, which created an anxious sense of personal insecurity. The disposable sanitary napkin also had an unmeasured effect on the woman's ability to work outside the home; indeed it probably did more to free women economically than has yet been appreciated. It may also have helped to modify the bulky feminine styles of clothing characteristic of the turn of the century, and in many ways must have given women a new sense of confidence. The sanitary napkin advertisements certainly featured this possibility. The exuberance of the roaring twenties may have been fueled at least in part by the need to celebrate this new freedom. The censuring public opinion toward that era was surely centered on the fear that women were breaking the mold of male domination and that traditional morality was being cast aside. When this new freedom was combined with the constitutional amendment in 1920 granting women the suffrage, clearly a new day and a new attitude were emerging.

Karen Horney, an early post-Freudian psychoanalyst, argues in her book *Feminine Psychology* that man historically had devalued woman's function in order to keep her out of his domain. He fashioned the social order deliberately, she suggests, to keep the male powerful and the female inferior.[26] It was important in that struggle for men to convince themselves and to convince women that women are biologically incapable of assuming positions of power. The number of women who opposed the Equal Rights Amendment is ample evidence that this tactic has been successful.

The relationship between men and women certainly appears to be based on the male's analysis and the male's suppositions about the female's power. Can we escape the inevitable conclusion one can learn from the behavioral sciences that no one goes to these lengths to dominate and control another unless one fears that other very deeply? Barely beneath the surface of our civilization, I believe, we see ample evidence that our social order is built on an unconscious fear that males have of females.

If this thesis is accurate, then a powerful control system had to be built and made secure to keep the female powerless and thus to keep the male fears of the female in check. In every civilization a major part of the control system has invariably been the organized religious life of that community, tribe, or nation. Basic assumptions about human life find their way into religious formulas. It is not long before they are written in stone, recited in the liturgy, and identified with the will of God. This enhances the permanence and security of such assumptions because it is difficult indeed for human rebels to challenge a system if God "himself" has created that system. Every religious tradition seems to have as one of its primary sociological functions the defining of sexual role models. Once the religious system makes that definition, then its enormous coercive power is employed to sustain its own definition.

From the male fear of women to misogyny is not a huge step. From superstitions about menstruation to a rigid system of control involving religious definitions is the route that I believe human thought and the development of sexual stereotypes has followed. It is a system that originated in prehistoric human life, but it has flowed without criticism into recorded history where it has been picked up, shaped, interpreted, and imposed on men and women by the institutions of civilization. How these stereotypes were received and conveyed in the Western world by the Christian church becomes the next stage where our examination must focus.

1. One source puts the statistic for monogamy in the various social groups in the world at 24%, polygamy at 75%, and polyandry at 1%.

2. C. D. Daly, "The Role of Menstruation in Human Phylogenesis and Ontogenesis," in *The International Journal of Psychoanalysis*, vol. 24, 1943, p. 151.

3. Others are the higher apes and the rhesus monkeys.

4. Dr. James Erwin, ed., *The American Journal of Primatology*, quoted in *Scientific Digest*, September 1982, p. 8.

5. Paula Weidiger, *Menstruation and Menopause*, New York, Knopf, 1976, pp. 92–95.

6. Janet Delaney, Mary Jane Lupton, Emily Toth, *The Curse: A Cultural History of Menstruation*, New York, E. P. Dutton, 1976, Chapter 2.

7. Sometimes the contrast is not the Virgin Mary and the prostitute, Mary Magdalene, but the Virgin Mary with the temptress, Eve.

8. Delaney et al., *The Curse*, p. 7.

9. Ibid.

10. Ibid.

11. Ibid.

12. Weidiger, p. 95.

13. William N. Stephens, "A Crosscultural Study of Menstrual Taboos," in *Cross-Cultural Approaches*, ed. Clellend S. Ford, New Haven, Conn. HRAF Press, p. 75.

14. Delaney et al., pp. 29–30.

15. Bruno Bettelheim, *Symbolic Wounds: Puberty Rites and the Envious Male*, New York, Collier, 1962, p. 137.

16. Sigmund Freud, *Three Contributions to the Theory of Sex*, New York, E. P. Dutton, 1962. Sigmund Freud, *Totem and Taboo*, New York, Vintage Press, 1946, provides a background analysis of the various sexual conflicts and taboos.

17. Alfred Adler, *Cooperation Between the Sexes: Writings on Women, Love, Marriage, Sexuality and Its Disorders*, Garden City, N. Y., Anchor Books, Doubleday, 1978, p. 310ff.

18. Nancy Friday, *My Mother, Myself*, New York, Delacorte, 1977, p. 120.

19. Delaney et al., p. 224.

20. Pliny, *Natural History*, vol. V, quoted in *Psychology Today*, September 1973, p. 44.

21. Karen E. Page, "Women Learn to Sing the Menstrual Blues," *Psychology Today*, September 1973, p. 44.

22. Ibid.

23. Ibid.

24. Edward Novak, "The Superstition and Folklore of Menstruation," *Johns Hopkins Hospital Bulletin*, #27, 1916, quoted in *The Curse*.

25. Recent court cases have lifted "premenstrual syndrome" into prominence as an extenuating circumstance in crimes committed by women.

26. Karen Horney, *Feminine Psychology*, Norton, 1967, pp. 78–79.

Chapter 7

WOMEN: LESS THAN FREE
IN CHRIST'S CHURCH

ORGANIZED religious systems serve many human functions that are not always conscious. A major function has been to define life and to exert the necessary control to see that all people adhere to that definition. One can thus study the religions of the world and through that means begin to understand the culturally assumed definitions of human sexuality and sexual roles allowed and blessed in the area where that religion is dominant.

To look briefly at the sexual implications present in the other religions of the world helps us to focus on the Western attitude toward women. In this process even assumptions we thought were innate and natural prove to be relative, and a new objectivity arises about how our own religious tradition has defined each of our roles and stamped us with our own sexual understandings.

The first observation that such a study reveals is that the religious systems that developed in the Western world are more intensely antifemale than are any other religious traditions. Judaism, Christianity, and Islam have an exclusively masculine understanding of God. No female divine figure is in the pantheon of any of these three religious systems. Hera, the wife of Zeus, or Juno, the wife of Jupiter, did not find a new incarnation in Western religious symbols.

In India, by contrast, the divine trinity, if we might use that phrase, is Shiva, the Father God; Shakti, his wife; and Vishnu, another male. Shiva and Shakti were often portrayed in Oriental art in passionate embraces so sensuous that modern-day puritans would be shocked.[1] There was no apparent need to deny or suppress the physical pleasures in Hinduism. Both the male and the female bodies were considered part of the human being, not separate from or over against the spirit. Fulfillment of the total human being and not the suppression of the body and its physical appetites was a dominating motif.

In Chinese philosophy the feminine principle is represented as an equal power in the dynamic tension of life that was pictorially expressed as the yin and the yang. The yin was feminine, representing the dark, mysterious, receptive, intuitive quality of life. It was contemplative and restful. The yin was identified with the earth, which was in most ancient traditions assumed to be feminine and called Mother Earth.

The yang on the other hand was the masculine principle. It represented the light of rationality and intellect. Action-oriented, strong, and aggressive, the yang was identified with the sky, the heavens, the creative powers. From the sky, the realm of the yang, the rain, thought to be the divine semen, fell to impregnate Mother Earth, the realm of the yin, so that life could emerge. The active dynamism of the yang always confronted the quiet, still, sagelike quality of the yin.

Despite the sexual typecasting present in these Chinese symbols, there was, in fact, no overt sense of superiority and inferiority between the yin and the yang. Theirs was the tension of equals, and a sense of wholeness was created by their mutual inescapability. They were both caught in a dynamic cyclical relationship, and each possessed within itself a bit of the other. Nothing was purely yin or purely yang, which is another way of saying that nothing was either purely feminine or purely masculine. The balance was perfect and the tension eternal.

I do not mean to suggest that the Eastern traditions escaped the misogyny that I submit was universal. Certainly the pattern of the wife walking three paces behind the husband and the cruel binding of the female's feet that served to create deeper dependency by curbing mobility are sufficient examples. In Japan the word woman is even used to apply to a slow and stupid man. The Chinese character for woman is the word noisy repeated three times.[2] The status of women in Eastern cultures does not appear to be enhanced by this theological inclusiveness. Nonetheless it is true that the Orient appears to have affirmed the value of feminine reality in its concept of God far more significantly than the West has ever done.

The sexual definitions in the Western tradition certainly reveal a vastly different and in many ways more hostile understanding of women. The negativity toward women so ancient in its origin was not countered by a divine feminine figure, and it became powerfully operative. Women were assigned a status that was less than fully human. A prayer in the Ancient Jewish Daily Prayer book said, "Blessed art thou, O Lord our God, King of the Universe, who hast not made me a woman." In contradistinction to the dynamic sexual tension of the East, the religious rhetoric of the West assumed that men formed the legitimate body of the community and that women were allowed to participate only when they assimilated themselves into the male society. Plato, in *The Timaeus*, wrote, "A man who led a good life might return to his native star; but if he did not, he might return as a woman."[3] Clearly to be a woman was punishment. The power of a curse still accompanied the woman, even in the lofty phrases of the great thinker Plato.

Aristotle, in *The Politics*, casually asserted woman's natural inferiority during a discussion of animal life. "Again the same holds true between man and the other animals. Tame animals are superior in their nature to wild animals. Yet for all the former, it is advantageous to be ruled by man since this gives them security. Also as between the sexes the male is superior and the female is inferior. The male is the ruler and the female is the subject."[4] Both *The Timaeus* and *The Politics* were frequently quoted by medieval scholars to justify the low status of women in later Western civilization.

The Old Testament meshed with these Greek opinions to form an uncritical tradition. In the Ten Commandments women were listed among male possessions together with slaves, cattle, and donkeys (Exodus 20:17). In the Garden of Eden story, sin entered the world through the weakness of a woman who was perceived as a secondary part of creation, lower than man while perhaps higher than animals, serving primarily as man's helpmate.

Into these prevailing attitudes the Christian church was born and these attitudes were filtered through, modified by, and given a special new emphasis by that tradition.

In its earliest years Christianity showed a remarkable openness to women. Jesus violated Jewish custom by talking with women and by allowing a woman of the street to wash and anoint his feet in a public place (Matthew 26:7ff). Clearly there were women in the disciple band

(Luke 23:27, Mark 15:40,41), though they do not appear to be num-
bered among the twelve. All four Gospels written between A.D. 65 and
100 preserve the tradition that the Resurrection of our Lord was first
announced to a group of women, with Mary Magdalene being the
central and consistent character in that drama[5] (Matthew 28:1, Mark
16:1, Luke 24:10, John 20:1). Luke tells us that "the women and Mary
the mother of Jesus" shared also in both the Ascension and Pentecost
experiences of the early church (Acts 1:14).

It seems clear that in the early period of church history women held
positions of leadership as prophets, teachers, and evangelists. Despite
our ecclesiastical arguments to the contrary, the threefold-ordered ministry of bishops, priests, and deacons had not yet developed. The Book
of Acts tells us of Priscilla's vital role not only as a supporter of Paul
(Acts 18:2, 18:18) but as the means through which Apollos, a male
evangelist, "understood the way of God more accurately" (Acts 18:26).
Paul called Priscilla "my fellow worker in Christ Jesus" and urged the
church "in her house" be greeted (Romans 16:3, 5). Paul commended
to the Roman Christians a woman deacon named Phoebe, urging them
to help her "for she has been a helper of many and of myself as well"
(Romans 16:2). Romans was written in A.D. 56, more than thirty years
before the Acts account of the choosing of the seven male deacons.
Paul also singled out for greeting a woman named Mary "who has
worked hard among you" (Romans 16:6). Cyril C. Richardson suggests
that the Junias whom Paul salutes as an "apostle who was in Christ
before me" (Romans 16:7) was, in fact, a woman, a point supported by
the recent research of Professor B. Brooten.[6]

In II Timothy the author indicates that Timothy's faith was a gift to
him from two generations of women—Lois, his grandmother, and
Eunice, his mother. Professor Wayne Meeks suggests that the phrase
"in Christ there is neither male nor female," which appears in Galatians 3:28, was originally a liturgical formula from an early Christian
initiation rite.[7] If that theory proves to be accurate, it would represent
a startling new consciousness that marked the early Christian
movement.

These illustrations are not meant to suggest that the early Christian
church escaped or even modified too significantly the sexual attitudes of that day, but it does indicate that the power of the Gospel was
so pervasive that life "in Christ" made all other barriers seem in-
significant, at least for a time. However, even then and certainly

continuing into our generation, the Christian church has consistently represented God in totally masculine terms as father, king, lord, master, ruler, and judge. Paul, speaking out of the traditional orientation of his time, argued that since God is male, only men, not women were created in God's image. Only man, therefore, "is the image and glory of God," he argued, while woman "is the glory of man." He continued to press this point by asserting, "Man was not made from woman but woman from man. Neither was man created for woman but woman for man" (I Corinthians 11:7–9).

Even this negative attitude, however, bore witness to the new consciousness, for one does not offer this kind of argument unless in answer to either a counterargument or a counterpractice. When Paul goes on to suggest that women must keep quiet in church, he reveals that he is in a polemic. Somewhere in the church women were, in fact, not keeping quiet, but rather were assuming a role and an authority in the church that bent if it did not break the male-imposed female role model.

By the end of the first century, however, this new spirit of inclusiveness was diminished by a strong antiwoman mood that ultimately won the day. The pseudo-Pauline letters to Timothy and to the church at Ephesus were accepted by orthodox Christians as genuinely Pauline. Both exaggerated the antifeminist element that was present but not quite so strident in the original Pauline corpus. "Let a woman learn in silence with all submissiveness," the letter to Timothy exhorted. "I permit no woman to teach or to have authority over men" (I Timothy 2:11ff). This author went on with some vehemence to blame women for sin and to suggest that a woman's salvation would come "through bearing children, if she continues in faith and love and holiness, with modesty" (I Timothy 2:15). He further defined the role of both a bishop and a deacon in such a way as to rule out women. The leaders of the church were to be picked from among those males who ruled their households well, to say nothing of being the husbands of only one wife (I Timothy 3:2). The author of Ephesians exhorted the wives to submit themselves to their husbands as unto the Lord, "for the husband is the head of the wife even as Christ is the head of the church" (Ephesians 5:23).

So far as the church could speak with authority, it proceeded to snuff out the early spirit of inclusive freedom and to lay a theological foundation that would establish beyond debate the secondary, subservient role and worth of women. In the name of a masculine God and in accordance with the will of this masculine God, the all-male hierarchy of the church had declared it to be so. From this definition there was no court of appeal. By making that claim good, the door was open in Western Christian civilization from that moment on for men alone to define not only God and human life but also to order worship, to establish sacred tradition, and to build the theological boundaries around orthodoxy without ever hearing, much less responding to, whatever insights women might possess.

The reasons are not certain for the shift against women toward the end of the first century of church history, but the reality is. One possible explanation is that Christianity began to move up the social ladder from the lower to the middle class. In the lower classes the labor of anyone able to work was needed, so the value of the woman could not be ignored. That pattern, in fact, still prevails even today in the Middle East, where only middle-class women, not working women, are required to be veiled.[8]

Elaine Pagels, in her provocative book *The Gnostic Gospels*, offers another possible explanation.[9] The gnostic groups, with whom the orthodox Christians appeared to be in competition, were universally more open to women than the dictates of the tradition and social order would tolerate. In the battle for supremacy that the orthodox bodies won, thereby winning for themselves the orthodox title, there was a general denigrating of any value associated with the gnostics. Some gnostic Christians and the orthodox Christians divided on their definition of God, with the gnostics viewing God as a dyad having both male and female elements. In the gnostic Gospel according to the Hebrews, Jesus spoke of "my mother, the Spirit."[10] The Hebrew word *ruach*, which was translated "spirit," was, in fact, a feminine word. In the Gospel of Thomas, Jesus contrasted his earthly parents, Joseph and Mary, with the Divine Father of Truth and the Divine Mother, the Holy Spirit.[11] The Gospel of Philip ridiculed those the author considered literal-minded Christians who mistakenly referred the virgin birth to Mary. "When did a woman conceive by a woman?" the author asks. "Christ was born from the Virgin Spirit" through the will of the Father, he asserted.[12] The humanity of Jesus was seriously questioned in gnostic circles.

These gnostic writings were rigorously attacked by the guardians of orthodoxy, and the fact that the gnostic groups seemed to have a powerful appeal to women, as noted even by Iraneus,[13] caused the orthodox attack to have increasingly militant sexist overtones. The gnostics were accused of being seducers of foolish women and purveyors of immoral actions. When the smoke of battle cleared, the gnostics had been routed, and with them the liberalizing attitude toward women in the church may have been destroyed. Tertullian spoke for what was to become the orthodox attitude when he wrote, "It is not permitted for a woman to speak in the church, nor is it permitted for her to teach, nor to baptize, nor to offer the eucharist, nor to claim for herself a share in any masculine function, least of all in priestly office."[14] The force of this statement indicates once again that women had, in fact, claimed for themselves each of the roles that Tertullian prohibited. No one prohibits that which no one had thought to do. But once the prohibition was pronounced, the justifying reasons were found and articulated. Inevitably the denigrating of the sexuality of women as something evil, unclean, and unworthy was offered to buttress the decision against inclusiveness. With this negativity abroad, it was not long before the church structures, traditions, theology, and liturgy all possessed a deeply pervasive antifemale bias.

One has only to scratch the surface just a bit to find that this negativity toward women was loaded time after time on the experience of menstruation. An unspoken argument against female ordination was and is the ancient fear of menstruation's power to pollute. This fear was recounted endlessly in medieval books. In many parts of the Catholic tradition today, little girls and old women are allowed to help in minor ways at church functions, while women in their prime are not.[15] The implication is clear. Even into this century some churches have taught that menstruating women were not to attend and receive the Holy Communion. Jerome wrote, "Nothing is so unclean as a woman in her periods. What she touches she causes to be unclean."[16] The ancient prejudice had clearly found expression in the new religion. Christianity inherited misogyny as a given and baptized this antifemale bias into its ongoing life. Christianity modified this negativity from time to time, but it never really escaped it.

The major Christian contribution to the prevailing and inherited sexual attitudes came through a school of philosophy known as Manicheanism. This philosophical system, which was related to the gnostic tradition,[17] emerged out of the Greek world but was grafted and incorporated so deeply into Christianity that people thought it was of the essence of the Gospel. Manicheanism added a new dimension of negativity toward women, and it had a marked impact upon both the church and the social order.

The philosophy of the Manicheans was based on the popular Greek dualistic view of reality that elevated what it called the realm of the spirit and denigrated what it called the realm of the material or physical. The spiritual aspect of human life represented the higher self, the source of lofty and pure thoughts. The physical aspect of human life represented the lower self, the body, the source of base and carnal desires. This dualistic philosophy tended to divide the human being at the diaphragm, pronouncing that which was above the diaphragm good and that which was below the diaphragm evil.

This point of view entered Christianity most specifically by way of Augustine, Bishop of Hippo, who had himself been a Manichean philosopher prior to his conversion. Augustine was the most powerful and influential Christian thinker and teacher for a thousand years, so his impact was vast. But the basic dualism of Manicheanism was also a pervasive and dominant attitude of Greek philosophy throughout the ancient world, and it interacted with Christianity at many points. It was the dualistic attitude which fed and continues to feed that ascetic tradition in Christianity that suggests that the Christian life can be achieved only when the physical body has been mortified of its desires and the sinful world has been escaped in the quest to find God.

Not surprisingly, when this ascetic tradition talked about the flesh, it found sin most devastatingly present in human sexuality. Furthermore, it identified the sensuous power and attraction of this evil experience primarily with the female of the species. If sex was evil, then that creature who was the desired object of sexual temptations had to be evil. Clearly one sees that the value system out of which these judgments proceeded was designed by men. Were it not for the woman's seductiveness and her tempting power, then the lordly male would not fall under her evil spells and therefore might escape the sins of the flesh. A breviary of love originating in A.D. 1288 put this concept into specific words when it said, "Satan in order to make men suffer bitterly makes them adore women; for instead of loving the creator, they sinfully love women."[18] These sentiments, informed by Manicheanism, constituted one more strand of the antiwomen mentality that fed Western civilization through the Christian church. It is not yet the whole answer, but its presence must be isolated and noted in any attempt to understand the broad and deep negativity that the West has historically felt toward the female.

Those who are uncomfortable admitting this antifemale bias which has come through the church offer as a counterargument that the importance given to Mary, the mother of our Lord, in Christian history tempered the negativity toward women in Western civilization. A closer look at Mary, however, calls this theory into serious question. The Virgin Mary that we meet in the tradition and in the mythology of the Western Catholic world is consistently man's version of what a woman should be. Mary is woman defined, circumscribed, and idealized by men who accept without questioning a particular male orientation. The male prejudice against women was so deep and so intense that man's version of the ideal woman was both dehumanized and desexed, and only by this process could she achieve that ideal status of female perfection. Women would never have defined woman this way.

Mary's humanity was irrevocably compromised by the assertion that she was immaculately conceived and bodily assumed. These two doctrines suggested that her entrance into life and her departure from life were abnormal and unhuman. She was rather a special visitor to the earth, not a part of the woof and warp of life. Her female sexual capability was removed from her by the stories of her virgin birth and the later tradition of her perpetual virginity. Even wilder stories circulated to build ever greater barriers around her potential sexuality. One legend suggested that her impregnation by the Holy Spirit was through her ear. Another suggested that the birth of our Lord was through her navel. Female sexuality had to be very evil in the minds of those who produced these myths and traditions.

Only one sexual function was allowed Mary in Western history, and even that proved to be short-lived. The breasts of Mary could produce milk. She could lactate, and to this product of her body were ascribed remarkable theraputic powers. An analysis of the medieval suckling stories about Mary show the gentle blending of many ancient goddess traditions of the pre-Christian world. The first nursing goddess appears to be Isis in Egypt, 1000 years before Christ. Later, in Greek mythology, the goddess Juno's milk was sprayed across the heavens one night while she was nursing Hercules. Because of this accidental spilling in the Greek myth, we call the heavenly bodies to this day the Milky Way; and even the word galaxy comes from the root *lac*, which means milk. In the thirteenth century, phials in which Mary's milk was preserved were venerated all over Christendom. John Calvin in his treatise on relics said, "There is no town so small or convent so mean that it does not display some of the virgin's milk. There is so much that if the Holy Virgin had been a cow or a wet nurse all her life, she would have been hard put to yield such a great quantity."[19]

Finally, however, even this human sex-related quality in Mary was repressed, and stories about the healing milk of Mary faded from the tradition. Sin, according to the Garden of Eden story, was punished in the woman by childbirth (Genesis 3:16). In the era before prepared baby formulas, nursing was an essential part of the childbearing experience. There was no continuity of life without breastfeeding. As the stories of Mary's sinlessness began to circulate, inevitably the stories of any sex-related function, including nursing, became inappropriate. The only survival of this tradition today is the popular German wine Liebfraumilch, which literally means dear lady's milk. The only indication of a body function left in the humanity of Mary was her ability to shed tears, and tears became the only product of her body that was not repressed. Somehow in our strange negative heritage we seem to believe that everything that comes out of the woman's body save for tears is evil.

The popular suggestion that devotion to Mary was translated into respect or enhanced status for women is simply without historic evidence. To the contrary, the church fathers who were extolling the virtues of the Virgin Mary were at the same time lambasting the sexuality of female persons. Tertullian in the third century and Chrysostom in the fourth century could be quoted at length. There is no historic correlation between the cult of the virgin and increased status for women that can be substantiated in Western history. Mother Church was, in fact, ruled by man; and Mary served the desires of those men who created this holy ideal of what they thought all women should be and then imposed it on their women.

Mary's chief role was that of intercessor, which was also not surprisingly the special role of the mother in medieval patriarchal family life. The mother was never the judge. She never made the power decisions. The judge was always the husband and father, who was the source of power, authority, and discipline. The mother's sole function was to intercede. She could plead for mercy in the handing down of punishment; but her only real power lay in her ability to move the lordly male to compassion and pity. The power structure of this family scene in medieval life was simply transposed in theological circles to the heavenly courtroom where the divine judge stood ready to punish sinners for their evil deeds. To ameliorate the sentence, the guilty party, reduced to childlike terror before the parental authority, would plead with the compassionate divine mother to pray to her son, the judge, on behalf of the penitent.

Marina Warner, in her provocative book *Alone of All Her Sex*, suggests that there is a historic correlation between the popularity of Mary and the low status of women even today.[20] In those countries where Mary still dominates the religious tradition of the people, the men still swagger and command and the women are more prone to submit and to withdraw. Machismo, Warner asserts, is the flip side of the sweet and gentle Mary who is not the ideal woman at all but the male ideal of what the submissive, powerless female should be.

Certainly the role of the woman in childbirth was recognized in Christian history by the church fathers, but they related to childbirth in a rather unusual way. Procreation was a necessary evil that ought to be escaped, they seemed to think. Their reasoning process went like this: women were inferior, so any attempt to elevate women had to be accomplished by removing the woman's sexuality, which was that human condition to which female inferiority was attached. This removal could be achieved only if women denied their sexuality. To express or to live out female sexuality was to carry on the sentence imposed on women in the Garden of Eden. So Cyprian, Tertullian, and Jerome urged women to remain virgins "so that you will not suffer the consequences of the fall."[21] The early theologians wrote extensively on the joys available to women in the single life. There was no husband to obey, nor a pregnancy to endure. The sorrows of conception could be escaped, and the marital condition could be avoided. Jerome asserted that only virginity could reverse woman's fall from grace in the Garden of Eden. He went on to say, "When a woman wishes to serve Christ more than the world, she will cease to be a woman and will be called a man."[22]

The importance of virginity hinged on the understanding of the female body generally abroad among the early church fathers. The virgin body was perfect and whole. Virginity, the status to which a woman was born, was created by God and was therefore holy. Ambrose suggested that for a woman to lose her "maidenhead" was to deface the work of the creator.[23] Marriage was tolerable, said Jerome, "only because more virgins were born as the result."[24] The church fathers made virginity the supreme image of wholeness and equated wholeness with holiness. Virginity thus was the only thing that separated humanity from the beasts.[25] Sexual union was believed to destroy the virgin body.[26] One vestige of this idea is still noted in that the French today call orgasm *la petite mort*, which means little death. Chastity thus became the only effective means available to a woman to combat the evil of her sex, and childbearing became the only possible compromise with human sexuality. The dualism of the Manicheans was assumed and was unquestioned.

If a woman chose marriage over virginity, part of the legitimate price she had to pay was submission to her husband, who ruled her by the same divine right that kings claimed over their domains. "Every man a king in his own home" is not a slogan of recent political origin,[27] but rather the experience of women historically in Western civilization. The church proclaimed that the woman who aspired to be ideal would be docile, gentle, and passive. After all, the ideal woman, the perpetual Virgin Mary, had responded to the annunciation, "Be it unto me according to your will," and that response became the required attitude the married woman had to assume toward her husband. Sex was allowable in marriage only for the purpose of procreation. Women were not only inferior, but childbearing was a divine necessary punishment they alone had to bear. Negativity toward sex was so great that sexual relations for any purpose other than childbearing was an unthinkable abomination. The condemnation of birth control today is a modern expression of this same attitude.

Through every medium this definition of woman was enforced by the church. Of the classical theological virtues only charity has historically been applied to women, not the more vigorous virtues of faith or hope. Of the cardinal virtues only prudence seems to have a feminine characteristic, not fortitude or justice or temperance. To be feminine was to be passive. Passivity was acted out both in the symbolic marriage to Jesus, which was the ideal that led to the life of cloistered obedience of the virgin nun, and in the actual marriage to a man for the sole purpose of bearing children and obediently serving the man's needs and comfort. The latter alternative, while allowable, was at best thought to be a compromise with sin and flesh. Women thus could serve husbands and children as wives and mothers, or they could serve priests and children as nuns. No other options were available.

Professor Suzannah Wemple of Barnard College argues persuasively in her book *Women in Frankish Society, 500 to 900* that nunneries served as vital female sanctuaries from male abuse.[28] The nunneries and convents of the early Middle Ages were the only places in Western society where women could exercise leadership and demonstrate ability. The abbesses and mothers superior guarded this freedom jealously, keeping it clear of male authority whenever possible. To these havens abused and battered women could flee to escape their male oppressors. This book gave me a significant new appreciation for the historic role of convents.

The male church leadership seemed to feel it was its sacred obligation to encourage the highest ideal of virginity for women and to minimize the number who would enter the compromised status of marriage. To assist in this process, the confirmation of little girls was portrayed as a kind of minimarriage to Jesus; hence the development of marriage symbols at confirmation for girls—the white miniwedding dress, the white miniwedding veil, even the wedding bouquet. A frequently cited slogan emanating from within the church proclaimed "Give me the child until she is six, and she will be ours forever." So, too, attitudes absorbed at a very young age lasted a lifetime.

By means of these traditions and attitudes, the church has imposed its sexual stereotypes on the secular order. Here they have remained in force as the common folk wisdom long after the institutional power of the church has waned. The church's definition of women was operative in 1873 when the Supreme Court of the United States declined by an 8-1 vote to allow a woman named Myra Bradford to practice law in the state of Illinois. Listen to the nuances of a strongly worded concurring opinion written by Justice Joseph P. Bradley:

> Man is or should be women's protector and defender. The natural and proper timidity and delicacy which belongs to the female sex evidently unfits it for many of the occupations of civil life. The constitution of the family organization which is founded in the divine ordinance as well as in the nature of things indicates the domestic sphere as that which properly belongs to the domain and function of womanhood. The paramount destiny and mission of woman are to fulfill the noble and benign office of wife and mother. This is the law of the creator. And the rules of civil society must be adapted to the general constitution and cannot be based upon exceptional cases.[29]

Justice Bradley certainly did not think of himself as anything but an "objective" judge, and yet his sexual assumptions were the products of his religious heritage. The only negative vote in that decision was cast by Chief Justice Salmon P. Chase, who did not put the content of his objection into writing.

The secular order is today in the process of challenging the sexual assumptions of the past and freeing itself from the power of those assumptions. But in many branches of the Christian church they still reign supreme, and in some instances are even as yet unquestioned. The hard line still followed in many church circles against the emergence of women from the stereotypes of the past arises from a historic inability of parts of the Christian movement to see women primarily as persons and not simply as creatures defined only by their sexuality as either virgins or baby-making machines.

Marina Warner, who was raised as a Roman Catholic, concludes her book *Alone of All Her Sex* by stating that the Vatican's inability to see women as people rather than mothers "underpins the church's continuing indefensible ban on contraception; a dualistic distaste for the material world reinforces the ideal of virginity; and an undiminished certainty that women are subordinate to men continues to make the priesthood of women unacceptable."[30]

The force of this longstanding and powerfully held position is massive. Social systems and social attitudes that are this immense point to an equally immense fear and force that have to be mastered and controlled. We in this rational, civilized, and enlightened era have not yet escaped these subliminal anxieties.

More than any of us recognize, we still harbor these ancient prejudices and we still victimize women in the service of these prejudices. Look at some of the symbols we employ. A sexual success is called a conquest as if in the nature of a war. Religious voices in our day have been raised in support of what is called "traditional family values," but when that term is defined by its advocates, it quickly loses its facade and is revealed as an antiwoman movement attached to traditional religious language. "Traditional family values" seems to be a modern version of the argument that "a woman's place is in the home." Church-related groups were most vocal in opposition to the Equal Rights Amendment, and they are highly emotional in opposition to abortion. These forces combined with the religious right to oppose the nomination of Sandra Day O'Connor, the first woman appointed to the

Supreme Court of the United States. In a letter to the editor of *Time*, one Sheila Walker from Colorado commented succinctly, "The new right will never be satisfied with any female appointed to the judiciary. Obviously a woman who respects 'traditional family values' would not have gone to law school or sought a career outside the home."[31]

Many of our marriage customs still reflect these suppositions of the ages. What are we saying in the wedding ceremony when one man gives the woman away to another man? Does this not imply that the woman is a piece of property that can be bartered or exchanged? Why is the groom not given away?

Our economic structures reveal a continuing active bias against women. In medicine the overwhelming number of doctors are male while the females are the helpful and less well-paid nurses. In business most executives are male, and the females are the indispensable but less well-paid secretaries. In the field of education the superintendents and principals are overwhelmingly male, while females still constitute the large majority of the essential but less well-paid teachers. Males are still primarily the dentists and the lawyers; females are the less well-paid oral hygienists and legal assistants. The priesthood is overwhelmingly male, while faithful women prepare the altars where the priest celebrates the Eucharist, and keep t'e priestly vestments clean and well pressed.

We still castigate males when we perceive what we think of as female characteristics in them. Our profanity and our sex talk are filled with crude and vulgar hostility that express a still-present subliminal negativity toward women. Sexist prejudice is enormous, and in many ways its major generator in history has been nothing less than the Christian church. We may well be able to trace these attitudes to their source, but we have yet to break their power over our minds. These facts pose a major question for Christians involved in the contemporary revolution of social consciousness. Can this same church that gave and still gives substance and value to sexual stereotypes now free itself from these stereotypes and help us to enter a new era of freedom without destroying itself in the process?

To me, this question points to incredibly important issues that may well carry with them the very future existence of Christianity. I am convinced that the ordination of women to the priesthood in the Episcopal Church, extra-canonically in 1975 and canonically in 1977, was the tip of an enormous reformation that offers a tiny new hope that the church might yet be able to survive and live in the brave new world of consciousness that is developing.

But the church as we know it will never be the same if that transition is accomplished. Sexual assumptions that are deep and still operative will have to be changed. Traditional role-enforcing mythologies will have to be abandoned. The Virgin Mary will have to be transcended and transformed so radically that her perpetual virgin status may well be seen as a sexist liability rather than a virtue. The ecclesiastical power formulas of the past will have to be rethought. The church has a choice to make, perhaps more serious than it has ever before had to make. If the church actively or passively insists on preserving or defending the attitudes of the past, if the church has not within itself the courage to enter this new world of sexual consciousness, then it must retire from history. Inevitably then, the quest for freedom from the sexual stereotypes of the past will move so far beyond the church that the church will become an antiquated group of guerilla fighters isolated in forgotten pockets, wondering why they are ignored and asking what happened to their cause. Our constituent members will be only those who could not embrace these changes. In my view there is no way the clock of sexual stereotyping will ever be turned back—not by the Vatican or the religious right or the scared conservative Christians in every branch of Christendom—though in the short run they will be much more secure in that stance than will those of us who will move ahead.

I cast my vote for a dangerous future. In that future we Christians must enter and embrace incredible changes, bear the dislocations of traditions, endure the death of symbols, and find the freedom to escape the debilitating prejudices and taboos of all those ages that have bound our consciousness and ill-equipped us for the revolution we now face. The greatest upheaval in Christian history, I believe, confronts us in the next century.

That we might know the full scope of the terrain into which we must venture, one additional piece of sexual consciousness needs to be opened. This too has been a significant factor in shaping the sexual stereotypes that have emerged from within the Christian church. I suspect that it will be the most emotional of all the traumas which will buffet the church in the near future. It was also a natural development in the patterns we have been tracing.

First there was the prehistoric male negativity that produced an almost universal misogyny. In Christian history this misogyny was filtered through the Manichean philosophy that continued to denigrate women and heaped scorn upon the flesh itself and the functions of the body, making sex the most heinous of sins. It also elevated abstinence, celibacy, and virginity to the status of the holiest of virtues. This, I submit, opened the door to the development of the next dimension of sexual thought in the church.

If it was evil to love a woman and evil to express one's natural sexual feelings toward women, then perhaps it would be better if men would turn their romantic attachments toward other men. This was at least the rationale that was used to interpret a major identification between Christianity, with its emphasis on "sexual purity," and the practice of homosexuality, for historically I am convinced that there has been a significant correlation between the Christian priesthood and a homosexual orientation. This correlation also contributed significantly to the prevailing negativity that continued to distort the church's understanding of women and their place in the church's life. It is not a simple subject to examine, but any attempt to explore the role of the church in setting historic sexual stereotypes without looking at the influence of homosexuality, particularly in the life of the dominant celibate tradition of the priesthood, would be hopelessly inadequate. So to that exploration our attention must now be turned.

1. Fritjof Capra, *The Tao of Physics*, Berkeley, Cal., Shambhala, 1975, p. 90.

2. Geoffrey Parrinder, *Sex and the World's Religions*, New York, Oxford Univ. Press, 1980, p. 117.

3. Plato, *Timaeus and Critias*, trans. H. D. B. Lee, London, 1971, p. 58, quoted in Marina Warner, *Alone of All Her Sex*, New York, Knopf, 1976, p. 177.

4. Aristotle, *The Politics*, I, II, 9. 11–12, ed. H. Rackman, London, 1949, in Warner, p. 178.

5. Since being a witness to the Resurrection was the only New Testament criterion for being an apostle, Mary Magdalene clearly qualified and may thus be considered the first woman in apostolic succession.

6. B. Brooten, *Women Priests*, New York, L. and A. Swidler, 1977, pp. 141–44.

7. Wayne Meeks, *The Image of Androgyne*, p. 180ff, quoted in Elaine Pagels, *The Gnostic Gospels*, New York, Random House, 1979, p. 61.

8. In the Moslem fundamentalist revival in Iran, after the fall of the Shah, all women were required to be veiled.

9. Elaine Pagels, *The Gnostic Gospels*, New York, Random House, 1979, p. 63ff.

10. Ibid., p. 52.

11. Ibid.

12. Ibid., p. 53 (The Gospel of Philip 55:25–26)

13. Ibid.

14. Tertullian, *De Virginibus Velandis* 9, in Pagels, p. 60.

15. In Warner, p. 76.

16. In Warner, p. 76.

17. The Rt. Rev. C. FitzSimons Allison, former Virginia Seminary church history professor, says, "If gnosticism is a dog, Manicheanism is a cocker spaniel."

18. Matfre Ermengand, *Le Breviarai d'Amor*, ed. G. Agais, in Warner, p. 153.

19. John Calvin, *Treatise on Relics*, in Warner, p. 200.

20. Warner, p. 183ff.

21. In Warner, p. 73.

22. Jerome, *Commentary on Ephesians*, quoted in Mary Daly, *The Church and the Second Sex*, Boston, 1968 (quoted in Warner, p. 73).

23. Ambrose, *Exhortatio Virginitatis*, quoted in Robert Briffault, *The Mothers*, 3 vols., New York, 1927 (in Warner, p. 73).

24. Jerome, *Letter 22 to Eustochium* (in Warner, p. 73).

25. Mary Douglas, *Purity and Danger: An Analysis of the Concepts of Purity and Taboo*, London, 1966, p. 186ff.

26. In Warner, p. 72.

27. This was a major theme in George Wallace's presidential campaign in 1972.

28. Suzannah Fonay Wemple, *Women in Frankish Society, 500–900*, Philadelphia, Univ. Pennsylvania Press, 1982.

29. Joseph P. Bradley, concurring opinion, U.S. Supreme Court, 1873, *Bradford v. State of Illinois.*

30. Warner, p. 338.

31. *Time*, Letters to the Editor, August 10, 1981, Vol. 118, No. 6.

Chapter 8

HOMOSEXUALITY'S INFLUENCE ON THE CHURCH'S DEFINITION OF WOMEN

WILLIAM James, in his monumental work *The Varieties of Religious Experience*, used a phrase that former President Jimmy Carter was later to borrow. He spoke of "the moral equivalent of war."[1] President Carter applied those words to his efforts to call the nation to an effective program of energy conservation and the development of new energy sources, but James used the phrase to apply to the disciplined life of the monastic community.

It was James's contention that part of the psychological reality in every male was his own sexual ambivalence. He believed that the male fear of his own potential homosexuality had to be put down or suppressed with effective and regular control. James argued that the violence of a periodic war provided a physical outlet for this pent-up male fear. There was actually, he suggested, an inner peace that descended on one who was involved in mortal conflict or dangerous battles because it calmed the anxiety about his sexual identity.

But what happens to this anxiety and its omnipresent energy in a protracted period of peace? William James believed that the rigorous, externally imposed order and discipline of the monastic community met in the male the same psychological need for the emotional outlet for sexual energy that was met in warfare. Hence the monastic community was for him the moral equivalent of war.

This fascinating observation suggests to me that we must at least admit the possibility that "priestly formation," which grew out of the monastic community, may really be a religious phrase used to describe the establishment of a powerful psychological control system to keep our unacceptable sexual ambivalence in check. That which we call "spiritual direction" originally may have been the priestly attempt to pass on a modified version of his own necessary psychological control system to the laity. At the very least the rigorous, disciplined life of the monastic community, which set the standards and expectations for the entire priesthood, historically seems to have appealed widely to those who were battling with the strongest sense of sexual ambivalence. When the priesthood is combined with the requirement of celibacy, the union of sexual ambivalence and priestly vocation becomes difficult to dispute historically.

I introduce this chapter with this thought-provoking vignette in order to startle our minds to a new sexual awareness that is beneath the level of our religious consciousness and beyond the ever-present sexual clichés. Our task has been to look deeply at the sexual attitudes which have shaped the Christian church and which continue to find expression in our theology, our liturgy, and in church practice. Yet most people will live a lifetime in the church without ever having their minds opened to this level of understanding.

To control unacceptable sexual feelings has been a major motif of the organized life of the Christian church. Fear has distorted our objectivity, and superstition born in ignorance has lived far beyond the time its originating misunderstanding could be adequately explained. Yet the sexual fears and mythologies lived on.

The ultimate targets of the sexual negativity in the church were women. But it seems possible, perhaps even probable, that behind the negativity toward women there was, in fact, a negativity toward heterosexuality. Women were evil. They were plagued with the menstrual curse. They excited the lust and desire that Christians believed to be the temptation of the devil. Women embodied the satanic power that called men to an awareness of the flesh from which their noble souls sought only release. Marriage was not an absolution for sexuality; it was a compromise with sin. That was a deeply held conviction.

The early spokesmen for Christianity were quite universal in affirming these attitudes. Jerome wrote, "A man who loves his wife very much is an adulterer."[2] The influential Augustine wrote in *The Soliloquy*,

"There is nothing which degrades more the manly spirit than the attractiveness of females and contact with their bodies."[3] As strange as these quotations might sound to us, they represent an attitude that has been pervasive in the Christian church throughout history. It found new expression as late as 1980 when John Paul II issued a statement in which he condemned a man who would "lust after his wife."[4] Subsequent Vatican attempts to explain this statement only succeeded in confirming the presence of this attitude of negativity toward heterosexual relationships save as the means of reproducing the race. Sex is for procreation only. Recreation is an illegitimate goal in lovemaking.

Another expression of this historic negativity toward heterosexual love is seen in that marriage itself was not declared to be a sacrament in the Western Catholic church until the Council of Trent in 1563. Prior to that time, matrimony was preferable only to promiscuity, but celibacy was certainly thought to be the higher calling. Legends that enforced this mythology abounded. A widely circulating tradition declared that sexual activity directly shortened one's life expectancy. One could choose a prolonged celibate life or a shorter, sexually active life. Obviously it was difficult to test this bit of folk wisdom; hence it was just repeated. Perhaps its truth lay in the fact that the celibate life only seemed longer.[5]

The official ecclesiastical attitude toward human sexuality was also unsuccessful in causing either sex or desire to die. This attitude did succeed, however, in making sexual activity the most negative aspect of all forms of human behavior, which in turn served two important purposes. First, it made guilt the daily fare of all sexually healthy people. Since the church was the only dispenser of forgiveness, to succeed in making everyone feel sexual guilt dramatically increased the church's power. Secondly, it opened the doors to a variety of alternative sexual outlets that found permanent lodging in both the conscious and unconscious levels of life. One such outlet that achieved popularity in the Middle Ages was found in the publication of books known as bestiaries. These collections of animal stories regularly transposed human sexual fantasies into the animal world. Many female animals were thought to be especially active sexually in a way that no proper woman would dare express. The mare, the female horse, was depicted in the bestiaries as the lustiest of all animals, always out to seduce a stallion. From that medieval concept the slang phrase "horsing around" entered our vocabulary.[6] Sexual activity or feelings unacceptable for men or women could find expression only in human folklore about the animal world.

The second outlet for sexual energy that also achieved both popularity and widespread practice was homosexuality. When the church adopted in A.D. 1123 the requirement of celibacy for priesthood in the Western Catholic tradition, it was merely endorsing what had been the majority tradition for centuries. The avoidance of a heterosexual relationship was therefore officially declared to be virtuous. The prevailing negative attitude toward women meant that sexual expressions that did not involve women could be viewed quite positively. This convenient combination of attitudes was thus used to provide a philosophical and moral rationale for homosexuality in Western Christianity. Sometimes this homosexuality was quite open; sometimes it exhibited only slight attempts at covertness; and sometimes it was hidden very deeply within the closet.

The impact of homosexual orientation and homosexual activity among the celibate male priestly tradition has not yet been accurately measured historically nor have the attitudes toward women of homosexual clergy throughout the history of the church been accurately documented. But in a social order where sexual consciousness is in flux, an exploration into this area of our Christian history is proving fruitful, and searching questions continue to be raised that are uncomfortable, but I believe necessary, for the Christian church to face.

In my mind a major resource at present to aid such a study is the monumental work of Yale University's social historian, Professor John Boswell, entitled *Christianity, Social Tolerance, and Homosexuality*.[7] I will lean heavily upon his research, which is extensive; yet perhaps a word of caution needs to be spoken.

While I am deeply in Dr. Boswell's debt and have had my conclusions shaped in large measure by his scholarship, my conclusions would nonetheless not be his conclusions. Boswell is a creative historian, and his book is a polemic to establish the place of homosexuals in the history of the church. In serving his purpose Boswell makes educated guesses and engages in brilliant speculations. The material he has to work with requires this treatment, for it is sketchy, private, and highly subjective. I have used his extensive and documented research to reach a set of conclusions that are mine, not his.

Boswell seeks to demonstrate the authentic presence in and contribution to the church's life of homosexual persons. I support that

conclusion with gratitude. I seek, however, to move beyond that conclusion to raise the question of whether the presence of large numbers
of male homosexual persons in the church's priesthood has been a
factor in continuing the antiwoman bias which, I submit, has always
marked the life of the Christian church. That is an issue which Boswell
does not address. Neither Boswell nor I can do more on this subject
than to raise the questions we seek to address.

I certainly do not claim to speak the final word in this debate. I wish
to raise these possibilities as provocatively and powerfully as I can, in
order to force them into the arena of conscious debate inside the life
of institutional Christianity. In this deeply sensitive, interpretive task,
room must be left for other points of view. To me, Boswell's book is
the finest piece of scholarship available today on this subject. His book
will and should be vigorously debated. I hope mine will be also. By
opening the subject of homosexuality in the priesthood of the church
to serious study, Boswell has performed, in my mind, an incalculable
service.

To explore this area of human sexuality is a delicate task. I have been
uncomfortably liberal when the subject of homosexuality has been
debated in the conventions of recent church history. My discomfort
comes from three identifiable sources: first, my own emotional attitudes, fears, prejudices, and upbringing; second, my inadequate knowledge of the causes and meaning of homosexuality; and, finally, my
supposition, which I shall seek to demonstrate, that, far more than
anyone has suspected, homosexually oriented clergy have been a major
influence on Christianity, shaping not only the church's sexual attitudes but its liturgy, its theology, its art, and its worship traditions. If
this supposition can be adequately documented, it might help us to
understand why negativity toward women is so much a part of the
whole Christian enterprise. I hope it might also move the church to a
new awareness of the need to have the whole spectrum of human
sexuality involved in defining God and human life, as well as setting
values, liturgies, and theologies.

To analyze and open these possibilities runs the risk of appearing
to be antihomosexual. I am not! A new era of homosexual prejudice
and persecution in the church would be the last thing to which I would
want to lend any support. I think of myself as for sexual wholeness
rather than against any mutually satisfactory sexual practice, but to
bring the church to a vision of sexual wholeness means combating

sexism in every expression. To the degree that one of the elements in the sexism of the church is a conscious and unconscious homosexual attitude, particularly among the clergy, that manifests itself in positions that are antiwoman, this investigation may be interpreted by some as an attack on homosexuality. I want to deny that charge categorically and express my regret if my words are ever used or interpreted in this manner. To remove an antiwoman bias and to replace it with an antigay bias would not be progress. The gay people of our day, both in the church and outside it, do not need one more voice adding to the pain that society seems to me to heap upon them. To cast judgment on gay people is not my motive or my goal. But to look at the Christian church's role in setting the sexual stereotypes, particularly of women, without examining homosexuality within the church would be impossible.

I do not regard homosexuality per se as a decisive factor in the acceptance or rejection of a candidate for the priesthood any more than I regard heterosexuality per se as a decisive factor. I also do not for a moment wish to imply that celibate clergy in general or any celibate clergyperson in particular is a homosexual person. There are certainly persons whose commitment to the priestly vocation is so absolute that no other commitment can share in that ultimacy. We are aware that repressed and angry heterosexuals have also been a factor in the Christian priesthood, viewing celibacy as a way to keep their feelings in check. Beyond that, there are many other reasons that one might choose not to marry. Certainly we are also aware that marriage itself is not always an indication that homosexuality is not present in one or the other partner. I do not want to pretend to psychologize or to judge anyone's motives or to cast doubt or suspicion on anyone's ministry. I do not even mean to suggest that if one is overtly homosexual his or her priesthood cannot be marked with beauty, effectiveness, and power. It is a fact that could easily be verified that the Christian church throughout its history, including our own day, has had clergy who have been homosexually oriented and homosexually active. Those of us in the priesthood have known them, and often our lives have been enriched by them. The recent debates on this subject in various national church bodies in the United States are misleading in their assumption that this is a reality new to the priesthood of the church.

I would argue, however, that a celibate priesthood, both monastic and secular, was first attractive to and then was deeply shaped, formed, and influenced by the homosexuality of significant numbers of its members throughout history. Statistics are impossible to cite, but evidence of the influence of homosexuality in the priesthood historically is so overwhelming as to point to percentages beyond what anyone has yet suggested. The rolls of homosexual clergy have included popes, archbishops, bishops, abbots, friars, monks, priests, and deacons. They have included names as well known as Lanfranc and Anselm, both Archbishops of Canterbury, and evidence points to the probability that this was the orientation of Hadrian IV, Leo IX, and Alexander II, among others from the See of Rome.

Homosexuality was certainly not limited to the clergy, and secular history may have turned on the alleged homosexual relationship between Richard the Lionhearted and the King of France. However, with celibacy as the norm, holy orders did offer a socially acceptable outlet for escaping heterosexual expectations. Such a sanctuary was periodically needed as social attitudes toward homosexuality ebbed and flowed throughout Western history. The priesthood also offered homosexual persons a community, a disciplined structure, companionship, respect, and love. The affinity that developed between homosexual persons and the celibate priesthood or the celibate religious life is easily understood.

For reasons that are not always obvious, a high correlation seems to exist between the religious diversity of a society and the acceptance of sexual variations. The fate of the Jews and the fate of gay people, for example, have been almost identical throughout European history.[8] When social attitudes are favorable, gay people tend to form viable subcultures. When attitudes turn hostile, gay people tend to become invisible.

If Professor Kinsey's statistics are accurate and can be taken as a norm for human beings, gay people have been an ever-present and influential minority in every generation. Kinsey suggested that 40 percent of American males and 20 percent of American females have some homosexual experience after puberty. He further suggested that 13 percent of American males and 7 percent of American females are primarily or exclusively homosexual for at least part of their lives.[9] There is no reason to think that America has either a higher or lower percentage than any other nation. Indeed Paul Gebhard, in a 1972 Department of Health, Education and Welfare background paper, asserted his conclusion that well over one-third of the American males have participated in a homosexual act.[10]

If the church's ministry historically has provided the primary institution in Western society where single people could live their lives without having to defend their single status, is it not possible, even probable, that those who were homosexually oriented and who did not want to deal with hostility or sexual ridicule would find the single-sex community of the priesthood or the nunnery highly desirable?

Professor Boswell asserts that there is a historic connection between those who are predisposed to spirituality or mysticism and those who are homosexually oriented that far transcends Christianity. He cites evidence to support this finding in Islamic Sufi literature and in Persian poetry and fiction, as well as in Christianity.[11]

Geoffrey Parrinder, in his book *Sex in the World's Religions*, mentions a tradition in Africa where religiously inspired men wear women's clothes and do women's work. They enjoy a position of honor in those societies.[12] This point of view is substantiated in an article by Charles and Cherry Lindholm entitled "The Erotic Sorcerers," which cites similar examples from Java, Mongolia, Siberia, and among North American Indians.[13] In each instance holy men are considered a third sex and are allowed to dress like women to perform their religious duties. Anthropological studies even suggest that the tribal holy man, the shaman or the medicine man, achieved his influence because, as a homosexual person, he was sexually trustworthy to leave with the women of the tribe when the men were away on a hunt. The concept of the Father God as the divine lover may suggest at least one psychological connecting point.

Margaretta Bowers, a former New York psychiatrist, in her book *Conflicts of the Clergy*, suggested that as a professional group the clergy exhibited deep patterns of loneliness and had a significantly high instance of sexual ambivalence and homosexual orientation.[14] James Ditts, studying clergy as a group, suggested that the profession is corporately marked by a passive-dependent personality profile, which historic studies reveal to be the personality role that males traditionally affirm as the normal behavior pattern for women.[15] This may be another means of explaining the affinity between religious vocations, sexual ambivalence, and homosexuality.

The language of romance frequently employs the diminutive words of a child when speaking of or to the desired lover—words such as "baby," "dear," "boyfriend," "girlfriend." In many still-existing communications from the Middle Ages between such people as the abbot and his monks and the bishop or priests and their lovers such words are regularly employed. Aelred, a priest who has been canonized despite the erotic letters he wrote to Simon, his lover, leaned heavily on this tradition.[16] Those who do not like to face this reality suggest that these writings reflected only the romantic style of the day and meant nothing more. No one, however, with our sexual consciousness could possibly accept that explanation once this massive amount of literature has been read.

Dr. Boswell traces the historic cultural attitudes toward homosexuality and documents the fact that homosexuality was widely practiced and almost unanimously approved in the Roman Empire until the third century.[17] Edward Gibbon, in *The Decline and Fall of the Roman Empire*, asserted that only Claudius of the first fifteen Roman emperors was entirely heterosexual.[18] An empire with a gay emperor was hardly likely to enact discriminatory laws designed to punish gay people. In this same period of history the battle between orthodoxy and gnosticism was being fought within Christianity. One cannot help but wonder how much of the favorable attitude toward homosexuality contributed to the overwhelming male orientation and to the consequent denigration of women that marked orthodoxy.

What little negativity there was toward homosexuality per se in this period of history did not seem to reside in a concept of sexual deviation. Rather it was yet another expression of negativity toward females. The homosexual act was thought to require a man to assume a female role, to act passively, which was considered to be an insult to his masculinity. If the passive role in the homosexual act was played by a boy or a slave or even by a social inferior, the negativity toward homosexuality itself was diminished. It was appropriate for women, boys, and slaves to be passive, to be politically impotent. Gradually the priest came to be added to that list, and passivity became a recognized and encouraged priestly virtue.

When one examines the behavior expectations of the priesthood, historically there is a high correlation of the behavior thought to be acceptable in a woman—weakness, obedience, submission, passivity—with the behavior thought to be acceptable in a priest. These characteristics in a male are not to be equated with homosexuality; there is, however, a strong correlation. Indeed the quality of unmanliness, a eunuch syndrome if you will, was looked upon favorably as a priestly virtue. Yet a masculine power title, "Father," was chosen for the priest, and a great necessity to keep the priesthood clear of any physical invasion by women became psychologically imperative.

Within the hierarchy of the church, from a very early time, an acquiescence toward homosexuality was so prevalent that it occasionally bordered on positive approval. When the Roman Empire fell, a result was a ruralization of the life of the people and their values.[19] Sexual variation and religious diversity both tend, even today, to be urban virtues, not rural virtues. Consequently this traumatic shift in the social order was accompanied by a powerful negativity in the society at large toward gay people. But the evidence reveals that this negativity was mitigated by the church time after time.

The church refused to impose the more severe judgments against homosexuals and declined to enforce the more stringent laws. Tacit approval of the presence of homosexual persons in both the church and the state was seen in the fact that homosexual prostitution was not only tolerated, it was even taxed by Christian emperors for nearly 200 years after Christianity became the official state religion.[20] It was not until the reign of Justinian in A.D. 533 that legislation was finally passed flatly outlawing homosexuality. No evidence exists that Justinian was supported by the church in this action, and records reveal that the only people known to have been punished under this law were prominent bishops.[21] Indeed almost all laws against homosexuality before the thirteenth century were erected by civil authorities with little support from the church.[22] Under the duress of social pressure the church would ratify these laws, but time after time they would soften the punishment. Clearly these civil laws were frequently aimed at the clergy, and the church took countermeasures for its own protection.

Still extant are a number of medieval penitentials published to aid confessors in assigning penances. These semiofficial church documents tended to treat homosexuality very mildly. The penitential of Pope Gregory III, for example, specified a penance of one year for male homosexuality but three years if a priest had gone hunting.[23] Peter Damian, a crusader for what he understood to be sexual purity who later was canonized by the church, complained bitterly about the widespread practice of gay priests confessing to each other to avoid detection and to obtain milder penances. He also alleged that many spiritual advisors had sexual relations with those entrusted to their care.[24]

The indulgent attitude of churchmen toward homosexuality in the early Middle Ages can hardly be due to ignorance of homosexuality.

It was specifically not ignored; rather it was treated quite mildly. John Boswell suggests that the reason for mild treatment was that homosexual relations were especially associated with the clergy.[25] He further asserts that many clergy turned the dominant negativity of the church toward female sexuality in the twelfth century into a positive assertion of the value of homosexual relations and celebrated them with an outburst of gay literature without parallel in the Western world.[26]

In the eleventh century Pope Urban II refused to take action against the installation of a man known only as John as the Bishop of Orleans, despite the fact that his sexual relationship with the previous Bishop of Orleans as well as with his chief sponsor, Ralph, the Archbishop of Tours, was widely known.[27] Popular songs were even composed about Ralph's homosexuality. This papal inaction could scarcely be carelessness or indifference. It must have represented tacit approval. To further document this conclusion, four years later Pope Paschal II intervened directly to depose a bishop named Etienne de Garland for adultery.[28] The comparison of these two responses is quite revealing. In A.D. 1102 the Council of London passed a resolution that sodomy, which by this time had become a synonym for homosexuality, must be confessed as a sin. But Anselm, the Archbishop of Canterbury, prohibited the publication of the decree, declaring, "This sin has hitherto been so public that hardly anyone is embarrassed by it. Many have fallen into it because they were unaware of its seriousness."[29]

This indifference to homosexuality in official church circles coincided with the strenuous effort that was being made to enforce clerical celibacy. Leo IX, who would not support Peter Damian's crusade against homosexual clergy, was the pope who finally took the decisive action against the marriage of clergy. The first Lateran Council of A.D. 1123 made celibacy a requirement for priesthood. There was clearly more than a coincidental relationship between the homosexuality of the clergy and the reforms effected during this century. Contemporaries were quick to note the enthusiasm among gay priests for the prohibition against clerical marriage.[30]

Literary evidence points to a power struggle between gay clergy and married clergy over whose predilections would be stigmatized. One document speaks of priests who are more apt to love gods than goddesses.[31] In some places the mere fact that a person was in holy orders rendered him liable to the suspicion of homosexuality. The astounding volume of gay literature which issued from the pens of clerics during the twelfth century reinforced that suspicion. This same period, Dr. Boswell suggests, "witnessed the first efforts to formulate a theology which would incorporate expressions of gay feelings into the most revered Christian lifestyle—monasticism."[32]

The relationship of David and Jonathan in the Old Testament (I Samuel 19ff) and Jesus and the beloved disciple in the New Testament (e.g., John 13:23) were the popular biblical reference points. St. Aelred, the Abbot of Rievaulx, gave love between people of the same gender its most lasting expression in a Christian context. As abbot he both allowed and encouraged the monks to hold hands and to express affection.[33] Opposition to homosexuality in the church at that time had come to a complete standstill. It was, in fact, tolerated among the highest-ranking prelates in the world. A twelfth-century Spanish Moslem writer, Ibn Abdum, concluded that Christian clergy were all particularly prone to homosexuality.[34]

Most of the gay relationships celebrated in the poetry of this era were between clerics. In some of these poems there would even be arguments about whether clerics or knights were better lovers. The clerics always won because they did the writing.[35]

As the twelfth century faded into history, a note of caution entered the gay literature of Western Europe. Baudri, the Archbishop of Dol, wrote to his beloved Peter, "The prudent lover disguises the deeds of love . . . If you can, keep your deeds above reproach; but if you cannot, at least keep your confidences to yourself."[36] By the thirteenth century a new intolerance was abroad that stifled in a dramatic way the flowering of gay literature. With the tremendous social unrest in the thirteenth century came a tightening of both central authority and religious intolerance. Anti-Semitism and persecution of those considered sexually abnormal people became virulent. Witchhunts, which are always directed toward women, abounded. Heresy trials and inquisitional behavior were encouraged, and whoever one's enemies were tended in the confrontation to be tarnished with the brush of sexual deviation. Many new laws against homosexuals were enacted in the thirteenth century. Once again the church was quite indulgent about enforcing them; but homosexual behavior was driven underground, obviously never to be annihilated but also never to flower openly again until our own day.

I do not mean to suggest that there were no voices in the church that condemned homosexuality. Certainly Aquinas in the thirteenth century could be cited. It is also clear that many a priest had a mistress and lived fairly openly in a heterosexual relationship. Luther strongly argued for a married priesthood in the sixteenth-century Reformation to make legitimate both the clergy-mistress relationships and the off-spring from those relationships. Many an illegitimate child of a bishop or cardinal received special favors and positions and titles of honor from an understanding and sympathetic hierarchy. Officially, however-er, the prevailing attitude was quite negative to the heterosexual sins of the flesh.

Romantic love between men and women in this period of history in fact received its primary boost not from the church but from a secular and pagan source. Alain de Lille, a poet, wrote "The Complaint of Nature" in which the goddess Natura complained about the violations of her sovereignty practiced by twelfth-century society in sexual mat-ters.[37] This was the only work at that time that encouraged and legiti-matized erotic heterosexual passion, and in some ways was the open-ing crack in the revolution against the sexual attitudes of the church, which revolution has reached its fruition in our generation. The divine Natura was the first voice in centuries in Western civilization to suggest that voluntary virginity was not natural, an idea that is commonly accepted today. It is not a long or difficult transition to move from divine Natura to Mother Nature to nature itself to justify the prevailing sexual attitudes in our day.

I trace this long bit of history (primarily with the help of John Boswell) not to raise horror specters about homosexuality in the church but only to show how the antifemale bias of the church came to be so emotional, so firmly written in stone, so hallowed by tradition, and so understood and blessed as the will of God. I would further suggest that these church-formed sexual stereotypes of women must be broken so that men and women both might be able to pursue their full potential and unique individuality as Christians, though to break them means a theological, liturgical, and ecclesiastical revolution such as no orga-nized religious institution has ever survived. The wild gales of change are blowing fiercely. These crucial issues will not be decided by church conventions where men still have enormous majorities. They will be decided outside church structures with the growing perception that the church with its distorted sexual symbols is no longer in touch with the truth by which men and women increasingly are living.

When the smoke of the sexual revolution has cleared, I suspect that we will discover that the Chinese philosophy is right: there is no yin apart from a yang; there is no masculine apart from the feminine. Human sexuality, I am convinced, will be revealed more as a continuum in which maleness and femaleness overlap significantly. I suspect that there is no place where men are men and women are women save in the fantasies of people who are sexually afraid. I believe that the woman who most needs to be liberated is the woman who lives in every man and the man who most needs to be freed is the one who dwells in every woman. I hope the church's sexual images, produced by a combination of misogyny, Manicheanism, and homosexuality, can now be examined with new and critical eyes.

As we have journeyed through these chapters, I have suggested that historically the church filtered misogyny through a Manichean dualism and then overlaid that negative attitude with a male priesthood that was in significant numbers homosexual. If that assumption is correct, the evidence should be found to indicate the effect this kind of sexual orientation has had on theology, liturgy, and the style of church life. This evidence needs to be presented not in order to pronounce it wrong and root it out so much as to open theology, liturgy, and style to some new and more inclusive possibilities where the sensitivities of women and a vigorously affirmed heterosexuality may also be heard. The old saw "Why do we call him Father when he dresses like Mother" needs to be examined from our new psychosexual perspective. Is it a historic coincidence that all male ecclesiastical vestments are dresses? Is the addition of lace to surplices and ruffles to rochets accidental? Does the emotional response to the women who now are assuming those vestments arise from rational objections or from the psychological fear that suddenly our shaky hold on masculinity is revealed? Can some of the hostility toward women priests be anything but a fear that sexually ambivalent male priests will be sexually exposed?

Is the shortage of clergy in those churches that require and enforce celibacy caused today by that requirement, as certain liberal theologians argue, or is it caused by the fact that in our modern world gay people no longer need the church as they once did as a cover to live full and creative lives? Has the exaltation by the church of both celibacy and virginity continued because historically it legitimatized the minority attitude, either misogynist or gay in origin, against marriage? Can anyone in the light of our new psychosexual consciousness still seriously identify celibacy or virginity with the ultimate will of God? Can the church on any level still suggest or believe that majority heterosexual desires are sinful? Do we not now recognize that antifemale prejudices, expressed in church bans on contraception, abortion, remarriage after divorce, clerical celibacy, and the prohibition of women from the priesthood and episcopacy, are a direct result of an ascetic negativity and psychological fear of women coupled with a powerful gay influence on church life? Have not these attitudes served men too well and far too long in their psychological need to keep the ever-threatening women down?

Are not our liturgical practices of kissing stoles, altars, Bibles, the blessed sacrament, reflections of a misplaced sexual function? Are not some aspects of our sacramental theology that literalize the bread as the body of Jesus that can be touched, fondled, broken, or worshiped, filled with psychosexual connotations? Does not any celibate, male-dominated institution that defines the ideal woman as a perpetual virgin finally wind up saying far more about the psychosexual orientation of those doing the defining than it does about the woman being defined or all women who are called to model that definition? Is the artistic portrayal of Jesus as a soft, rather feminine male figure an accurate portrayal or an expression of the desires of those in the church who dominated and controlled the art images through the ages? Is the popularity of the almost nude Christ on the cross that adorns the wall of many a monastic cell devoid of any erotic connotation?

I pose all of these questions just to be pondered. They are not of equal merit, but they do seem to forge a consistent pattern that needs to be explored.

In our day of new sexual awareness, either we Christians will ourselves open our historic sexual prejudices honestly or others will open them for us. Hope seems to me to find expression only when the full spectrum of human sexuality can be called by the church into the task of shaping the sexual images of the future. I yearn to be a part of a Christian community that can celebrate the variety of life-giving sexual options in the human experience. I yearn to avoid the stance of resisting the sexual revolution in an attempt to preserve stereotypes which do violence to many and which are deeply destructive. I yearn to see the church explore and open every oppressive bit of prejudice, including prejudice against homosexuals, that would bind any life into another life's expectations. I do not believe the Christian church can ever again with credibility speak in the name of God unless it speaks with the voice and experience of a full sexual humanity. I do not want to further the experience that women so often have had of being denigrated and humiliated in the name of a Father God by a Mother Church in which only men have positions of power.

I lay out these concerns publicly and at some personal cost because I want to be a responsible leader in this battered but still beloved church of ours. I believe that an open, honest raising of questions will bring together into a community of faith those scattered persons who understand these issues and who are capable of being the church's saving remnant in the crisis of our time. I see the future of the church as bright, not dark, but that bright vision must sustain us with enormous courage as we walk through the threatening and fearful uncertainty that is our present time of transition. There is for me strength in the realization that as I journey toward that vision, I shall discover again and again that in Christ there is neither male nor female, that all our human divisions can be transcended. When that is equally true in the life of the church of this Christ, then the battle for the freedom of the souls of men and women will be over and the victory will usher in a new and fascinating day of full and deeply Christian creativity.

1. William James, *The Varieties of Religious Experience*, New Hyde Park, N.Y., University Books, p. 367.

2. Vincent of Beauvais, *Speculum Doctrinale: A Popular Manual of Moral Doctrine in the Middle Ages*, quoted in John Boswell, *Christianity, Social Tolerance, and Homosexuality*, Chicago, Univ. of Chicago Press, 1980, p. 164.

3. Augustine, *The Soliloquy*, p. 1. 40, in Boswell, p. 164.

4. Clearly, using a spouse as a loveless sex object is not a privilege of marriage. Rape in marriage can be as real as rape outside of marriage. The Vatican was certainly correct in condemning this in their attempt to interpret the Pope.

5. Since so many women died in childbirth, there was, in fact, statistical evidence for this if women were included in the statistics. Also priests and monks were not killed in battle, were fed well, and drank only in moderation; so the statistics had credibility even if the interpretation of the statistics did not.

6. Anne Clark, *Beasts and Bawdy*, New York, Taplinger, 1975, p. 81.

7. John Boswell, *Christianity, Social Tolerance, and Homosexuality*, Chicago, Univ. of Chicago Press, 1980.

8. Ibid., p. 15.

9. Kinsey, *Sexual Behavior in the Human Male* and *Sexual Behavior in the Human Female* (Chapters entitled "Homosexual Outlet").

10. Paul Gebhard, HEW Publication #72-9116, pp. 22–23.

11. Edward Carpenter, *Intermediate Types Among Primitive Folk*, London, 1914, Part I (in Boswell, p. 27).

12. Geoffrey Parrinder, *Sex in the World's Religions*, New York, Oxford Univ. Press, 1980, p. 146.

13. Charles Lindholm and Cherry Lindholm, "The Erotic Sorcerers," *Science Digest*, September 1982.

14. Margaretta Bowers, *Conflicts of the Clergy*, New York, Thomas Nelson, 1963.

15. James E. Ditts, *When People Say No: Conflict and the Call to Ministry*, San Francisco, Harper & Row, 1979.

16. Boswell, p. 223.

17. Boswell, Chapter 3.

18. Edward Gibbon, *The Decline and Fall of the Roman Empire*, ed. Dean Milman et al., London, 1898, p. 313.

19. Boswell, Chapter 5.

20. Boswell, p. 131.

21. Joannes Malalas, *Chrographia* (in Boswell, p. 172).

22. Boswell, p. 174.

23. Boswell, p. 180.

24. Boswell, p. 182, 211 (ref. Liber Gomorrhianus).

25. Boswell, p. 187.

26. Boswell, Chapters 8 and 9.

27. Boswell, p. 213.

28. Boswell, p. 215 (ref. Fliche Le Regne, p. 441–42).

29. Boswell, p. 215.

30. Boswell, p. 217 (See especially the long poem "We Married Clergy," p. 398ff).

31. Boswell, p. 217 (ref. to Note 34).

32. Boswell, p. 218.

33. Marc Daniel, *Hommes du Grand Siècle* (in Boswell, p. 225).

34. Boswell, p. 233.

35. Boswell, p. 256.

36. Boswell, p. 246.

37. Boswell, p. 310.

Chapter 9

FACING NEW QUESTIONS IN THE SEXUAL REVOLUTION

THE revolution goes on. Sexual roles are in flux, sexual stereotypes are in transition. The church, as a major historic institution in setting standards and determining values, is undergoing its own internal traumatic shifting. But while we wait for the smoke of battle to clear, decisions in human lives about sexual behavior have to be made. To shout the authority of the past at the issues of today is doomed to failure.

Three different issues need to be addressed in this whirlwind of change that is upon us. First, what help is forthcoming from the church to assist teenagers and young adults to find sexual values by which they can be guided prior to marriage? These values must be true to the realities in which their lives are lived and at the same time must give expression to the ultimate Christian affirmation that individual life is sacred. Second, what does marriage mean, and what is the essence of sexual fidelity in marriage in this revolutionary age? Third, what are the standards and the norms that would reflect a Christian ethic for those who must make sexual decisions in a postmarital stage of life, whether it be by way of divorce or death? Fitting into this category would also be the mature single adult. I will certainly not be authoritative or exhaustive, but I will seek to point my readers toward the task of seeking new values in the sexual revolution.

To enter the first arena, I would like to share with my readers an existential attempt to communicate as a Christian bishop with the concerns of very real teenagers. It began when the council of youth leaders of the Diocese of Newark asked me if I would speak to their annual winter conference. No content was mentioned. I was flattered to be asked, and so I accepted. Two weeks later they told me that the theme of their conference was human sexuality and asked if I would address that subject. Once again, I agreed. Then I received a letter from them informing me that they had conducted their own discussion group to frame questions they would like me to address. They enclosed their questions, and I reproduce them here:

Why is sexuality a part of our being?
How do we express our human sexuality?
What moral issue is involved in masturbation?
What is the church's view on premarital sex?
Is it OK to live together before marriage?
What is the responsibility of a person under eighteen who decides to have sexual intercourse?
Do people have a right to be gay?
What expressions of my sexuality are acceptable? What are unacceptable?
At what point am I responsible in having sex?
What are the risks to my being when I express my sexuality?
What is the difference between lust and love?
Who is responsible for the decision when abortion is being considered?
Is oral sex immoral, and if so, why?

I was trapped. Their questions guaranteed that I would be real. They had closed the door on the possibility that I might try to hide behind pious platitudes or escapist rhetoric. If I had harbored any doubts that the revolution in sexual consciousness was all-pervasive, these questions finished off those doubts forever. These young people were asking me about things that from my Southern, repressed, moralistic background had never occured to me that I would ever address publicly. I may be the only bishop in any church who has been asked by an official body within his jurisdiction to speak to a church gathering on oral sex and masturbation.

In a very real sense they had honored me. Aided by skillful and sensitive counsellors and advisors, they had developed a direct kind of honesty that bordered on the audacious. I knew that if I or any institutional representative of the Christian church was going to enter their world, the presentation had to be equally honest, equally bold. We will never speak to this generation from ivory towers or from the safe ecclesiastical systems of yesterday. This revolution is real.

Who are these young people? How typical are they of young people today? I submit that they are, in fact, a representative segment of today's teenage world. They come from all parts of the Diocese of Newark, which is as diverse as any other unit of the Episcopal Church in America. This diocese serves all of northern New Jersey, an area that includes some of America's most depressed inner-city ghettos as well as some of America's most beautiful and affluent suburbs. It also embraces little country towns in its northwestern corner that are as isolated, as ingrown, and as skeptical of strangers as small towns in the South and West tend to be. There are also high-rise communities like Fort Lee and Secaucus that house the transient, upwardly mobile New York commuters. There are ethnic communities like Union City with its dominant Cuban population, Ringwood with its Ramapo Indian people, and Hoboken with its large Puerto Rican contingent.

The people in northern New Jersey are a veritable United Nations in national background. There is a Portuguese section of Newark and a German section of Jersey City. The area has received constant waves of immigrants. They came from England originally, but then from France, Spain, Italy, and other parts of southern and eastern Europe. Many were Jews fleeing oppression. Later came the "American migrations" as blacks arrived, first seeking to escape slavery and then, after the Civil War, seeking opportunity in the rapidly growing manufacturing industry. West Indian blacks and Puerto Ricans followed. People from the Orient came, especially after World War II and the wars in Korea and Vietnam. All of these immigrant waves were superimposed upon the native American population we call Indians, who left their indelible mark in the names of many of New Jersey's towns, valleys, lakes, and streams. Each new migrating group brought with them their values, their traditions, their religious convictions; and there was a gentle and mutual sharing that gives this area depth and integrity that is very special. The questions came from young people who had roots in many of these diverse backgrounds.

When I prepared to address these young people, I was convinced that three things had to be clear in my presentation. First, I am a

Christian. That must be implicit and explicit in everything I say. These young people were not addressing their questions to me because I was a sociologist, a historian, a philosopher, a psychiatrist, or just another adult. They were asking their bishop who in some way represented Christianity to them and who was perceived in some sense to speak for the church as well as for himself. Second, it is apparent, but nonetheless once more necessary to state, that I am a man. I cannot, therefore, view sexuality except as a male. My masculine limitation must be understood, and a woman's viewpoint must challenge and correct this presentation. A man cannot escape his maleness, and a male view of human sexuality is only half of the sexual perspective. Third, I must be real. To some degree I had to escape my hangups, the sensitivities of my generation, and the cultural taboos that may no longer be appropriate. Only my audience could judge whether or not I succeeded.

In many ways the questions the teenagers posed are the most difficult, the most emotional, and the most controversial that one who wants to be both a Christian and a citizen of the twentieth century could possibly face, for human sexuality is at the heart of our humanity. It touches everything we do and say and are. It is intimately tied up with love and with normal biological yearnings.

Psychiatrists tell us that sexual feelings are generalized at birth so that the touch of a loving parent bathing, drying, powdering, and massaging with baby oil are all sexually satisfying moments to the infant. The mouth is the first locus of sexual feeling, and the process of nursing, eating, drinking, and sucking are connected in our conscious and unconscious minds with our sexuality. Oral gratification is a need in the life of every one of us from infancy on. Clearly there are adult ways of achieving oral satisfaction. Eating is one; smoking is another; kissing is still another. All have a sexual dimension.

This oral phase of human sexuality feeds the breast consciousness of adults. The female breast is a sex symbol because it awakens not too deeply hidden memories of the joy of oral gratification. In the life of the woman, I am told, nursing an infant is also a deeply gratifying experience, as the action of breastfeeding causes the same hormones to be released into a woman's body that orgasm releases. Sexuality has always had oral components. From infancy on, oral sexuality has always been a part of lovemaking. I suspect that it will always be so. My personal feeling is that at the very least, inside the private sanctity of a marriage, any sexual practice that is mutually desirable and that is voluntarily and lovingly shared cannot be wrong. Obviously that includes oral sex. Outside of marriage it would depend, as would all sexual activity, on the quality of the relationship; and that will need much further defining as this thesis is developed.

As the child grows, other parts of the body are added to the self-consciousness of sexuality. In the early years of life following toilet training, the biological process of bowel movements makes the anal area a sexually alive erogenous zone. Bowel movements are regarded by children as creations of the body analogous to giving birth. Children not infrequently have been known to invite their friends in to view what they have created. Toilet jokes become the favorites of little children up to about ten years of age. The more subtle descendants of these toilet jokes still amuse the adult population, while the cruder descendants lodge permanently in our vulgar language or our profanity. It is interesting to see just how much of our profanity has a toilet content. Sexuality never fully escapes this anal focus, and the frequently given invitation to "kiss my ass" emphasizes the connection by combining a sexual lovemaking oral act with the anal region. In normal adults anal stimulation recedes in importance, but it never disappears. Otherwise the advertising campaigns for designer jeans would not have the obvious appeal that they have. Indeed, tailored jeans deliberately present the anal region as a sexually stimulating area. Fannies are obviously "in" today.

With the onset of puberty, human sexuality achieves its dominant focus in the genital area as the innate power of creation prepares human life for reproduction. This driving biological urge becomes a major force in life, and its power is exciting, dangerous, compelling, and fearful.

Genital sexuality has been celebrated in human worship in ancient fertility cults with temple prostitutes, both male and female. It has been denied and repressed in human worship in such things as the requirements of celibacy for the priesthood and in the suggestion, noted in the previous chapters, that the ideal woman is a "perpetual virgin." It has created the romantic literature of the ages including ancient Greek mythology, the story of Tristan and Isolde, the adventures of King Arthur and Gwenivere, and Hamlet and Ophelia. It soars to the heights of the English language in the sonnets of Robert and Elizabeth Barrett Browning and descends to the pedestrian level of love comics, which I suspect some of my teenage audience had read. The power of sex has been the source of political intrigue in such episodes as David and Bathsheba in the Bible, Antony and Cleopatra in Rome, and the more modern story of Edward VIII, whose love for Baltimore divorcee Wally Simpson caused him to give up his throne in England in 1936. This power fills the biographer's need to expose the sexual appetites of important people as well as to name their lovers. No public figure, not even the paternal President Dwight Eisenhower or the popular theologian Paul Tillich, has escaped this treatment.

The biological drive of genital sexuality undergirds both the institution of marriage and also houses of prostitution. It creates those marvelous pictures of wrinkled couples who are celebrating their golden wedding anniversaries, as well as the various sexploitation businesses that flourish at Times Square in New York City. All of these and many others are the manifestations of the enormous power of human sexuality.

It is easy to understand the twin emotions of desire and fear that surround human sexuality. Desire drives us toward a legitimate way to express, enjoy, and appreciate our sexuality. Fear drives us toward a legitimate way to control, bridle, or repress so dangerous a force. Sexual mores have always sought to move creatively between desire and fear. The goodness of the desire must be affirmed, or we deny the essential goodness of God's creation. The reality of the fear creates the necessary controls so that a constructive expression of human sexuality can be achieved. Many of the facets of sexuality that we have to deal with today are present because the control systems of yesterday have been dismantled. It is not that the control systems were wrong; it is that they became irrelevant.

In an era when sexuality and procreation could not be separated, the whole society had to organize so that the goodness of sexuality would find expression only inside that unit of society that could manage effectively the birth of a new life. So marriage became the only legitimate doorway into the fullness of sexual expression.

The sanctity of marriage was affirmed in all of the wedding traditions. The father, who had been the protector of the female virtue, gave his daughter away to the man who would now assume that role as the sole recipient of her feminine charms. The wedding dress of white symbolized the purity of the virgin bride. The other customs—the hope chest, the symbols (something old, something new, something borrowed, something blue), the bachelor's party, the decorated wedding car, the jokes, the carrying of the bride over the threshold—all supported the social concern that sex was allowable only inside marriage. Even the wedding ring symbolized the sexual union. The ring was the female sex symbol, the finger the male sex symbol; the placing of the ring on the finger was the pledge of fidelity in physical love. It was the absolute social conviction in the world that created these traditions that only inside marriage could children be born and have a chance to grow up in a stable social order, being nurtured by a male and a female.

To guard the sanctity of marriage, vast social pressures were applied to uphold the standards. A woman who had a child out of wedlock received a condemnation so total that excommunication from the social order would not be too strong a term to describe it. Since the "wild passions of the flesh" were both known and feared, every effort was expended to keep sex in bounds before marriage. In nineteenth-century Western courtship patterns, holding hands was forbidden prior to engagement, and kissing was a serious offense. Elaborate chaperone systems were devised. The society was not particularly mobile in those days, and eligible daughters were guarded, watched, and accompanied everywhere they went.

The chaperone system functioned between puberty and marriage, a time span that a century ago was quite brief. Puberty today starts some five or six years earlier than it did in the early nineteenth century. Marriage also occurs today, especially for women, much later than it did a century ago. Very few women in the nineteenth century had the benefit of higher education or the opportunity to pursue careers outside the home, so the time between puberty and marriage for most young women was relatively brief in that era. Marriage was a woman's primary destiny. A woman who did not marry had very few options. She could become the maiden aunt who lived at home and was the ready chaperone for the next generation. The only professions open to unmarried women were teaching, nursing, or becoming a nun. These female vocational activities also produced a rigidly controlled living system, and no respectable woman would live outside such a system in that day.

Today's teenagers lack the historical perspective to embrace the newness of the facts they take for granted. The automobile as an adjunct to almost every family is a very new part of American life, scarcely fifty years old. The familiar suburban living pattern, complete with gigantic shopping centers that make cars essential, is a post-World War II phenomenon. In the nineteenth century, neighborhoods were the places we lived, not the places we slept. The system devised to control human sexuality was not born in our kind of world. In that era there was almost no way a romantic young couple could escape the immediate gaze of an authority figure. When young women did begin to go away to college, college administrations became, in fact, alma maters—nurturing mothers—and the control system continued to live. If today's college students would examine the dormitory rules of a women's school fifty years ago, they would be amazed, aghast, and amused. That world could not have conceived of our world of automobiles that seek out and find lovers' lanes, vans that rock in the night, coeducational dormitories, or college administrations that refuse to be involved in the task of chaperoning.

The widespread opportunity for sexual expression or sexual experimentation has existed but a few years, relatively speaking. This means that the grandparents or great-grandparents of today's teenagers had to make very few sexual decisions. Most decisions were made for them, and it did not occur to that generation to question the process. Theirs was a rigidly controlled world. Since the whole social structure dictated that children could be managed only inside marriage, so sex which produced children could be allowed only inside marriage. That was the clear, logical assumption on which sexual behavior rested before sexuality and procreation were separated.

It should not be surprising that Christianity was interpreted as securing and blessing the control system. When the history of Christianity is studied, it is clear that the church viewed sexual sins as the worst sins imaginable. Adultery was a crime punishable in earlier days in this country by death. Because medicine in that era had not yet associated infections with germs, the social diseases were viewed as quite simply the punishment of God upon those who violated the moral norms. Most people today are not aware that before the advent of penicillin, victims of advanced syphilis (which attacks the nervous system) were the primary inhabitants of mental hospitals, and this fact helped to form the bitter, prejudiced pattern of the society toward people in mental institutions.

When all of these factors are put together, it is easy to be aware of the massive control system set up by the society to manage the powerful drive of human sexuality. To ensure that children were conceived only inside marriage, a negativity of large proportions toward sex was built and undergirded by the determiners of value in the society. The power of the church was employed to scare people into righteousness. The fear of contracting an incurable social disease curbed sexual appetite. A rigorous chaperone system reduced opportunity for indiscretion to almost zero. The role of women was so clearly circumscribed that until very recently women could not escape the imposed definition of what a woman must be. Sex was understood, experienced, and acted out in that kind of world.

Then came the revolution. It was not a moral revolution first, but rather a technological revolution. Sexuality and procreation were effectively separated by the development of birth-control devices.[1] When that happened, the whole superstructure of control came tumbling down—not all at once, but its doom was certain.

The primary reason sex had to be controlled was that the birth of children needed to be within a married union or the whole structure of society would topple. But suddenly sex and childbirth were separated. Miracle drugs cured infectious diseases. Women began to break out of the male-imposed stereotypes. A culture based on the automobile and the nuclear family developed. Women began to live alone; divorce rates skyrocketed; living patterns changed. Marriage itself began to be questioned. The old fears were rendered impotent, and the joy of sexual expression rose to prominence. The goodness of sex as a natural part of God's creation began to be celebrated.

In our rush to escape the fear motives of the past and to inaugurate a new sexual freedom, new values were espoused and new freedom was achieved, which means that questions like the ones the Diocesan Youth Group asked me abound, and answers like the ones that I received in my day no longer suffice. The time has come in the sexual revolution to search for guidelines that affirm values to which we can be committed so that we might develop standards that are appropriate in our world. Yesterday's repression has lost its power, but today's sense that anything goes is morally inadequate. If the church does not take seriously the sexual realities of this moment of history, or if we try to give artificial respiration to yesterday's system of repression and control and to impose it anew, we will simply lose our credibility. But if we as a church have no values to share, no guidelines to offer, no verities to affirm in this vital area of life at this revolutionary moment, then we are no longer worthy of anyone's attention. So let me try to build a value system that can be discussed, clarified, and perhaps adopted.

I start with some positive statements that arise out of my understanding of Christianity. Human life is good. Personhood is good. Sex as a part of human life is inseparable from our personhood. So sex is good. It was created to find expression in loving relationships that enrich and enhance life. Sex is powerful and touches life at its very depth. Sex is more than physical thrills. It is an emotional, a psychological, and even a spiritual experience. Sex is meant to be shared. The sex act requires a deep commitment to mutual responsibility and well-being. Male sex organs need female sex organs to be completed. Female sex organs need male sex organs to be completed. So sex is giving and receiving, loving and being loved, completing and being completed. When these qualities are present, sex has the potential to be good.

Obviously, so sacred, so emotional, and so deep a commitment cannot be achieved in a casual relationship. If sex and love are ever separated, the result, I believe, is destructive to the sacredness of personhood. No one can use another person without turning that person into a thing. No one wants to be a Hertz Rent-a-Body to gratify another's need. No one wants to be manipulated, fed a line, made a conquest. Those activities do not create or enhance life.

For sex to be a creative and life-giving experience it must be limited to a proper relationship, which means that "a proper relationship" needs to be defined and sexual behavior needs to be appropriate to that relationship. It is important to know that every human relationship has a physical side. The context and the quality of the relationship determine the proper physical expression. A handshake is a physical symbol. So is an embrace, a kiss, a pat, a touch. So is sexual intercourse. But clearly some of those physical expressions are not appropriate in every relationship.

We think of holding hands as a very casual kind of physical symbol. But if a teenager began to hold hands with someone he or she barely knows, the high school principal for instance, it would be an inappropriate physical symbol. Even the same physical expression has different meanings in different contexts. On Sunday afternoon before 75,000 people in Giants Stadium in the New Jersey Meadowlands, and before millions more on television, a 250-pound linebacker will walk back and forth swatting 270-pound tackles and defensive ends on the posterior. No one seems to think that strange. But if an acolyte went up and down the communion rail doing the exact same thing to worshipers in church, we would not think that appropriate behavior. The physical symbol is identical, but the context of the action makes one seem so normal as to be unnoticed while the other would appear to be bizarre. Physical symbols must always be appropriate to the context and to the nature of the relationship in which they are employed.

It is appropriate in some relationships to hug, but not in others. It is appropriate in some relationships to hold hands, to kiss, to pat, to touch, to hold; but it is not appropriate to do any or all of those things in every relationship. Sexual intercourse is clearly an appropriate means of expressing love in some relationships and equally clearly not in other relationships. The question then becomes not what is right, or how do I express my sexuality, or what is my responsibility if I am under eighteen and decide to have sex, or what expressions of my sexuality are acceptable; but rather what kind of relationship must I have to make the expression of the various parts of my sexuality appropriate, life-giving, and good? What kind of relationship is required for me to be certain that sex is loving and reciprocal and not using and self-gratifying? What responsibility do I have to control my biological yearnings so that they are positive not negative, enhancing life not destroying it? Only in response to these probings can we determine standards that affirm biological reality and the Christian commitment to the holiness of each individual life.

I cannot speak for everyone, but I can share my convictions and I can seek to interpret the church's teaching on some of the issues that the young people of our diocese have raised.

When is sexual intercourse appropriate behavior? For me, it is appropriate inside a relationship to which an enormous, perhaps an ultimate, commitment has been made. It cannot be casual and still be moral. It cannot be separated from deep and abiding love without being cheapened. It must be special, the culmination of much time together, during which the personhood of each partner is progressively revealed and received by the other. It must be acted out only under the circumstances where each is capable of being responsible for all aspects of the action, including emotional, psychological, and spiritual aspects. It must be sacred, private, an exquisite moment to be shared with no one else. It cannot be a subject for gossip or bragging and still be loving. It cannot be filled with fear. Fear is the recognition that one is not capable of being responsible for one's action and therefore must slip or sneak or hide.

For me the normative relationship in which all of these elements are present is still marriage, which is a public pledge under God that a man and a woman have chosen to be responsible for all that their relationship can be, "for better, for worse, for richer, for poorer, in sickness and in health, until we are parted by death."[2] For me marriage remains the norm, the ideal in which the deepest sharing of human sexuality finds its fullest and most complete outlet. Here the potential is present for expanded life, the greatest love, the most complete sexual fulfillment. So I would have to say that it is clear to me that premarital sex in most circumstances would not be considered the ideal, the norm of the Christian church.

But is it evil? Is it wrong? Is it never an alternative? Is it biologically possible to separate puberty from marriage by ten to fifteen years as we have done in Western civilization and still limit sexual intercourse to marriage? Under such circumstances could not the vigorous maintenance of the ideal actually be destructive by imposing a standard that is counter to the normal drives of normal people? Cannot sexual intercourse, now separated from reproduction, be viewed in less ultimate ways? Can it not be an intimate and mutually satisfying expression of love that gives a new dimension to deep friendship? My younger friends make this case. Without endorsing that possibility, I must at least seek to understand it and recognize that it is the ascending norm, while the ideal I seek to maintain is, at least statistically, the declining norm of yesterday.

Nonetheless I remain convinced that, at the minimum, sexual intercourse separated from any love or commitment is destructive to personhood and is therefore immoral. So the boundaries are set with an ideal that may be unachievable on one side and a practice that appears immoral on the other. Between the ideal of married love and the immorality of loveless sex, there is a vast gray area, and in that area today's young people live their lives and make their decisions. The only guidelines I can offer them are the ones that lead me to affirm marriage as the normal context for the fullest expression of our sexuality. If sexual intercourse is practiced before marriage, I would hold that a deep, significant, committed relationship is necessary if such sexual activity is to be called moral. If that commitment is present, then sex shared in that relationship may not be ideal; but I for one can no longer say it is immoral. Whatever conclusion or action plan at which today's young people arrive, life must be seen as holy and personhood as sacred. Holy life and sacred personhood to me are the irrevocable, bedrock positions of Christian morality. Each decision must affirm these bedrock positions if that decision is to reside inside Christian morality.

Let me speak briefly to some of the other specific questions asked me by the Diocesan Youth Group.

Masturbation

In my book *The Living Commandments*, published in 1977, I said:

> I want to make it clear that I do not in any sense regard masturbation as evil or destructive. I consider it a natural part of the discovery of bodily joys. Harm comes from masturbation only because of the fear and negativity with which past generations have regarded it. I am impressed by some recent studies that seem to indicate that better marital adjustments are made by those who had regularly engaged in adolescent masturbation than by those who had not. Danger arises when one limits his or her own sexual desire to this level, substituting a solitary act for the sharing of life which I believe is inherent in sexuality and is potentially the deepest human experience of community.[3]

I see no reason to change that attitude today, except to be even more positive that these conclusions are right.

Abortion

Abortion is too great and complex a subject to be treated in a cursory manner, so all I would like to do is set the parameters in which I believe abortion decisions need to be made. If abortion is used as a means of birth control, I regard it as highly questionable. That is one parameter. Human life, either actual or potential, must always be regarded as sacred. An unborn fetus and a senile elderly person must both be regarded as holy. A cavalier treatment of life that denies human sacredness must be opposed by a Christian who believes in a God who creates us in God's own image, who redeems us in Jesus Christ, and who sanctifies us by the Holy Spirit. A sexual act that runs the risk of pregnancy outside the context of a marriage in which the life of a child can be properly nurtured is irresponsible, insensitive, and unloving, no matter how much we surround that act with moonlight and roses. Anyone who is incapable of caring for the life of a baby must not act in a manner that runs the risk of giving birth to a baby. That is not positive behavior. To plan to use abortion consciously to rectify previous mistakes becomes for me not within the sphere of moral decision-making.

Having said that, I still would assert quickly the other side of my set of parameters. Abortion must always be a legal alternative for women. There are clearly circumstances where the decision to have an abortion can be made responsibly, though that is never easy and seldom ideal. Everyone whose life is affected by the decision should be a party to the abortion decision. The mother, the father, the web of relationships in which they live, their doctor, the unborn child, the church must all be considered in seeking the best alternative under the less than ideal circumstances in which human life is lived. But when all is said and done, the fetus is in the body of the mother, and every woman must, I believe, have the right to make the ultimate decision about her own body in all matters, including this one.

If a couple decides that they are going to live in an active sexual relationship outside of marriage, then responsible love seems to me to require effective birth control. Inside marriage, effective birth control, used to ensure the physical, emotional, spiritual, economic, and psychological well-being of the entire family, is not just beneficial but its absence, in my mind, borders on being immoral. This clearly does not exhaust the abortion issue, but a more complete treatment is outside the scope of this volume.

The Gay Issue

Once again, a profoundly complex issue cannot receive the attention it demands, but when the young people asked for my views, I responded in this manner:

There is no unanimity of opinion in the social order or in the church on the question of homosexuality. There are many theories but few universally held convictions. So long as that is the case, I believe it behooves all of us to act in charity and compassion on issues we do not understand. For example, a hundred years ago, before we had the benefit of psychological thinking, the Christian church condemned suicide and refused to allow anyone who had committed suicide to be buried from the church. Today we understand depression, mental illness, the self-destructive human urges; and we are embarrassed that we ever could have been so cruel to the suffering suicide victims or to their bereaved families. In many ways the church seems to me to be repeating this mistake whenever it assumes a rigid position on homosexuality without adequate knowledge.

Homosexuality is publicly discussed today, but it has always been a fact of life, with varying attitudes toward it prevailing from time to time. The general wisdom of the social scientists today asserts that homosexual persons have in every generation been a silent but ever-present minority. The question is whether homosexuality is genetically produced or environmentally produced. Is it a valid part of the continuum of human sexuality? Is it a perfectly normal but minority aspect of human life, like left-handedness, for example, or is it a distortion of human life, a sickness? Are people born homosexual and have no option to be otherwise, or are they shaped by environmental forces such as distorted parents or deviant relatives? Can homosexual school teachers or homosexual clergy seduce heterosexual children into being homosexual, or is homosexuality a preconditioned state that environmental forces cannot manipulate?

Those questions must be answered with authority before we can speak to such questions as: do people have a right to be gay or is it Christian to be gay? If homosexuality is an environmentally produced distortion of human life, then we need to root out those twisting forces and seek to overcome the distortions in the human being so that the full humanity of every person who is homosexual might be restored. If that proves not to be possible, we need to be sensitive and humane to those who are so victimized. If, on the other hand, homosexuality is a genetic reality, a normal minority experience of human beings, then we must say that homosexuality is no more non-Christian than is heterosexuality, and the only moral issue that needs to be addressed is the way in which our sexuality is expressed. The weight of recent scholarship seems to point toward the genetic origin of most homosexuality, but final, conclusive data are simply not yet available. So the stance of the Christian church toward homosexuality must be, I believe, open, sensitive, life-giving, and nonjudgmental; for every person is the child of God, holy and acceptable to God regardless of his or her sexual orientation.

The fact remains that, regardless of the original cause, homosexuality is today considered by most psychiatrists to be an irreversible orientation. Homosexual persons need friends, community, love, mutual commitment, and physical expressions as much as any other human beings. I do not want to be in the position of saying that loving relationships are moral only for heterosexual people. I would hope that soon the church would design a liturgical service whereby gay and lesbian couples might make a public pledge to each other and have that pledge blessed by the church. I do not believe that marriage is the appropriate word to use for gay and lesbian relationships, but a liturgical act of mutual dedication to each other would, it seems to me, be a loving and supportive stance for the church to take. It would move us beyond a primary concern with the morality of sexual intercourse so that we could begin to address the far more destructive and serious moral issues of rape, child molesting, prostitution, and pimping which are present among both heterosexually and homosexually oriented people.

I conclude this chapter by reiterating that we are living in an era of history when yesterday's moral and sexual guidelines have been widely abandoned and tomorrow's moral and sexual standards have not yet been established. It is a dangerous time and a difficult time. I do not believe that the Christian church can say with the assurance of yesterday that certain practices are always right and certain practices are always wrong. But we can say that human life is always sacred. We can say that the full expression of the unique personhood of every child of God is both holy and the final goal of our life and behavior. Every act in which we engage must answer these questions: Does this act make explicit the sacredness of human life? Does this act enhance my personhood and the personhood of everyone involved, or does it deny and repress personhood? Starting here, I believe we can and will create new standards of behavior. They will be far more flexible than the standards of the past, but they will not sell out to the hedonism of our time. They will have the power to elicit our commitment and will prove worthy to be called "Christian" by our generation.

1. Madonna Kolbenschlag, *Kiss Sleeping Beauty Good-bye*, New York, Doubleday, 1979, p. 16ff. Kolbenschlag argues persuasively that the pill was, in fact, woman's great emancipator.

2. *Book of Common Prayer*, 1979, p. 427.

3. John S. Spong, *The Living Commandments*, New York, Seabury, 1977, p. 90.

Chapter 10

MARRIAGE:
A CHANGING INSTITUTION
POSTMARRIAGE: A NEW REALITY

THE attitude of the church toward marriage has been, as we have seen, inconsistent in history. The prevailing understanding has been determined by many factors. Yet there is a sense in which people with short historical memories assume that what they have traditionally associated with the church's view of marriage has, in fact, been universal in time and assumed in history.

For us to talk about new possibilities in thinking about marriage patterns in the future demands a consistent concept from which new ideas would deviate. For my church and, I suspect, for most branches of Christianity, that would best be seen in the liturgy of a marriage service in each tradition.

The Episcopal Book of Common Prayer, 1979, states:

> The union of husband and wife in heart, body, and mind is intended by God for their mutual joy; for the help and comfort given one another in prosperity and adversity; and, when it is God's will, for the procreation of children and their nurture in the knowledge and love of the Lord. Therefore marriage is not to be entered into unadvisedly or lightly, but reverently, deliberately, and in accordance with the purposes for which it was instituted by God.[1]

The solemn vows that are exchanged emphasize the eternal, irrevocable nature of the commitment:

> Will you have this man to be your husband; to live together in the covenant of marriage? Will you love him, comfort him, honor and keep him, in sickness and in health; and, forsaking all others, be faithful to him as long as you both shall live?
>
> Will you have this woman to be your wife; to live together in the covenant of marriage? Will you love her, comfort her, honor and keep her, in sickness and in health; and, forsaking all others, be faithful to her as long as you both shall live?[2]

In the prayers offered for the married couple, the Prayer Book says:

> Make their life together a sign of Christ's love to this sinful and broken world, that unity may overcome estrangement, forgiveness heal guilt, and joy conquer despair.[3]

These illustrations from the liturgy seem to me to express the view that most of us have identified with the concept of Christian marriage. It is a concept that has never been static or fixed, but not in recent history has it been subjected to the pressures that today and tomorrow are certain to bring.

If our understanding of human sexuality and sexual stereotypes is in radical flux, then marriage, which certainly has a sexual component, will also be in a spinning state of transition. The symbols of that transition are abundantly clear and are, to many, deeply disturbing.

In our day many couples do not get married until they have tested their relationship in both formal and informal living-together arrangements. Marriage itself has shifted from being a unit within an extended family into being a nuclear unit. The role and place of the woman within that nuclear unit is radically different today from previous generations. The pressures on that unit in today's society are so intense that divorce occurs within almost one of every two marriages. This has served to create a significant number of persons in our world who are "postmarriage people," a category that our great-grandparents would have thought of only for widows and widowers.

Postmarriage sexual patterns are clearly different from the past, but so are the sexual patterns in marriage and the sexual patterns in the premarriage period. The revolution is real. There is a desperate need for the church that wants to be part of the future to address these realities of human life, to help people find value and meaning within the new patterns, and at the same time to bear witness to the ideal of marriage as Christians continue to uphold that ideal. That is not an easy task.

If the church were to undertake a public program to help divorcing people to walk through that experience with a minimum amount of scarring, a ministry which desperately needs to be developed, the leaders would be whiplashed by certain religious voices who would see in this effort nothing but the church endorsing divorce. When the patterns of sexual behavior in a society deviate so completely from what we think of as Christian standards, the explanation may be that the whole society is sick or sinful and therefore unworthy of attempts at redemption. That was the judgment the Bible made about the cities of Sodom and Gomorrah (Genesis 18 and 19).

But it also may be that the so-called Christian standards are no longer sensitive to or understanding of the dynamics and pressure under which our people are living. In this chapter I want to raise that latter possibility and examine some alternative styles of human relationships that perhaps ought to be embraced and blessed by the Christian church.

Before moving into that provocative area, however, I want to hold up the pattern of monogamous, faithful marriage and to say that in my mind this still is the ideal, even if statistics reveal that it has ceased to be the norm. As a pastor, my desire is to meet people where they are, to practice the art of the possible, to help them achieve the good that is available to them within the brokenness of their particular human lives. But as a person, I still believe that ideals need to be stated and lifted up, not to judge that which is not ideal but simply to keep before us everything that human life can be. The Bible reminds us that life in this world cannot be equated with life in the Garden of Eden. We all live east of Eden. I only want to make sure that we never forget what Eden was and what Eden can be. So let me begin with a personal witness.

In my deepest being I remain convinced of the truth that the highest development of human character and the greatest potential human joy are finally the results and by-products of the total commitment of one person to another in a holy marriage. This kind of commitment begins for me in a public pledge of a husband and wife before "God and this company." From that moment, which for many, if not most of us, is so shallow, so naive, and so immature, nevertheless a life together starts to grow, a corporate history begins to be written. In no time at all thousands of ties emerge to bind the couple. Some of these ties are large, but most of them are so tiny that to many people they are not significant at all.

In every marriage there are peak moments of special joy: the wedding itself, the honeymoon, the first home, various anniversaries and birthdays, the first pregnancy, the birth of each child, favorite vacation spots and moments. There are also crises that must be faced and overcome: the decision to move, failures, sickness, the breakup of a friendship, the death of a loved one. There are emotional moments of transition: high school and college graduations, the engagement and marriage of grown sons and daughters, the arrival of grandchildren, business changes, promotions or firings. There is the death of the couple's own parents, which makes them realize that they are now the senior members of their family. All of these experiences become the shared mountaintop memories that make two lives so deeply one that if they are severed or ripped apart, the pain is not unlike radical surgery.

On a less conscious or significant level, however, there are also millions of hair-thin threads that bind a married couple together more steadfastly than Gulliver was ever bound. These threads consist of habits, styles, special food (not fancy but uniquely part of a particular marriage: salmon croquettes and corn muffins made without sugar, it is for me), a memorable restaurant, a hallowed place. There are even ties in those irritating habits that become marks of the relationship about which family jokes are made. Growing old together when the mutual life of the couple has been fed with this constant living stream of memories and has been bound with millions of shared moments seems to me to be the charted route toward the development of a new and full personhood in each of the partners of such a marriage.

There is, I am convinced, more potential for the realization of all of our humanity in this pattern than in any other lifestyle. It is in this life pattern, I believe, that character is best shaped and defined. Here also a resonant joy is discovered that becomes strong enough to embrace the inevitabilities of human life and transform the sadness, the sickness, and finally even the death of one's spouse into victories, not defeats. This kind of marriage is still possible, I believe, but it takes a single-minded dedication on the part of both partners. It does not come if happiness is one's primary goal, but its rewards strike me as eminently worth the effort.

No matter how our standards change in an effort to accommodate a radically changing world with compassion and sensitivity, there must still be a goal and an ideal. For me, faithful monogamous marriage where both partners grow as their relationship grows is that ideal. I lift it high. I salute it. I believe in it. But with the norm fully stated, the ideal compellingly presented, we still must be sensitive to those human circumstances that may well be beyond human control which time after time render the ideal impossible or unachievable. Any ethical system based on the sacredness of life must embrace the exceptions.

The first exception is that marriage in our day does not in many instances inaugurate the sexual relationship. Formal and informal living-together arrangements are a rising phenomenon of our times. Generally the church officially has viewed this pattern with judgmental disfavor. There is, however, a positive side that needs to be stated. Today's young generation does not seem to feel that the satisfaction of sexual desire is an adequate reason to enter a marriage. As a marriage counselor, I totally agree. Many of today's young people, disillusioned by the marriages they have witnessed, seek a wiser choice, a more knowledgable commitment, a deeper experience of compatibility. They want to test marriage before they enter it. In some ways that is their tribute to the sanctity of marriage.

This is a new phenomenon, relatively speaking, that has emerged as the old sexual pressures of the prerevolutionary world began to die. When sexuality was separated from procreation, when the time between puberty and marriage was stretched to ten or more years, when the stereotype of a woman that placed her on a pedestal and proclaimed that she was a prize to be courted, won, kept, and protected was challenged, then it was all but inevitable that some sexual sharing in a relationship of equality prior to marriage would in time become the norm. In our generation it has almost become so. But is it bad? Is it immoral? I want to be on record as saying that I do not think it is always so.

Suppose that fifty years from now we discover that couples who marry after they have lived together for a period of time have a significantly lower divorce rate than do those who do not. If living together causes two people to decide they are not congenial enough to enter marriage, is that not a positive achievement? It has been my experience that couples who decide after living together that they want to be married approach that marriage with a seriousness and a dedication that is not always apparent in their more traditional counterparts. Maybe this arrangement is not ideal, but neither is the present system that pretends that this is not happening and has produced our present marital instability.

No less a figure than Geoffrey Fisher, the former Archbishop of Canterbury, after his retirement called on the Church of England to develop some liturgical service of mutual dedication for a couple to enable them with the church's blessings to enter something he called trial marriage, or what others call an informal living-together arrangement. Needless to say, his conservative ecclesiastical colleagues dismissed the idea as the product of an aging mind bordering on senility in their former primate. One wonders now how it was that the Archbishop could have been so far ahead of the thinking of his own time. I believe this is an idea that will increasingly find support.

This liturgical recognition would signify that the relationship is an act of mutual commitment, though short of a legal marriage. It might carry such elements as pledge of fidelity, a pledge not to have children, and a specific time for evaluation. Short of this, I see nothing except increasing indiscriminate sexual experimentation. I do not believe that biologically active young adults in our mobile society, with no cultural restraints, will postpone sexual intercourse until they are married when birth control is readily available and when marriage is separated from puberty by the span of time that is the case today. If they do, there will be a price to be paid in emotional capital and mental health. For the church to bless the mutual dedication of a couple not yet ready to make a lifetime commitment, and give some order to the sexual experimentation that is now the rule and not the exception, would, in my opinion, be a sensitive pastoral act.

Perhaps the choice for young adults today is becoming either sexual relations where deep if not ultimate commitment is present or sexual relations outside any significant commitment at all. If that analysis is correct, then I urge the church to meet people where they are and bless the new arrangements with sensitivity to their values and understanding of their development. A radical suggestion, some will say. Before another generation has passed, I submit it will be normative.

The ideal for me is sexual fidelity in a monogamous marriage. But what can we say to the marriage patterns of our day when the ideal is impossible and the pain is unbearable and the choices are quite narrow? Our traditional understanding of marriage was forged in a world where the extended family was a reality, where the stereotypical role of the woman as resident homemaker was unchallenged, where the assumption that the childbearer would be the childrearer was universal. No one in that era could conceive of a husband refusing to accept a promotion because it was detrimental to his wife's career, or the category "househusband," or the legal ramifications of maternity leaves, or shared domestic duty. These are all symbols of the revolution, and they have impacted marriage dramatically.

When I weigh these pressures with an open mind and a sensitive spirit, my surprise is that one of every two marriages seems to succeed. How compromised the nondivorced marriage is by infidelity, discontent, cold war, neurotic attachment, or economic dependency that precludes divorce we may never know. What emerges as an obvious fact, however, is that few marriages come close to that ideal of mutual satisfaction, mutual growth, and mutual fidelity. Marriage is for most not a dream but a struggle, and sex, even in marriage, is not necessarily a symbol of fulfillment. Sexually frustrated, sexually hungry, and sexually hurting adults—both men and women—are numerous today. Many of them are living inside the institution of marriage. Changes in mores, moral attitudes, and sexual practices mark marriage today as surely as they mark the premarriage patterns.

So long as the marriage is operative to any degree, I believe that there is a moral obligation to seek sexual fidelity. Marriage is worthy of such an effort, and a single-minded sexual commitment is, I believe, a part of the mutual responsibility of the couple. To split off one's sexual affection from one's spouse and still seek to save a marriage is not a positive response, I am convinced.

Yet we must be open to the possibilities and the pressures that now surround us. No man or woman ever seems to have had all of his or her sexual needs met inside a single relationship. Please note that by sexual needs I do not necessarily mean to imply sexual-intercourse needs. In the extended family of the previous century, the husband and the wife had many contacts that had sexual components and that greatly enriched their individual lives. Very seldom, however, did these contacts result in infidelity. The man, for example, would relate intimately to his mother, his mother-in-law, perhaps a maiden aunt, his sisters and/or sisters-in-law, his daughters, and his nieces. The woman on the other hand would relate to her father, her father-in-law, perhaps a bachelor uncle, her brothers and/or brothers-in-law, her sons, and her nephews. There woud be appropriate physical contact on many levels in each relationship. For some it might be a hug, for others a kiss, for others even a pat. There would be mutual emotional stroking, intimate advice-giving, deep emotional sharing. Different feelings would be communicated to different people in that family constellation at different times. The husband and the wife did not carry each other's whole emotional load. Love was an emotion that embraced a community. The marriage was a unit lived in and supported by the extended family.

Sexual exclusiveness could be maintained, I submit, far better when sexual needs on a less ultimate level than sexual intercourse were met legitimately and openly in numerous other interfamily male-female relationships. When those ceased to be normative, spouses were forced to look first to each other with an emotional expectation that was doomed from the beginning. Then in desperation they began to look to other relationships across sexual lines. They were seeking the non-sexual-intercourse levels of intimacy that they once had found in the extended family, but they found it increasingly difficult to receive the strokes and emotional feeding without having the relationship become an intimate, clandestine, sexual-intercourse relationship. Before we become moral judges, we must become sensitive understanders of human reality.

While I regret marital infidelity, I no longer consider it to be a legitimate reason for the breakup of a marriage. Adultery is not a proper cause for divorce. It is rather an invitation to examine the needs that both the wandering spouse and the nonwandering spouse are revealing in and through their behavior. It is an opportunity to look at the quality of the whole relationship including its sexual component, but it is not a sufficient reason to destroy a family's unity. The cuckolded husband and the macho male are both images that need to be explored in the light of the sexual revolution, as are the hurt wife and the seductive female. All of these roles are models of a previous mentality that are increasingly anachronistic.

We can never return, I would guess, to the pattern of the extended family. We do need, however, to study ways and means to develop the gifts the extended family once brought to an individual marriage.

Community building, group dynamics, small circles of deeply committed friends, even group therapy might offer some hopeful clues. When I was a pastor serving a congregation and engaged frequently in marriage counseling, the first thing I tried to help a struggling couple do was to identify their support group, or if a support group did not exist, to help them see the necessity of creating it. "Who are your mutual friends?" became a regular and early question.

Some people have ventured far beyond this frontier to argue the proposition that significant relationships of deep and real love that involve sexual intercourse can be had by married people with someone other than their spouse without it hurting or even violating their marriage. These intimate sexual moments are not carried out with potential new spouses, they say, and are entered into with no intention of breaking the person's own primary marriage bond. This point of view would maintain that these extramarital relationships enrich rather than detract from the marriage. They save marriages, these people argue, rather than destroy them.

Statistical data to support this thesis are obviously not available. The human need to rationalize the fulfillment of any desire may well be operating. But nonetheless people whose lives are deep and rich and whom I admire as human beings have brought this point of view to me with considerable force. I do not dismiss it out of hand as I once did, but I regard it as quite dangerous at the very least to the sacredness of life and to the sacredness of solemn vows. Human emotions are so fragile and sexual feelings so intense that I suspect if this can be a positive option at all, it could be so only for a very few who could somehow manage creatively the emotions involved.

Yet I have known and been pastor to married people whose spouses were the victims of an illness that rendered them sexually incompetent. Sometimes the remaining spouse, obviously still married, decides after careful and long deliberation to enter an extramarital sexual relationship. For that decision to be called positive and moral, some factors, I believe, need to be present. Included would be that no one else's marriage must be violated by the new sexual relationship. The relationship must share many things before sex can be shared with meaning. This extramarital relationship must be loving, tender, exclusive, and, above all else, discreet.

In those situations where this experience in life was shared by others with me as a pastor, my first response was that moral judgment was not appropriate. But the older I get the easier it is for me to say that this exceptional relationship, extramarital and irregular by traditional standards, can nonetheless be positive, life-giving, moral, and even virtuous. I say this publicly because I think the church is perceived so often only in negative, moralistic terms by so many hurting lives. I only hope no one will read these words and justify thereby an irresponsible act of sexual behavior. That is always a danger when exceptional cases are raised to public consciousness.

I take great strength and comfort in the discovery that no less a person than Martin Luther reached this same conclusion. In his treatise entitled "The Babylonian Captivity of the Church" written in 1520, Luther argues that a woman who finds herself wed to a hopelessly impotent man, though she is nonetheless "desirous of having children or is unable to remain continent," shall give herself to another man.[4] Should children result from that union, they are to be ascribed to the "so-called putative father," Luther asserts. Such a person, Luther contends, would still be in a "saved state," for "the woman is free through the divine law and cannot be compelled to remain continent." If the legal husband would not agree to this arrangement, Luther counseled the woman to flee the marriage and enter a second marriage in "parts unknown" without benefit of divorce, which for a woman in that day was not available.

Luther was certainly a pastorally sensitive situationist in his ethical thinking. The rules of normal ethical and moral decision-making most often serve the cause of both love and justice. There are exceptions, however, and Luther sought to let Christian charity decide, as I too have intended to do. Luther concludes, "This have I set forth to the best of my ability for the strengthening of anxious consciences, being desirous to bring my afflicted brethren in this captivity what little comfort I can."

Finally, let me address the situation of postmarital sexual expressions. Once again, the ideal of married love is not possible. Circumstances, whether of death or divorce, have intervened. Many of these people do not want to be remarried. A marriage in which a new partner has to be integrated into an already existing family with its complicated web of relationships may be too difficult emotionally for some to risk. Sometimes divorce leaves scars that are not healed for years. Sometimes bereavement renders the surviving spouse incapable of making a new total commitment. Certainly no competent marriage counselor would recommend to the widowed or divorced person to remarry immediately so that one's intimate sexual needs might be met. The single life may well be the best option for some individuals.

In the days before sexuality and procreation were separated, sexual abstinence may have been, if not the only, at least the most loving alternative. But is it today? I have known situations where clearly it was not the best alternative. One's sexual needs do not die with the death of one's spouse or the death of one's marriage. All human beings need to be cherished, stroked, touched, kissed, embraced, held inside a relationship of love and trust. If children are not born of the union, if responsible discretion is observed, if intimacy is so sacred that it is not hinted at or alluded to outside the privacy of that single relationship, if no other marriage is violated by the relationship, if it is within a relationship of significant if not ultimate commitment, then I believe that such sexual activity can be good not evil, moral not immoral, life-affirming not life-denying. Although I have not spoken directly to the situation of the bachelor or the woman who never married, I think the principles enunciated here could equally well be applied to that circumstance.

In the old days before the revolution in sexual consciousness, the rules were clear, and no decisions had to be made except whether to obey the rules and be pronounced a moral person or to disobey the rules and be pronounced an immoral person. Life today is far more complex. Freedom carries with it a heavy responsibility. Decision-making is an arduous and mature process. Values and standards may be different; but they are not absent, and they need to be found and affirmed in the flux of our current life.

Sexual roles, sexual preconceptions, sexual stereotypes are all in transition. So indeed are sexual rules, sexual expectations, sexual standards. For the Christian the only thing that is not debatable or capable of compromise in my mind is that each human life is sacred and is called to achieve its own fullness in the midst of our bent and broken world. Serving that basic Christian position will take courage to battle the forces of repression, whether they be sexism and moralism on one side or the forces of moral anarchy and moral irresponsibility on the other. To join that struggle, frightening and dangerous as it is, must be the call of the church if we wish to share in the shaping of the life of our world in the twenty-first century.

1. *The Book of Common Prayer*, New York, Church Hymnal Corporation and Seabury Press, 1979, p. 423.

2. Ibid., p. 424.

3. Ibid., p. 429.

4. Martin Luther, *Three Treatises*, Philadelphia, Muhlenberg Press, 1943, p. 221ff.

Section III

MOVING BEYOND TRIBAL IDENTITY

Chapter 11

THE THIRD FRONTIER:
CHURCH AND TRIBE,
INTERDEPENDENCE AND DEATH

T HE third frontier toward which our generation is being propelled is as subtle as the crossing of it will be traumatic. The original passageway to this frontier was the death of religious or theological certainty, about which the first section of this book was concerned. But there is another dimension to this revolution that is uniquely the experience of the latter part of the twentieth century, and it will be, I am convinced, the pervading reality of the human spirit in the twenty-first century. I refer to the death in our day of tribalism and of the tribal mentality that feeds such powerful emotions as nationalism and patriotism.

As the world shrinks in size, the provincial loyalties and prejudices are the first to begin to fade. As that shrinking process continues, even the national loyalties begin to wither. That is what has happened in our recent experience; it is continuing to happen at this very moment; and it will happen in the future with accelerating intensity.

Far deeper than any of us is consciously aware, our religious understandings are informed by our tribal identity. When tribalism dies, a tradition-shattering revolution in our religious understanding will be inevitable, and an anxiety-producing human insecurity of vast proportions will be loosed upon the world; for tribalism is a primary means by which we form our self-identity. Never before in history has human life been asked to embrace emotionally a barrier-free world or to live without identifiable limits that serve to keep us from feeling alone. The vision is frightening, for when we scratch this surface, we discover that no human emotion—not sex, not love, not even selfishness—is stronger than tribalism; yet its power is frequently not even a part of our awareness. To force that tribal identity into our consciousness and to seek to separate Christianity from it will be the focus of this volume's concluding unit.

Tribalism is the source of the hatred and fear that one nation articulates toward another nation or group of nations with which it competes for economic or military advantage. Tribalism is the content of our nationalistic propaganda. It is the basis upon which the world is divided into armed camps with each side being willing to spend itself into poverty to "defend" itself against the other. Tribalism is so powerful that it transcends both forms of government and economic systems. Hedrick Smith, a *New York Times* international political commentator, in his book *The Russians*, documents this quite clearly by showing that the foreign policy of the Soviet Union and the foreign policy of the czars over a period of centuries is basically the same policy representing the same national yearnings and national goals.[1] The tribal mentality has a constancy that finds new incarnations in each moment of history, and through varying social and economic systems.

It is tribalism that makes us feel more secure when our weapons systems reach the absurd level of sophistication that will enable the efficient killing of every person in the world more than twenty times. It was tribalism that created in 1982 an atmosphere of Hollywood-like unreality over a rock formation in the South Atlantic called the Falkland Islands or the Malvinas. Only the power of a tribal identity could motivate young Britons or young Argentines to journey so far from their respective homes for the sole purpose of killing each other in the attempt to build up national pride. It is tribalism that causes the erection of tariff laws to protect one tribe's well-being from another's economic invasion. It is tribalism that creates slogans like "54-40 or fight" or that compels us to view national boundaries as barriers so great that at their edges human concern is allowed to cease, progress is stopped, and economic advantage is protected.

Buckminster Fuller, in his book *The Critical Path*, argues that the world's standard of living would rise dramatically if national boundaries could be ignored. Fuller maintains that if electric gridwork could be shared by hemispheres that alternate between summer and winter as well as among those various parts of the earth that have night while others are having day, the entire world could be electrified and the standard of living for all people could be raised with less electrical generating capacity than it takes now just to power the energy demands of the advanced nations.[2] Tribalism is a major factor in the inequitable distribution of the world's resources. A part of every religious system is an attempt to interpret these inequities, yet tribalism is so much a part of our identity that it remains almost unquestioned.

Some time ago, I read the letters and papers of Field Marshall Erwin Rommel, the "Desert Fox" of Adolf Hitler's Afrika Korps in World War II.[3] I had previously read many volumes by both the major war figures and the recognized historians regarding that war.[4] I had also lived through the war, reading the newspapers daily and avidly listening to the news on the radio. Still, I was not prepared for the shock that I received from reading Rommel. Suddenly I was faced with an account of World War II from a German perspective, filtered through none of my tribal biases, freed of my own nation's conscious and unconscious propaganda needs. It was like reading about a different war.

We have previously made the case that there is no objectivity in human language. Certainly there is no objectivity in telling the story of human history. History is written by the winners, the survivors of human conflict. They impose their subjective interpretations onto history. The losers or the nonsurvivors are not present to question official views, to counter prevailing assumptions, or to balance impassioned patriotism.

When tribalism or national identity is properly fanned, this force can muster incredible reserves of human energy to endure hardships that are almost unbelievable. Harrison Salisbury graphically describes this elemental human power in his book *The 900 Days: The Siege of Leningrad*.[5] Tribalism can fuel a national effort that could successfully land a team of explorers on the surface of the moon. It is this same force, however, that has the power to turn an entire nation of people into hate-filled killers who can rejoice in body counts and in the massive destruction of its enemies, yet always perfuming such inhumanity with noble slogans and virtuous goals. This tribal mentality infects human life deeply and binds each of us into a system of identity that is basic, irrational, and emotional.

This very tribalism, however, is being buffeted today by gigantic forces that no one will ever turn back. Our world, once thought to be so vast, is now perceived as one tiny spaceship floating alone in an alien universe. We who inhabit the various regions of this planet once could enjoy the security of a limited vision. We knew our place in the provincial realm that was complete with local prejudices, local stereotypes, local accents. One brief century ago, the vast majority of the people of the world were born, wed, and died within fifty miles of the place of their origin. Today one can visit an international airport such as the one in Quito, Ecuador, nestled 9,300 feet above sea level in the remote Andes Mountains, and watch planes come and go daily to all of the major cities of Europe, North and South America, Africa, Japan, and Australia.

No one in our generation lives very far from the crosscurrents of the world. Only two nations of this earth, I am told, are today without television as part of their internal and external communications systems. A local conflict in some remote region, which in previous eras would not have been noted in any other part of the world, can today be the powder keg that sparks the final conflagration on our tiny globe. Our world economy is already interdependent, as we have learned to our surprise and distress by the roller coaster prices of gasoline and energy, and that interdependence will continue to increase. Those resources that people share in common, such as the precious air we breathe and the mighty seas that feed us, are today threatened by our selfish misuse. No one nation alone can attack these problems effectively. The very existence of atomic weapons and their rapid proliferation among the nations has also made nationalism wither perceptibly.

Clearly there is growing in our time a human rebellion, worldwide in scope, which is accompanied by an enhanced consciousness against the narrow claims of nationalism. This rebellion was first just a trickle in history, but in our time has become a mighty tide. Its actual beginning may have been as ancient as that moment when the realization dawned that the world was not flat space of infinite dimensions but a self-contained, closed, and finite sphere. Tribalism was doomed from that instant, but centuries were to pass before we were emotionally forced to face the implications of its demise.

The abortive League of Nations was the first international political start in this new direction. It failed, but it represented an idea that was inevitable. The somewhat stronger United Nations inched us another step or two along the way in our perception of one world. This emerging consciousness and new learning continued to grow in such remote areas as Vietnam and Afghanistan where the great powers discovered that they could not impose their wills on even tiny nations, nor could they police the entire world.

Other signs of tribalism's weakening power include the new awareness of the fragile nature of our environment; the antiwar passion that produced peace marches, East and West; the growing world clamor against the production and deployment of atomic weapons; the increasing recognition that in this one world there is but one human family who constitutes its citizens. When these ideas become dominant, suddenly we will realize that every war in human history was and is a civil war, for it divides in conflict the one solitary human family. National self-interest is destined to become a category of the past.

There may be more violent outbursts of nationalism in our immediate future or many twitching responses before the rigor mortis of nationalism sets in, but a long-range view of history must conclude that tribal identity is even now sick unto death. National boundaries and tribal thinking simply cannot survive into the future on this radically interdependent globe. When nationalism dies, however, one must wonder what will happen to organized religion, for one of the major historic sociological purposes of organized religion in every tradition has been to uphold nationalistic interests.

An intimate connection between religion and nationalism has always existed. All religious systems find their origins in tribal worship practices. Every national concept of being "the chosen people," every theory of the divine right of kings, every claim to be "one nation under God," are nothing but later historic examples of tribalism and tribal deities influencing the minds of the people. Each of these concepts has been a major influence in shaping our civilization from both a religious and a national perspective, and the two are intimately bound together.

Echoes of tribalism in organized religion are overt in Christianity, both in local liturgical usage and in the proliferation of denominational structures. National flags fly in most of the Christian churches in this world. In Europe legally established and governmentally supported churches have historically been the rule, not the exception. Even the American concept of "separation of church and state" is deeply compromised by laws granting tax exemptions to churches, by the use of government-paid chaplains in the armed forces as well as in the Senate and House of Representatives, by invocations at public meetings, by the motto on our coins, and in countless other ways. National holidays in every land are regularly observed with liturgical expressions in the churches. None of us finally escapes some variation of the thought that God will bless our nation, or that the sun really rises in our country, or that we are a people of destiny directed by God.

Beyond these relatively superficial connections, the historic divisions of Christianity today appear to be far more the result of tribal identity than of religious conviction. It is the wedding of Christianity and tribalism that results in the fact that the Anglican Communion is deeply shaped by the English milieu. The defeat of the Spanish Armada in 1588 was widely interpreted throughout the English realm as a victory for the English version of Protestant Christianity over the Spanish version of Roman Catholic Christianity.* Indeed that war produced such a surge of nationalism in England that it was almost an act of treason to be a Roman Catholic Christian in that country at that time. This attitude is still written into the behavior expectations of the royal family. Those realities in turn helped to shape the theology, the liturgy, and the organized life of the Church of England, which became a world religious force only because England became a world military power.

At the same time, a visit to a Lutheran church in the United States will reveal a strong German or Scandinavian ethnic presence. The Reformation that Luther ignited on the Continent was joined to the political power needs of some of the German princes, and Lutheranism became the official state religion of many parts of Northern Europe, thereby incorporating tribal understandings into the Gospel itself.

The various Lutheran traditions in America are divided not so much by theology as by national origin. The particularly separatist Missouri Synod Lutherans combine the Reformation tradition of the Continent with the revival tradition of frontier America. This religious identity was forged with an intensity that enables the Missouri Synod today to endure in splendid isolation from the mainstream of Lutheran and, indeed, American life. Their claim to certainty is inviolable and is a prerequisite for being part of their community of faith.

---

*The pope at that time called on all Roman Catholics in England to rise up against the established government, an action that certainly fed the religious hostility in that moment of history.

John Calvin's thought was established and institutionalized in Geneva and in the Dutch Reformed tradition, which later took root in a peculiar form as the religion of the Dutch-related Afrikaners in South Africa where it is intensely nationalistic. Calvinistic Christianity also found expression among the French Huguenots and in the nationalistic yearnings of the Scottish Presbyterians. In each case the result was an interesting blending of Christianity with nationalism, religion with tribalism.

Orthodoxy became the name used in the Eastern rite of Greek-speaking Christians who incorporated into their Christian understandings, as if they were original to Christianity, the thought forms of the Greek mind. As Orthodoxy marched into the Balkans and Russia, it was newly shaped and formed by the understandings and tribal mentality of each national group.

Catholicism was the word employed by the Western rite of the Latin-speaking Christians, and it always reflected the legalism and hierarchical structure of the Western world. Ireland and Italy were particular strongholds of an unchallenged Roman Catholicism and in both cases incorporated their national yearnings and biases into the religious life of the people.

In Ireland, the nationalistic yearnings require an identification of England with the oppression of Irish people and the denial of Irish independence. Inevitably those feelings find expression in the religious wars that have rocked that nation for generations.

Until John Paul II, the papacy had been for centuries the special fiefdom of the Italian religious hierarchy. No one looking at history could doubt that even in the Catholic tradition national differences have made the Roman Catholic Church in the United States different from the same church in Poland, or Spain, or Holland, for example. Religion and tribe are deeply related.

Superimposed on the national religious patterns are various cultural and sociological differences within the nations. Pentecostal groups, for example, tend to appeal to that segment of the population that feels outside the social mainstream. Methodism made inroads into England's blue-collar population that the class-conscious established Church of England found difficult to touch.

Methodism has the best claim, I believe, to being the primary indigenous church of the newly independent United States. Methodism was English enough to appeal to the English identity of the majority of the citizens when our nation was new, but it was also distanced politically from England in a way that the Episcopal Church was not. Most of the Episcopal clergy and leading lay people were Tories during the American Revolution, which made them rather suspect in the new nation. Once more, tribal identity proved a powerful force in the shaping of Christianity in another nation. Methodism, as the new church of the working classes, carried very little formal structure or established hierarchy into the New World, so that it could quickly become indigenous in that world, accompanying pioneers and settlers in the westward expansion of this nation. In that process, needless to say, Methodism's character was once more shaped by its tribal history, becoming emotional, evangelistic, and moralistic as the rugged life of the American frontier seemed to require.

Later in the history of the United States, the Civil War once more divided the religious population along political lines so that we had such unique forms of American Christianity as Northern Baptists and Southern Baptists, the Presbyterian Church in the United States of America (Northern) and the Presbyterian Church-United States (Southern). Racial variety also added a distinctive note to the religious life of this nation and was recognized in the formation of the specifically African churches (African Methodist Episcopal and African Methodist Episcopal Zion) and the various black Baptist denominations.

Once any group of Christians was separated from the larger body, each tended to develop somewhat independently, serving the identity and social needs of its own constituency. Vance Packard surveyed this variety in American religious life when he wrote a chapter entitled "The Long Road from Pentecostal to Episcopal" in his book *The Status Seekers*.[6] In an isolated area in the premodern world, a group of Christians, unburdened by a vision of a wider expression could give full expression to their religious prejudices; and they did and they still do. Ecclesiastical one-upmanship has historically been a popular religious game.

However, that mentality finds a smaller and smaller audience in our smaller and smaller world. Tribal distinctions are fading under the impact of radical interdependence. Christianity is today being viewed with new eyes, from new vistas, with a new consciousness. Intellectually we have moved beyond certainty; ancient sexual assumptions are being abandoned; and the emotional ties of tribalism are being loosened. We are being stretched to embrace a universalism that will challenge the comfortable definitions and threaten the deepest and most elemental of the human systems of emotional security.

To explore these implications means that much of what we have understood to be the essence of Christianity may fade in relative importance. In this section I want us to look at how this consciousness has begun to emerge among Christians, both positively and negatively. This will involve us in an analysis of such traditional activities as evangelism, the ecumenical movement, world mission, interreligious dialogue and cooperation, and the emerging future shape of the church. All of these topics will, I submit, look radically different on the far side of the barriers that this volume suggests we must cross to enter the future. Specifically the barrier of tribal identity, when transcended, will force disturbing new understandings into these particular concepts.

In many ways this will be the most painful part of the journey for traditional believers. It has been painful for me. It is a journey, however, that I am willing to take because I believe the survival of Christianity as a viable force in the world requires this pilgrimage. Ours is not a day for leadership of limited vision or for business as usual in the life of the church. The call that the world must hear cannot be compromised to protect the sensitivities of those who do not see or comprehend the issues. It must be a compelling invitation to the open, the honest, the courageous, the daring. Someone must lead us through this wilderness and into the whirlwind of change and dislocation. It is not by avoiding the whirlwind but by walking through it that the Christian church is going to find a new day of hope. Discipleship in such a time may well prove to be possible only for the valiant.

The church of the future will be different. The arrogance of the past will be impossible. Time, like an ever-rolling stream, rushes us all toward a new century. There we will discover that only a Christianity which is uncompromised by tribal needs will emerge from out the carnage to a new life. That part of Christianity which remains tribal will disintegrate and die. Since there is no place to hide from that which is to come, the journey must continue.

1. Hedrick Smith, *The Russians*, New York, Quadrangle, 1976.

2. Buckminster Fuller, *The Critical Path*, New York, St. Martin's, 1981, p. XXXIV.

3. Erwin Rommel, *The Rommel Papers*, ed. B. H. Liddell-Hart and Manfred Rommel, New York, Harcourt, Brace, 1953.

4. I refer especially to: B. H. Liddell-Hart, *History of World War II*, New York, Putnam, 1971; Winston Churchill, *History of World War II* (six vols.), New York and London, Harper, 1948; Alan Moorehead, *The March to Tunis*, New York, Harper & Row, 1967; Dwight Eisenhower, *Crusade in Europe*, Garden City, N.Y., Doubleday, 1948.

5. Harrison Salisbury, *The 900 Days: The Siege of Leningrad*, New York, Harper & Row, 1969.

6. Vance Packard, *The Status Seekers*, New York, McKay, 1959.

Chapter 12

EVANGELISM AND
MISSION STRATEGY IN A
POSTTRIBAL WORLD

EVANGELISM is an intriguing word. It captures in its nuances
the battle that is being waged between those whose minds
are basically premodern in their thought forms and those whose minds
are postmodern. To look at this word helps us to examine the emerging
new consciousness that will finally deliver us from regional and provincial thinking, which is a necessary transition before we can embrace
the frontiers of the world where tribalism is now dying. If one cannot
move out of a local and provincial mindset, the wider questions will
never be raised. So let us bring this rich word "evangelism" into focus
for examination.

Some years ago when the national Episcopal Church was experiencing what they thought was a communications problem, an elaborate
plan for consultation with diocesan decision-making bodies was un-
dertaken. The problems facing the church at that time were complex,
but the symptoms were easily discernible. Contributions to the national church's program were down. There were widespread protests in
conservative church circles directed at the social involvement of the
church in the quest for civil rights, in the antiwar movement, and in
environmental and consumer affairs concerns. There was a noticeable
decline in the number of Episcopalians in the United States. We sank
below the 3,000,000-member level that at least one publication used as

the benchmark to distinguish a church from a sect. To counter these problems, a program of consultation was designed to let "the grass roots people speak" and to set the future priorities for our church. I regarded this activity then and I continue to regard it now as a highly dubious exercise in the abdication of effective leadership.

Not surprisingly, the results, published in a national church pamphlet entitled "What We Learned From What You Said," listed evangelism and Christian education as the top two priorities for the church, according to the grass roots people. The national structures of that church then moved to respond to their survey. One step involved the creation of a position for a staff officer for evangelism in the national office and the launching of evangelism programs and promotion.

No one in that process sought to determine whether the vote for evangelism was positive or whether it was a vote against programs of social involvement. Evangelism was a familiar word, and it had a pious ring. No one asked the people in the several dioceses what they meant by the word evangelism or why it was their first priority. Since no standard definition was agreed upon, the value of the data-gathering process was even more questionable, and all of us are left to speculate on what it meant and to whom. Evangelism-oriented groups around the country had their own definitions, one of which was adopted as the official definition of evangelism by a later General Convention. It goes as follows: "Evangelism is the presentation of Jesus Christ, in the power of the Holy Spirit, in such ways that persons may be led to believe in him as Saviour and follow him as Lord within the fellowship of the church."

The interesting thing to note about the General Convention action adopting this definition of evangelism is that the resolution received a unanimous vote, which usually means that it falls into the category of a "motherhood" resolution. Since not one of the terms was defined, they were obviously not debated. This would indicate either that a common understanding of the meaning of these words was universally agreed upon or that no one considered the resolution to be of great import. Since the former is certainly not so, the latter might fairly be assumed.

It also seems clear that many people concerned with declining church membership and church attendance saw evangelism primarily in terms of church growth, and anything that added sheep to the flock had to be good. Our grass roots church leadership, reeling under budgetary cuts and declining congregations, seemed sure that this was their great-est need. But is it? And if it is, what does it mean?

When the word evangelism is used, it conjures up images and defini-tions that beg all kinds of questions, and if those questions are not addressed, evangelism will remain the private possession of a special variety of Christian response to the premodern world. For far too many, that is quite simply what it is today.

The word evangelism makes a number of assumptions that reveal a limited vision. It assumes, for example, that the one doing the work of evangelism has something that the one who is being evangelized needs, or wants, or should want. Historically the motive for evangeliz-ing was born in the altruistic concern of Christians to save the souls of the lost from perdition. Those who believed they knew Christ and who therefore possessed salvation felt they had a duty to make Christ known to those who did not know him and who were therefore with-out salvation. Efforts toward evangelism were fueled by the promise of a heavenly reward both for the newly converted and for the one who brought the message of salvation. The status of the evangelist was both romantic and genuinely admired.

Behind these attitudes resides the highly nationalistic concept of "Christendom." Christendom meant that Christianity and the social order of the entire Western world were identical and inseparable. In "Christendom" there was a cultural assumption that only Christianity was true, and therefore the Christian church had not only the right but the obligation to share, even to impose, its truth on those who did not have it. Since there has not been for hundreds of years a single, unified church, inevitably each separate branch of the church had its own version of what was real Christian truth.

As hard as it seems now to believe, the real religious battles in nineteenth-century provincial America were over the relative merits of various Christian denominations. Roman Catholic Christians seriously discussed whether Protestants would get to heaven, and the Roman Catholic consensus was that they would not. This is why Roman Catholics were not allowed to enter Protestant churches and why today they are not officially allowed to receive the sacraments from non-Roman Catholic altars. The present ecumenical posture of Rome is not so much the birth of a positive attitude as it is a lessening of this overwhelmingly negative, imperialistic claim that ultimate authority rests finally in Rome, and Protestants who were previously lost sheep are now seen only as misguided sheep.

Nineteenth-century American Protestant Christianity, not to be out-done in sin by the Catholics, was equally negative in its view of the Roman Church, raising questions as to whether Roman Catholics were really Christians or idol worshipers. In more isolated communities in the rural South and West where Roman Catholics were few and far between, the real battle was over whether God was a Baptist or a Methodist. Jokes about Baptists or Methodists thinking they were the only inhabitants of heaven were born in a very real attitude. The Jews were still called Christ-killers and were thought to be doomed. As late as 1980 Dr. Bailey Smith, president of the Southern Baptist Convention, informed us that "God Almighty does not hear the prayers of a Jew," and we become aware that this provincial attitude is not yet dead. Since most people in the nineteenth century knew little or nothing about other religious traditions, they were lumped in the general derogatory category called "heathen" and were generally ignored unless a traveling missionary happened to come by seeking support. Those within our civilization who had no church identity were simply dismissed as sinners.

In nineteenth-century America, Christianity was still identified with social respectability. Dominant community pressure made church membership not only a necessity but also the mark of civilization, good manners, and decent living. The Episcopal Church was perceived in America in that era as the best church for the educated, the cultured, and the refined people to attend. Episcopalians deliberately cultivated the image of exclusiveness. This was our power, and our growth was almost totally among the upwardly mobile. Overseas missionary work was supported, but active programs of local evangelism were not encouraged in the Episcopal Church; they did not have to be. We had social prestige going for us, and that provided us with all the new members we really wanted. But many of the other denominations were perceived as a means to respectable Christian living instead of a life of dereliction; hence for them evangelism, understood as soul-winning, became a central concern. An annual feature in local communities was the revival, which was designed to lower the number of sinners in the area and to raise the number of Christians. There was always great rejoicing when the town drunk was "saved."

Not many people in that day agreed on what was the truth, but they all seemed to agree that Christians had "the truth" and non-Christians did not; and so the Christian had a responsibility to give the truth to

the non-Christian. That was an unquestioned presupposition of organized church life.

Evangelism as a working concept was born in this kind of world, and
it was defined by this kind of world. I would submit that it has not yet
fully escaped either the definition or the preconceptions of that context. Evangelism tends still to assume that there is a single definition
of God, an exclusive Christian truth, and that the end of sharing that
truth justifies the means, no matter how imperialistic. It certainly does
not comprehend the tribal element in the life of organized religion. For
these reasons active programs of evangelism flourish most in those
churches where the provincial consciousness still is in vogue, while in
the mainline churches evangelism tends to reside in splendid isolation
as a special interest of a limited group who are more subjective in their
approach to God and who have not yet been forced to stand on the
wider frontier of human thought.

Yet the word "evangelism" is surrounded by such holy sentiments
that to oppose it feels like one is opposing the spread of Christianity
itself. So it is generally not opposed. It is simply not engaged, or it is
kept peripheral, or it is tolerated, or it is ignored. I remember hearing
an Episcopal bishop, when he had finished reading the long list of
people he was appointing to the Evangelism Committee of his diocese,
declare, "If you can't save the world with all those people on the
committee, it must be hopeless." His comment clearly revealed his
attitude about the irrelevance of this group in the first place.

The emergence of a concern for evangelism in the Episcopal Church
reflected many crosscurrents. The decline in numbers was certainly
one. Suddenly the primary source of new members for the Episcopal
Church began to dry up. The upwardly mobile were opting for no
church identification in the secular society instead of opting for Episcopal identification. That was at least the conclusion reached by William
Coats of Pittsburgh in an article in *Plumbline*.[1] When the primary
source of new church members begins to diminish, institutional survival needs come to the surface. Evangelism had worked for others; we
hoped it might work for us, so it became the first priority. A retreat into
yesterday was apparent, for to deal with the inbreaking power of
tomorrow was too painful.

Most of us are no more than one or two generations from the religious traditions of rural or small-town America. We still carry the
religious nostalgia of our past in our subconscious minds. This nostal-

gia is revived periodically. There is much evidence that our time is one of the revival periods. Not surprisingly, the reviving groups call themselves evangelicals.

This is part of the obvious appeal of popular evangelists like Billy Sunday and Billy Graham. It also clearly is operating in that recent alliance of evangelical groups with right-wing politics which has been quick to link religion with patriotism, yesterday's family values with Christianity. These new devotees of evangelism are as imperialistic as those committed to evangelism always are, attacking any who deviate as secular humanists (read "pagans") and demanding conformity of its adherents under the pain of excommunication (read being targeted for defeat in the next election).

Evangelism as an activity of the church seems to require for its very existence a sense that those who evangelize possess certainty. Its vital nerve is cut by relativity. Its appeal is inevitably limited to those who share particular attitudes and convictions. Many people who are strong on evangelism tend to have a strong bias against intellectualism. They cannot embrace the dynamic pluralism of our post-Christian world. They frequently encourage Bible study, but they seldom accompany that with serious biblical scholarship. Consequently, those in the church who do not share their presuppositions or their conclusions are made to feel uncomfortable at best, inadequate at worst. There is a tendency among evangelically oriented people to stick to their own group for mutual encouragement rather than to expose themselves to those who might be critical. It is really a reaction on the part of many who cannot walk into the beckoning world of posttribal consciousness.

Inside the establishment of the church, the position of evangelism is usually given more lip service than real commitment. No one is opposed to evangelism, prayer, or church growth, but the evangelism activity seldom has significant support or makes a serious impact on the life and policy of the mainline church bodies. It consumes its energy in planning conferences on evangelism or on prayer. It encourages the new packaging of old revival techniques in such activities as the Charismatic Movement or the Faith Alive Movement.

Evangelism offices and commissions gather and affirm the various groups that identify under their broad banner; they sponsor workshops on church growth, offering helpful techniques on how to make church life more inclusive than exclusive, how to bring back those who drift away, how to incorporate new members more quickly, how to set up and carry out community-building activities such as lay visitation. But, at the deepest level, this program of evangelism is, I believe, addressing only the Christian "in" group or fanning the religious nostalgia of the past. The vision of Christianity to which it calls people is by and large a narrow view of the way things used to be. Evangelism as it is presently constituted does not address the central missionary and evangelical questions of our post-Christian world, which are far more radical than those who are committed to evangelism seem to recognize.

These questions are: How can we talk about Christ in a pluralistic society where "the truth" is not believed to be the possession of any person or any tradition? With the exclusive claims of Christianity gone, can we still proclaim the Gospel? With religious certainty surrendered, can we still possess power? If there is not "unchanging truth," what do we evangelize about? Can evangelism, growing out of a simpler world, ever become sophisticated enough or refined enough finally to escape its basic attitude of imperialism? And if it can, should it? Can we separate tribal thought from religious conviction? If we admit that we do not possess the whole truth, can we be evangelists for our partial understanding of the truth of Christ? If we admit that our truth is partial, not whole, we quickly discover that our power as a church is directly related to the myth of our certainty. It is true that the only churches that seem to be growing today are the churches that claim and proclaim certainty. That reflects a tension within our consciousness far more than it is a commentary on our understanding.

What reward do we offer to entice nonbelievers into believing? Is that reward legitimate? Is it honest? Is it real? Do any of us today really believe that heaven is reserved for those who think as we do, who believe as we do? Even if we say that believing in Jesus is necessary to be saved or to gain heaven, do we agree on what believing in Jesus means? Whose theological understanding of Jesus do we accept? Is a Unitarian a believer in Jesus? A liberal Protestant? Is Hans Küng a Christian? Or Edward Schillebeeckx? Are Jews going to be saved? Do we dare limit God's grace or God's action by our creeds, our scriptures, our theology? Yet if we do not so limit God, will the unique revelation of the Christian Gospel disappear? In our day of expanded sensitivity to the religious yearnings of the people of the world and expanded consciousness of the variety of the religious experiences of the people of the world, must we revive the power of yesterday's limited religious certainty as the only means to avoid having Christianity join the gods of Olympus as a footnote in the religious history of the human race?

There is ample reason to believe that these questions have been answered unconsciously by the institutional church, but they have not yet in most instances been faced consciously. Does the fear of punishment in hell or the promise of heavenly reward motivate many people today? Comments like that of the Rev. Dr. Bailey Smith were heard with discordant pain in 1980 even by the religious establishment, yet one hundred years ago his statement was the working presupposition of almost all evangelistic activity. What sounds like religious bigotry today was the conviction that fueled the efforts in evangelism yesterday. That conviction no longer exists. If we no longer claim that conviction, that power, that certainty, can evangelism survive? Is not this realization, even this fear, the reason that evangelism groups continue to claim the conviction of yesterday on some basis? Is it not the claiming of this conviction that creates the very reason many others are uncomfortable with evangelism groups today? To the degree that evangelism is rooted in the certainties of yesterday, it will always be an ineffective and even discordant tool for the church eager to enter the world of tomorrow. The struggle between premodern tribal thinking and postmodern, posttribal thinking is rising in our consciousness.

Look for a moment at the questions that church expansion and growth within our own domestic world raise about evangelism. Then perhaps we can view the issues that "foreign missionary activity" raises on the international scene.

In the pluralism of Christianity in the United States, a new church is founded in a community where our particular branch of the church has not been before. Other Christian churches are present, so why do we locate an outpost of our denomination there? On some level we want to be present to serve those who are already our constituents who may move into that area. On other levels we may believe that our particular church will meet some people more effectively than another church will, which is another way of saying that we believe we offer something unique; but we are frequently hard-pressed to define that uniqueness. Episcopal churches throughout the country vary among themselves so widely that the unique thing we believe we have to offer in one place would be unrecognizable as the possession of our church in another place. On still other levels we are not immune to empire-building, and like every business we cannot resist the temptation to open yet another branch office in an area that looks promising. In this illustration the pluralism of the Christian church is faced, but we are forced to entertain the anxiety of asking the deeper question of why we are in business as a church in the first place. Life has a way of raising issues that are real, whether or not we like them raised.

A different question on a slightly deeper level is drawn in the inner city where old churches struggle to find new reasons for existence. Why do church hierarchies want those churches to stay? It certainly is not the same reason for opening a new church in a new suburb. Whatever is unique in the Episcopal Church, for example, would be even more difficult to define in the inner city. Not many inner-city residents are worried about apostolic succession, valid sacraments, or Henry VIII's sex life. So rationales abound. We stay in the city to make a witness, we say, to offer hope, though hope for what is not always clear. We announce our intention to identify with the poor and dispossessed, but frequently the poor and the dispossessed are not aware that we are identifying with them and seem uninterested in identifying with us. We state our desire to build, through the church, a sense of community, though sociologists tell us that effective community in the inner city is usually built around an issue, not a building or a tradition.

We see sincere people operating from storefronts with varying religious traditions, all claiming Christ but still manipulating people with fear, superstition, or the promise of heavenly peace and glory in another world. They have an appeal, but in all honesty we want to avoid that image. We are also fearful of being guilty of the Marxist charge that we are an opiate for the people. Sometimes we meet that fear by pretending, at least verbally, to take the cause of the people as our cause, by seeking to be a voice for the voiceless. We also want to avoid the charge on this side that we are producing "rice Christians," bribing into church membership those we can win with promises of material help.

In the inner city we must quickly abandon the culturally conditioned concepts of the Episcopal Church or we do not survive. "The Tory Party at Prayer" will not appeal to many urban dwellers. If anything matters here, it must be Christ, not the Episcopal version of Christ, but Christ. But how is that to be understood, articulated, lived? Some answers emerge. Christ must be incarnate in that world, indigenous to those people; or he will be, as he has been before, another agent of colonial oppression.

The evangelical style from another century, with its promise of glory, its anthropological view of human depravity apart from Christ, its respectable definition of Christianity, becomes part of the problem, not part of the cure, in the inner city. The questions we need to address here are not generally addressed by proponents of evangelism. What is Christ's essence? What will Christ be like when he is indigenous to this world? How is Christ met? How does Christ love, forgive, feed, nurture, encourage? Can evangelism take the form of community organization, rent strikes, public protests, street demonstrations and still be evangelism? Can Christ be real in the city, and if he can, how does that reality relate to the Christ evangelism groups talk about? In response to these probes, we might begin to separate evangelism from the world that produced its traditional definition and approach a new definition of evangelism for our time. I suspect it would have little to do with what is now called church growth.

Consider one more situation. A declining church sits in the shadow of a massive high-rise apartment building that brings hundreds of new residents to that community each year. The residents in the high-rise are a cross section of the secular society of our generation. They are not church related and are not even nostalgic about a past that may have included the church. They are transient, rootless, and highly mobile. They are swinging singles, living in formal and informal relationships, with wide ethnic and cultural diversity and equally wide sexual and moral mores. They are married couples (perhaps divorced more than once), oriented not at all to the community in which they sleep but rather to the city in which they work. The evangelistic tactics of the church that would call them back to the world view of yesterday, a world view they left ages ago because it no longer made contact with their lives, are doomed to failure.

They listen to the new religious conservative movement calling for "a return to the traditional family," which seems to include the defeat of the Equal Rights Amendment and the ban on abortion. They hear organized religion affirming a view of women as domestic creatures who will do all those chores yesterday's frontier women used to do. But that frontier stereotype collides with a new feminine consciousness that refuses to accept the ties which bind them to Old World images. They live in a world organized in a radically different way. In that world the suggestions that birth control is evil or that women are biologically incapable of being priests strike them as quaint at best, ludicrous at worst.

These modern, secularized apartment dwellers could not care less whether we are Protestant or Catholic, to say nothing of whether we are Presbyterian or Methodist. They are engaged in trying to make sense out of their lives, and in that effort they do not see the traditional church speaking, save in the accents of yesterday. A church dominated by its own institutional struggle to survive and grow simply does not touch their lives. A church clinging to a narrow certainty from yesterday's simple world is not appealing in the churning, insecure world they know. Yet they are looking for something. Underneath the busyness of their lives, there is an echo of emptiness. It is experienced when the endless variety of sexual partners gets boring, when the alcoholic consumption rate gets heavier, when the depression cannot be crowded out by togetherness. What does evangelism mean here? What is that essence of the Christian Gospel that we might offer in this world?

In these three vignettes wherein the church is confronting the world, we are forced to think anew about what we who are Christians have to offer and how it can be offered in a pluralistic, increasingly alienated, and post-Christian world like our own. If evangelism means offering the Gospel to the world, how can we do that in a secular society that is less and less nostalgic, less and less oriented to take seriously traditional religious claims, and less and less willing to be bound by the barriers of the past?

The same discomfort that accompanies the evangelistic efforts on the domestic scene also permeates the offices of world mission in the Christian churches of our generation. Once again the issue when the content is cleared away is a struggle between those who inhabit the post-Christian world and those who continue to operate on the basis of the premodern provincialism of the past. Today the Episcopal Church in the United States has only sixty-six missionary appointees serving around the world. The style of even that limited activity is vastly different from the style of the nineteenth century. The difference is the direct result of a growing sense of universalism and a dying of tribal identification.

Kenneth Scott Latourette, in his monumental history of the expansion of Christianity, identifies the nineteenth century as the high-water mark of worldwide Christian missionary activity.[2] It was in this century, he argues, that the consciousness of Christian Europe and America became aware of the peoples in what we now call the Third World who were known as pagans or heathens. Hence those who lived in what they thought of as Christian civilized nations felt compelled to carry both their Christianity and their civilization to these benighted savages. These feelings caused a wave of religious missionary fervor to demand activity designed to save these doomed native peoples. To civilize and to evangelize were twin goals that no one seemed seriously to divide.

Following the flag of colonial nationalism, the missionaries fanned out across the world. Subtlety was not a trait of the nineteenth-century missionaries. They were going to save souls, whether the people to whom they went wanted to be saved or not. Many missionary hymns grew out of this attitude. Hear the premodern tribal mentality that finds expression in their words:

> From Greenland's icy mountains, From India's coral strand
> Where Afric's sunny fountains Roll down their golden sand,
> From many an ancient river, From many a palmy plain,
> They call us to deliver Their land from error's chain.
>
> Can we, whose souls are lighted With wisdom from on high,
> Can we to men benighted The lamp of life deny?
> Salvation, O salvation! The joyful sound proclaim,
> Till each remotest nation Has learnt Messiah's name.[3]

Or again,

> Some work in sultry forests Where apes swing to and fro,
> Some fish in mighty rivers, Some hunt across the snow.
> Remember all God's children, Who yet have never heard
> The truth that comes from Jesus, The glory of his word.
>
> God bless the men and women Who serve him over sea;
> God raise up more to help them To set the nations free,
> Till all the distant people In every foreign place
> Shall understand his kingdom And come into his grace.[4]

Alan Moorehead, the English historian, has chronicled the result of this mentality upon the culture, the values, and the civilization of South Pacific Island people and Australian aborigines in a book significantly entitled *The Fatal Impact*.[5] S. L. A. Marshall, the esteemed military historian, records the contact between American natives known as Indians and the civilized American nation, including Christian missionaries, in his book poignantly named *Crimsoned Prairie*.[6] It was a wise Indian philosopher who said, "When the white man arrived, he had the Bible and we had the land. Now we have the Bible and he has the land." James Michener, perhaps the most widely read novelist of recent decades, created a fictional but nonetheless historically accurate portrait of missionary activity and arrogance in his book *Hawaii.*[7]

It did not occur to people in the nineteenth century to think that there might be truth, integrity, or value in a religious tradition other than Christianity. The world was neatly divided into Christians, pagans, and Jews.

These tactics have been rendered inoperable by the thought processes of our interdependent world. They do not fit our comprehension of reality. They create discomfort when we meet one who takes them seriously. If we cannot move our religious convictions beyond these concepts, then we either retreat with our convictions intact into the realm of private piety or we abandon our religious convictions altogether. Examples of both responses are visible today.

The new pluralistic post-Christian consciousness is pervasive and inescapable. The premodern tribal assumptions are loosening and dying. Christianity will die with them unless we can separate the essence of Christianity from the assumptions of the past and enable it to live in the emerging posttribal world of the future.

Now perhaps we are ready to reconstruct what evangelism and missionary activity can mean to a Christian in a posttribal world. My starting point must be the assertion that radical honesty will have to be the primary manifestation of all Christian proclamations in the future. To be wrong is forgivable, given the vastness of truth. To be dishonest, however, is to be religiously manipulative. Dishonesty is apparent every time we claim too much for our partial grasp of the truth of God, every time we presume that God is limited to our understanding of God, every time we limit salvation to those who share our vision or participate in our revelation, no matter how broadly we define that vision or that revelation. Dishonesty comes from claiming wholeness when all we possess is the partial, as surely as it comes from any other bending of the truth. Yet this dishonesty is insidious because it serves the power needs of institutional religion, and its presence has therefore been overt in Christian history. The protection of the power base of the church has become in the church a higher priority than the truth. That is sin. The church is guilty.

Erasmus, whose books were banned by Pope Paul IV because he did not support the Vatican's static and exclusive claims, once wrote, "To call the new learning heresy is to assume that the old orthodoxy is ignorance."[8] To be honest in our day is to embrace relativity as a virtue and to recognize that absolutism is a vice—any kind of absolutism, whether it be ecclesiastical, papal, biblical, or the absolutism of sacred tradition. To embrace relativity is to end for all time the imperialism that has far too often been a mark of religious endeavors, but it is also to be honest.

In the short term, I am convinced that this honesty will cause the church as an institution to lose power, missionary activity to be curtailed, the blurring of our purposes to be experienced, and, in the minds of many, it will be to lose our credibility as Christians. I am also convinced that when Christians give up the claim of certainty, the church will decline numerically. I am also sure that church leaders who dare to face these issues openly and publicly will be attacked and abused by those who need what an honest church cannot give. We cannot give easy answers, the simplistic guarantee of heaven, visions of certainty, the security of escape from the essential, never-ending quest for meaning that is the mark of those who are in touch with the spirit of our century. We cannot give what we do not have. Certainty has never been our possession. It has always been our illusion. We do not have the whole truth of God. We never have; we never will. What we really have to offer our world is a companionship on a journey and hope that the reality of God will be at the journey's end. But in this life the journey will never end.

Yet as soon as all that is clear, there is a positive word that can be spoken. When we say that we do not have the whole truth of God, that must not be heard to mean that we have *no* truth of God. St. Paul said, "We see through a glass, darkly" (I Corinthians 13:12 KJV), but he did see. And so do we. And what we see we must share, not because others need it to be as good as we are, but because love demands that we share with others the gifts that bring meaning to our lives. In this lies the clue that will salvage the word evangelism from the abuses of the past.

Note the operative word "share." There is a note of reciprocity about that word. I share only with one with whom I have some relationship. There is a receptivity in the other which makes sharing possible. If I try to share with a stranger, he or she would experience not a gift but a burden, not a sharing but a dumping. If I try to give another what the other has not requested or does not want, I am clearly meeting my needs, not the needs of the other. If I imply that I have something the other needs in order for the other to be a better person, I am playing the game "I'm OK, you're not OK," which Thomas Harris suggested in his book cannot be received as anything other than hostility.[9] If what I have to share gives the object of my sharing only the choice of rejection or conversion, it cannot be loving, no matter how pious or holy my rhetoric about it might be. If I seek to force another to acknowledge the meaning I have in my life without being sensitive to the meaning by which the other lives, I am not proclaiming the Gospel.

But when I have been touched by a fascinating book or enjoyed a good movie or read a penetrating editorial or been delighted by a new recipe or been moved by a provocative sermon, the people I know learn of these enriching moments; for in the course of human relationships, these joys are shared with excitement and enthusiasm. They are both offered and received. Sharing requires both actions.

The experts of Madison Avenue tell us that the most effective advertising is by word of mouth. So it is with the sharing of the Gospel of Jesus Christ. It must be honest, not phony; integrated into my being, not peripheral; shared naturally, not unnaturally; given as an offering in love, not as a manifestation of my superiority; without calculation or ulterior motives and without any hint that my word is the final word to be spoken on the subject.

My Christ may not be ultimate, but he is real. My Christ may not be definitive, but he is operative. This for me, therefore, must be the most distinguishing mark of posttribal Christianity. Sharing Christ finally involves us in the sharing of our being, not our doing; and when it becomes something that we do rather than part of who we are, then honesty is battered.

If sharing our being is the primary means of spreading Christianity, then the one who would be an evangelist has got to be radically open, unthreatened, capable of listening deeply, enormously sensitive, able to risk, possessing the ability to embrace vulnerability and uncertainty as the marks of life in Christ. The one who will witness to Christ must be marked by the gifts of Christ: love, joy, peace, long-suffering. The pious certainty, the ready and unquestioned definition of evangelism, the thin smile that so often covers the hostile being of the insecure Christian who seeks to impose Christ, the words of love that scarcely veil the judgmental attitude of those who profess to be evangelists:

these are not the marks of Christ but are rather the marks of human brokenness. Yet these are what many see in those who would elevate evangelism into a program. Evangelism in our day must be done on a basis far more radically honest and more deeply integrated than that.

I believe that the only reward Christ offers is the Christ life of openness, vulnerability, expansion, risk, wholeness, love. Nothing else: not success, not heaven, not an escape from hell, not friends, not security, not peace of mind. I feel I must beware of evangelistic Christians who come offering rewards. I am frightened of those who want to do something to me or for me "for my own good." I am appprehensive when I meet those who would limit the divine and expansive Christ to the historic life of Jesus and who suggest that we have to "carry Christ" to someone or someplace where in our frail judgment Christ does not dwell, as if somehow Christ is limited.

The frequently voiced opinion suggesting that the church, in order to show its commitment to evangelism from national to local levels, must have an evangelism committee or officer or program is in my mind nothing but intimidating, pious rhetoric. Evangelism is of the essence of every church activity or it is nothing.

Examples of this attitude abound. I believe that all church structures must assist people in the art and practice of prayer, but this must be done by those who do not deny the reality of the world we live in by calling us into patterns or practices we cannot possibly adopt without serious, mind-bending exercises. Prayer must be part of the definition of evangelism, for I cannot share a presence of God I have not personally experienced; and this is the essence of prayer.

Churches need help in the task of community building so that lives might be attracted to the quality of love, acceptance, forgiveness, and inclusiveness that I believe must mark the people of God. When people touch the life of the church, they want to feel power, the power that comes from lives that are real and honest and loving—the power of being open, accessible, and embracing. Those qualities cause people to inquire into their source and meaning. Evangelism is the inner power of community building.

Churches need to be teaching centers, synagogues if you will, where faith and tradition can be explored, where truth can be pursued without authoritarian clichés like "the church teaches" or "the Bible says" being employed to stifle the questioning process. The bearers of our deepest understanding of the Gospel inevitably both capture and distort the Gospel. The Bible, the creeds, the sacred traditions are only pointers to God that must be opened, transcended, explored in the light of each new day; for as the hymn puts it, "Time makes ancient good uncouth."[10] That opening is the essence of the church's teaching ministry to both children and adults. The teaching ministry of the church is thus an arm of evangelism.

The church's prophetic word must be heard in the public sector, in searing judgment against those actions, both individual and systematic, which continue patterns of oppression based on strength or race or sex or tradition. A church that talks of salvation but does not battle for social justice will be dismissed as phony. A church that shuns controversy for fear of upsetting its membership has ceased to be the church and has become a club. No program of evangelism will save it.

I want the church's prophetic word to be turned upon itself as well as on the world. I want the church to address its own denominational idolatry as well as the tribal idolatry of the secular order with which we are so totally identified. I want the church to address its own prejudices, whether against blacks, women, suicides, divorced people, homosexuals, Jews or other religious bodies, as well as the prejudices of the secular order that we in the church had so much to do with both creating and supporting. Let us not forget that both slavery and segregation were blessed by the institutional church. Anti-Semitism was birthed and fueled by the institutional church. Heresy hunts and inquisitions are our own children. The systematic oppression of women we still encourage at worst, tolerate at best. Evangelism is the primary thrust and meaning of the prophetic ministry. It is the proclamation of the Gospel exposing the darkness of human evil. Any program that ignores this dimension of the church cannot possibly be called evangelism.

If evangelism is separated from these dimensions of church life, it becomes empty, pious rhetoric. But if evangelism is incarnate in each of these dimensions, it becomes the essence and core of everything the church does. Effective evangelism then is the all-embracing thrust of the total life of the church. Evangelism cannot be a program or an emphasis. It cannot belong to a narrow sliver of church people who like to sing Gospel songs and pray extemporaneously and witness publicly. It cannot be based on an assumption, conscious or unconscious, that we have the truth and others do not. It cannot be arrogant or other-worldly or ignorant of the vast new insights and realities of the modern world. It cannot be a nostalgic attempt to return to yesterday's religious security. Rather evangelism must be an open, honest, radical, risking willingness to face our limitations in a brave new world, and to be in that world a presence, a leavening in the lump, a flickering candle daring to push back the world's darkness.

I do not believe that the church will grow for long by clever manipulation. I do not believe a church grows in worthwhile ways by trying to grow. Church growth must be the by-product of the church being true to its deepest calling to be the body through which the infinite mystery of God is confronted and all life is freed from bondage and expanded to its fullness. It must be achieved in the willingness to live in risky vulnerability without defense or security. I am confident that such a quality of life would find a way to be shared and received and that in this way evangelism in the modern world might be done with integrity, with effectiveness, and above all without planning to do evangelism.

1. William Coats, *Plumbline*, a publication of the Episcopal Society for College Work, 1979.

2. Kenneth Scott Latourette, *The History of the Christian Church*, 7 vols., New York and London, Harper, 1941. Volumes 3, 4, and 5 are entitled "The Great Century, 1800–1914."

3. *Hymnal 1940*, #254.

4. *Hymnal 1940*, #262.

5. Alan Moorehead, *The Fatal Impact*, New York, Harper & Row, 1966.

6. S. L. A. Marshall, *Crimsoned Prairie*, New York, Scribner's Sons, 1972.

7. James Michener, *Hawaii*, New York, Random House, 1959.

8. Erasmus, *Increditio de Fide*, 1515, trans. Craig Thompson, New Haven, Conn., Yale Univ. Press.

9. Thomas Harris, *I'm OK, You're OK*, New York, Harper & Row, 1969.

10. *Hymnal 1940*, #519.

Chapter 13

THE COPERNICAN
REVOLUTION IN THEOLOGY

WHEN we move beyond the concerns of evangelism, we move beyond the realm of denominational thinking and traditional missionary concerns, if not yet beyond the bounds of Christianity itself. The next level of consciousness that must be engaged is represented by the growing ecumenical movements. Whether admitted or not, the ecumenical movement in Christianity is a result of seeing the relativity of truth, experiencing the loosening of barriers, and digesting emotionally the shrinking size of the world. Tribal and provincial divisions cannot possibly be maintained when these dividing lines are blurred by constant proximity. Not surprisingly, when ever-widening contact is achieved among groups of Christians, progress toward ecumenical unity is increased.

The Evangelical United Brethren and the Methodist Church came together to form the United Methodist Church in 1968. Various Lutheran bodies have begun to transcend their national origins and identities and to merge, as have various Presbyterian bodies. The Bishop of Rome and the Archbishop of Canterbury, breaking centuries of alienation, held a historic meeting and prayed together in England in 1982. The Church of England entered negotiations with the Methodists, and later with a combination of the Free Churches of England, aimed at unity; but in both instances the Church of England proved unwilling to compromise its dominance of that island's religious life and backed away after both the Methodists and the consortium of Free Churches had agreed to the merger plan. That temporary setback will not finally prevail.

Whether successful or not, there was in this ecumenical activity a new awareness that truth was not the sole possession of any branch of Christianity. Only the dominant Roman Catholic Church has found it difficult to translate ecumenical negotiations into concrete action, for at stake would be the admission of relativity into their understanding of ultimate truth, an admission that their infallibility claims make quite difficult. So dialogue that has involved Roman Catholics requires hours to be spent on minuscule matters that result in agreements to appoint new study commissions—and even these minimal agreements receive a cool hierarchical reception when they are completed. Roman Catholic rank and file clergy and laity, however, ignoring the hierarchy, have already in large measure made a public admission of that very relativity. It is quite clearly just a matter of time before the hierarchy tumbles into this new consciousness.

However, what even the most enthusiastic ecumenist does not yet seem to grasp is that this very consciousness in which the ecumenical movement is finding fertile soil to flourish is but the dawning of a vastly more revolutionary consciousness that will not just bring separated Christians together but rather will, in time, separate all religious thought from its tribal identity. This will finally force on all Christians a worldwide awareness of religious unity that will be deeper than anything the ecumenical movement has yet contemplated. In another hundred years one wonders if the great religions of the world will not seem as similar in their essence as the various denominations of Christianity seem today. When the tribal identity needs are stripped from organized religion, when the culturally and politically imposed variety is removed from religious systems, when the increasingly indefensible idea that certainty in articulating the truth of God lies exclusively in one's own faith tradition has lost its power, what will remain? These seem to be the inevitabilities of our world.

Lesslie Newbigin, the great missionary bishop of the Church of South India, in his book *The Open Secret*,[1] struggles to balance the competing forces of his particular Christian claim with the dawning consciousness of a universal mentality. He finally comes down on the side of his particular Christian revelation by saying that the primacy of Jesus as the source of all salvation must be preserved.[2] But in the process he bends the particularity of Jesus significantly and opens the doors to a possible new universalism. "If Jesus is God present in the fullness of being, if Jesus is the Word through which all things came to be," he argues, "then Jesus is the life of all that is, whether acknowledged or not." The presence of Jesus cannot therefore be confined to those places where his name is recognized. "Every person," he continues, "must be encouraged to go toward where the light shines for him or her. If one turns his or her back on the source where light is found, then the result can only be deeper darkness. . . . Something is clearly wrong with us when we belittle the light that is shining in others."

Despite Bishop Newbigin's attempt to be inclusive, he is nonetheless articulating only the liberal fringe of the traditional conservative position. Even so, it is far ahead of the religious mentality that was dominant just a few short decades ago. In his words the dawning posttribal consciousness is making a tentative appearance, even in the conservative tradition.

John Hick, the British philosopher-theologian, in his book *God and the Universe of Faith*, takes a far more liberal view and in the process relativizes the ultimate claims of any particular religious tradition, including Christianity.[3] Hick attempts to separate the central affirmations of every major religious tradition from the methodology employed by each religious body. "The methodology," he argues, "is highly subjective, offering rich, poetic elaborations and explanations and concrete cultic expressions which have grown up alongside of and have interwoven with the central affirmations." Through these methodologies the central affirmations have been subjected to tribal needs, cultural prejudices, and environmental and linguistic influences. The central affirmations of every religious system may be examined and compared by philosophers and theologians as to their truth or falsity, he maintains, but the cultural accretions surrounding the various affirmations are not in the same sense either true or false. They reflect rather the wide variety of human styles and existence, various aspects of civilization, values and taboos. They are part of the glue of tribal life and need to be understood, not compared in respect to truth or falsity.

To study and compare the central affirmations of various great religious systems demands what Hick calls a Copernican revolution in theological thinking. The pre-Copernican or Ptolemaic view Hick defines as the conviction that one's own religion is the center of the religious universe and provides a touchstone for the truth of all other faith commitments. In this Ptolemaic system the Christian would assert that

Christianity is the gateway to salvation through which all must come. Other religions are dismissed either as positively harmful, by traditional religious conservatives, or as less full and less complete than the ultimate truth of Christianity, by those who claim to be open, modern liberals. The conservative response comes primarily from those who have not recognized the geographic distribution and tribal content of various faiths and hence admit them only as a mission field to which the church is called. The liberal response comes from those who are conscious of the world's infinite religious variety and have begun to make peace with that fact and with their own tribal thinking without compromising their claim to possess the essential and final truth. But, Hick believes, the more one experiences and learns about the nature of the world's religious systems, the less any of these conclusions, conservative or liberal, will seem ultimately plausible. The result, he maintains, will finally be a Copernican revolution in religious thought. That revolution will overwhelm all formal religious systems, he asserts.

The Copernican revolution in theological thinking that Hick proposes requires a radical shift in one's traditional religious convictions. The ultimate position to which one's deepest commitments and beliefs are usually consigned must be modified so that the believer might view all religious convictions, including his or her own, not as complete in and of themselves, but as various overlapping aspects of the same final reality. Any particular understanding of God, any particular religious system can thus no longer be equated with the ultimate truth. Rather all systems of belief will necessarily fade into being parts of a single system, orbiting in various ways around the truth of God to which they all point. In post-Copernican theological thought, no religious system can ever again assert that the truth of that system shares an identity with the truth of God or the will of God, nor can that system presume that in its creeds and articulations the fullness of God has been exhaustively proclaimed. No religious spokesperson, standing within his or her own tribal identity that has dramatically shaped the religious convictions held by the tribe, can dismiss someone else's faith content as cavalierly as was once the rule and practice of religious persons. No religious system can continue to ignore, to condemn, or to view other religious systems as pagan candidates for conversion. The realization of the truth of these insights will strike body blows at most traditional religious claims.

Most Christians are woefully ignorant of the truth and beauty of other religions. Our ignorance breeds a prejudice that is coupled with our emotional need to be certain, and religious bigotry is the inevitable result. In the service of that bigotry, we make interesting and shallow comparisons. For example, we are frequently heard to say things like, "God is personal in Christianity and impersonal in Buddhism." But a closer view of Buddhism can discover a deeply personal concept of God, and in the ontological concepts used to define God in later Christian theology, a nonpersonal concept of God can certainly not be excised from Christian history. Paul Tillich's definition of God as the "ground of all being" and the ancient definitions of God as Father and anthropomorphically human so prevalent among the early church fathers provide a wide range for thinking about God theologically within Christianity. That range of understanding between the personal definition of ultimate reality (father) and the nonpersonal definition (being) can, in fact, also be found in most religious traditions.

In all religious systems the primary level of religious experience exists quite apart from the attempt to think theologically and philosophically about that experience. Inevitably, in the process of time, the experience is subjected to different historical and cultural influences within the limitations of a tribe, a nation, or a region. Over the centuries every one of the world's religious systems became distinctive, variegated, and many-branched as it was more and more localized and indigenous to a particular part of the world.

Hinduism, Buddhism, Islam, Judaism, and Christianity all have within them wide variety and highly developed separate schools of thought. These differences are clearly more cultural, psychological, environmental, and political than they are theological.

But what a posttribal world is beginning to embrace is that what we have heretofore thought to be the insuperable barriers that divide the world's great religious systems may not be insuperable at all. Those differences, thought once to be eternal, may turn out to be only relative differences. To entertain such a possibility would be a revolution in religious thinking indeed, yet I believe it is inevitable. To see the tribal content in the religious systems of the entire world becomes a doorway into this revolutionary perception. Let me turn first to the tribal origin of our own Christian faith.

The tribal setting of the Old Testament is obvious even to the most cursory reader. Yahweh, Israel's tribal god, hated all those whom the

Israelites hated. Yahweh went before Israel in battle. In Israel's wars Yahweh fought with the tribal deity of Israel's enemies, while Israel's army fought with their armies. In victory Yahweh ordered the Egyptians drowned (Exodus 14:26ff), the Amalekites slaughtered (I Samuel 15:1ff), the Edomites reduced to servitude (II Samuel 8:14). Universalism was not a concept that came easily to Israel. When taken into captivity in Babylon (596–586 B.C.), the Jewish people believed themselves literally to be taken away from their God who was wedded to the actual soil of their nation, causing them to wonder how they would sing the Lord's song in a strange land (Psalm 137).

Slowly in that captivity, as happens in all movements of historic transition, the tribal limitations on God were eased or broken. Led by the unknown prophet we call Second Isaiah, a tentative universalism began to dawn. In the writings of this prophet, there was a new, broader vision that was rare in the Hebrew scriptures. The return to Canaan under Ezra and Nehemiah in the fifth century B.C. was, however, the occasion for the momentary loss of even this small vision. Universal thinking always seems less satisfying than the tribal security system. Postexilic Judaism was marked by a new rampant ethnic purity which enforced the traditional Jewish claim to be the exclusive chosen people of God (Ezra 9).

By the time Christianity broke into world history out of the womb of this same Judaism, the popular religions of the Mediterranean world were in a state of advanced decay. There was an emptiness at the heart of life filled only by a variety of mystery religions and cults on the popular level and by elevated philosophical systems on the level of the elite. Christianity struggled against the limitations of its Jewish tribal origin. Some felt that Christianity should remain firmly within the traditions of Judaism. The battle was intense and is referred to in Galatians 1 and in the Book of Acts. Acts 15 records a temporary solution between these warring ideas, but the historic fact remains that Christianity became more and more a gentile body and Judaism became less and less capable of absorbing Christianity. The final break was a bitter one, and its intensity is heard especially in the anti-Jewish polemics that echo with regularity throughout the pages of the Fourth Gospel.[4]

By A.D. 313, when the Emperor Constantine issued the Edict of Milan, an overwhelmingly gentile Christianity had become a legal religion in the Roman Empire. By A.D. 384 it had become the only legal religion by decree of the Emperor Theodosius and as such was used as a powerful ally in the task of unifying the empire. Christianity had become, in fact, the new tribal religion of the Western world, destined to overpower every religious competitor and to extinguish them all except for the tiny continuing Jewish minority that clung tenaciously to its own tribal deity, even without a homeland, from A.D. 70 until 1948 when, in the form of Zionism, it reasserted its tribal demand for a space that it could call its own.

Because most people in Western civilization throughout history were blissfully unaware of the other peoples of the world, they assumed that their religious convictions were universal or catholic. There was great security in such relative ignorance. It was, however, destined not to endure forever.

A late-developing religious system formed by the prophet Mohammed challenged Christianity's hegemony for a while even in the Western world, but Islam was finally checked and turned back in the Battle of Tours in A.D. 732. Christians continued to fight against the "infidel Moslems" in romantic but inconclusive battles known as the Crusades. This, however, did not prevent Islam from becoming established as the tribal religion of the Arab and Middle Eastern world, spreading as far east as Pakistan and Indonesia and as far south and west as Africa, and even making minor inroads among certain oppressed racial minorities in the United States in our own day.

Basically, Christianity's sphere of influence and Islam's sphere of influence remained separate after the Crusades. The two religious systems settled down in a stance which ignored each other until the vastly smaller interdependent world of the twentieth century produced economic pressures that caused both knowledge of each other and dynamic tension to erupt anew in the energy crisis. Once again nationalism merged with religion to produce such a figure as the Ayatollah Khomeini in Iran, and the Western world became aware again of the power of Islam as a tribal religion, especially when the Islamic tribes controlled the vital oil reserves on which the Western world had become so dependent.

Tribal Christianity dealt with its unabsorbable Jewish minority in a way that is scandalous to the faith the Christians profess,[5] but it is shamefully true to the way tribal religion has always acted historically. Even people known as saints and heroes in the Christian tradition, from John Chrysostom[6] to Martin Luther,[7] paved the way for the vehement and murderous anti-Semitism of Adolf Hitler in the twentieth century. Tribal religion can live in relative peace alongside another religious system with which it interacts little if at all, but it tolerates poorly a minority presence within its tribal sphere, for that presence erodes its claim to sovereignty, infallibility, or the certainty of its truth.

It was not until Marco Polo (1254–1324) that a positive consciousness of the Orient first began to dawn on the Western Christian world. Earlier Western responses to the East had been filled only with fear and loathing by the sweep of the Genghis Khan (1162–1227) and his Mongol army into Russia, Eastern Europe, and Turkey. There was, however, even after Marco Polo, very little attempt to understand or to appreciate the religious thought of the East. It was dismissed as pagan and was therefore viewed as a fertile missionary field. After the Orient was opened to trade, the Western nations moved quickly to share in the wealth of those intriguing new markets. As was always the case, the tribal religion of the West moved with them.[8]

Generally, the peoples of the East were able to avoid the religious system of the economically dominant West. Wherever political pressure did, however, force the Orient to adopt Western religions, the Oriental power to absorb enemies and ideas and to syncretize them seemed to operate. It is not an accident that Chinese Roman Catholicism is even today fiercely independent of the Vatican. With the twentieth-century resurgence of China as a world power, only a non-Westernized, nonimperialistic form of indigenous tribal Christianity could possibly survive in that land. Subservience to a Western ecclesiastical structure could prove a serious liability to life itself. The Orient never really became a successful missionary area for Christians, and the tribal religions of the East have remained indigenous to the people in that region of the world.

This very brief analysis points out amply, I submit, the tribal nature of all religious systems including our own. It calls us to consider the fine surgical task that will be required to separate the essence of faith from the form of faith, a form which has been compromised by the political, social, economic, and psychological needs of our tribal identities throughout our history. The inevitable conclusion is that every human belief system, every value system, every creed, every theology has significant tribal content.

With the dawning of this realization, urgent questions arise demanding answers. What then is that core to which all the accretions have been added? What is our essential Christian truth, and what are our acculturations? We cannot fail to acknowledge that Christianity has been used time and again in Western history as a tool and weapon of conquest. We note with some embarrassment today, for example, that there are places in Africa where Victorian morality has been imposed in the name of the Western tribal god upon the indigenous values of the local tribal people. We have seen native family life destroyed by the "Christian" standard of monogamy superimposed on a society where the women outnumbered the men significantly. The otherwise unprotected women who were forced out of the polygamous family patterns had to resort to prostitution in order to survive. That is a strange conclusion to which our "moral standards" have forced us.

Today a new religious consciousness is emerging. In part it results from a secularization that has eroded the power of all religious systems. The knowledge explosion has forced us to walk beyond the security of yesterday's certainty, but the even greater driving force has been the technological revolution that has shown us how small and interdependent the world really is. The great religious traditions of this tiny planet can no longer ignore one another. They have proved incapable of converting one another or even in making significant inroads into one another. One could find evidence to support the argument that there is more Eastern penetration of Western life today than vice versa. Many of the popular forms of meditation in the Western world today are Eastern in origin. Eastern gurus have vast followings, and conversions to some form of Eastern spirituality are not uncommon in the West. This trend may well prove, in time, to be nothing more than a spiritual rebellion against an empty Western materialism, but it does point to the fact that options for the West can emerge out of the East today in a way that would have been impossible a century ago. However, even when all such examples are cited, the mutual penetration among Eastern, Mideastern, and Western religious systems is minuscule.

It is not just conceivable, but increasingly evident that in our earliest and now-forgotten religious origins there was far more syncretism among various religious ideas than we now admit. Even in the formation of the tribal God of Israel there is today the recognition that no religion grows up in a cultural vacuum. In the early diverse names for God in the Old Testament—El Shaddai (Genesis 15), Yahweh (Exodus 3), and Elohim (Genesis 1 and 6)—there was the gentle blending of differing traditions. In the merging of the Abraham stories (Genesis 12–15), the Isaac stories (Genesis 25–27), and the Jacob stories (Genesis 28–50), there was a merger of the originally separate worship traditions at Hebron (Genesis 23), Beersheba (Genesis 26), and Bethel (Genesis 35) into a consistent narrative. Most Old Testament scholars view the biblical attempt to portray Abraham, Isaac, and Jacob as three generations of the same family as an ingenious later effort to merge the separate traditions of these three shrines. In later history Israel certainly did not endure enslavement in Egypt without having Egyptian gods shape its understanding of Yahweh, nor did they endure their captivity in Babylon and their later alliance with Persia to end that captivity without being influenced by both Babylonian and Persian thinking. The dualism of Zoroastrianism can be found in Judaism, for example, only after the Babylonian exile was over.

Christianity also cannot claim a pure history of simply developed revelation. The mystery religions of the Mediterranean world clearly shaped early Christian theology and worship. There has been a gentle blending of legend, liturgy, and creed wherever Christianity has spread. As we noted earlier, Isis of Egypt and the Virgin Mary have been the bearers of similar legends.

When the Hebrew *YHWH* entered the Greek language as *theos* and became the New Testament word for God, it was inevitable that the Greek concepts behind the word *theos* would also enter Christianity. Beyond that, Lesslie Newbigin has reminded us that the word *theos* has, in the history of Christian missionary expansion, been translated by thousands of local tribal words that meant God to those people long before Christianity arrived.[9] Surely the Christian concept "God," when translated by the pre-Christian tribal word for the deity, did not preempt all the local meaning that the name of their deity held for them. Wherever different peoples have met, whether as friends or as foes, whether conquerors or conquered, mutual influencing has taken place. As life became more and more interdependent, great systems of thought began to unify regions of the world. Included in these systems were religious concepts that gathered people into large, loosely related families without obliterating national or tribal differences (or denominations) but nonetheless creating a sense of common identity.

This does not mean that there were no titanic struggles or civil wars within those families. Certainly, in recent history, both World Wars I and II, at least in their European focus, can now be viewed as regional civil wars within the Western family of nations. The older struggles between France and England, England and Spain, France and Prussia, can be similarly viewed. Today the economies of those countries are so interrelated through the European Common Market that war between those nations has become almost unthinkable. The skirmishes since World War II have tended to pit different cultures and civilizations against each other: America against China in Korea; France first, and then America against Vietnam; Russia against Afghanistan.

More and more we are having to deal with ideas and relativities that come to us from other people. The ancient human divisions of language, nationality, and ethnic origin are fading in the realization that our humanity is shared and that this humanity transcends all other differences. Religious imperialism is giving way, first to mutual forbearance, then to interaction, and finally to mutual enrichment. Ultimate truth and one's primary commitments are being separated from the cultural elaborations that created our belief systems. Belief systems are today being analyzed, evaluated, studied in depth. The great issues in human life that those systems were created to address are being understood. In the process every religious system, including Christianity, is going through a vigorous reevaluation in which the wheat and the chaff are being separated, revealing that much we once considered wheat was really chaff all the time.

It is a deeply threatening time to those who are the guardians of traditional religious truth. But it is also a time that is inevitable. The only way to stop this process is to divide the world again into isolated regions, cease all interregional cooperation, and recover the innocence of our lost provincial ignorance. Those of us who take our religious convictions seriously are discovering that, in J. B. Phillips's words, our God is too small.[10] When we allow this God to grow toward a closer approximation of what surely this God must be, then we will discover that our creeds are also too small and finally incapable either of defining God adequately or binding God.

Arnold J. Toynbee, the esteemed historian, in the Hewitt Lectures, argued that the religious system that survives into the future will be the one that proves capable of expanding and evolving in such a way as to embrace the essential truths in the other religious systems.[11] He dismissed the possibility of an eclectic future pantheon on the pattern of the B'hai tradition as unnatural. Evolution, he argued, always works by growing out of the old into the new, not by picking up and choosing from available options to create a new construct.

Toynbee hoped that Christianity would prove to be this elastic, and thus might, in some different but continuous expression, be the embracing religious system of the future. Toward the end of his life, however, that hope began to diminish, for he saw Christianity hardening into a brittle, defensive posture, making final and ultimate claims for its present understanding of the truth. Time alone will tell whether Toynbee's early hope or later fear proves to be accurate.

To be catapulted into a world beyond tribal identity is also to be catapulted beyond every religious definition into a world of dreadful religious insecurity that cries out in the darkening void in the hope that there will be a responding divine voice. In that place the interdisciplinary religious conflicts of the past, the differences among Christian groups that still seem so important to so many, the ecumenical movement that seeks to address these differences, will all seem like irrelevant carryovers from a premodern consciousness. They will all finally be ignored as unworthy of much human energy, for larger issues will confront us. Christianity's future life may well depend on the Christian ability to respond to those larger issues, for that response will force a degree of change which will give us the possibility of achieving the evolutionary expansion that is the key to survival.

In such a world it is inevitable that Christianity's proclamations will seem more and more tentative and honesty will require searching questions to be raised inside our community of faith.

Some of these questions will be:

What is truth? Who is God? Do the absence of religious certainty and the loss of tribal identity mean the death of God? Are there ways to walk into this brave new world, this radical new consciousness, with a human integrity that is real and a faith commitment that is honest? Will those of us who want to live in this world with all of its fearful wonder be able to do so and be Christians still? If so, what kind of Christianity will it be? What does the Christ claim mean in this arena? Will there be enough continuity with our faith of tomorrow and the faith of our fathers and mothers to claim a continued identity? When we step beyond tribal Christianity, what remains? We must attempt to speak to these questions, for on our answers, I believe, the future of Christianity and the future of all the religions of the world now balances.

1. Lesslie Newbigin, *The Open Secret*, Grand Rapids, Mich., Eerdman's, 1980.

2. Ibid., p. 197ff.

3. John Hick, *God and the Universe of Faith*, London, Macmillan, 1973.

4. This insight is especially well developed in Raymond Brown's monumental study of John in the Anchor Bible Series. It is also highlighted in John Koenig's book *Jews and Christians in Dialogue*, Philadelphia, Westminster, 1979.

5. John S. Spong and Jack D. Spiro, *Dialogue: In Search of Jewish-Christian Understanding*, New York, Seabury, 1975. This is chronicled beautifully in a preface to this book by the distinguished head of the Religion Department of the University of Richmond, Professor Frank Eakin.

6. Roland deCorneille, *Christians and Jews*, Harper & Row, 1966, pp. 20–21.

7. Ibid., pp. 36–37.

8. I suppose Christian missionaries have never been more romantic about any mission field than they were about China. So deeply did Christian missionaries shape the image of China in America that this became a powerful force binding America emotionally to the Chinese people in World War II and was referred to by Winston Churchill in his volume *The Hinge of Fate*. It still finds political expression in what is known as the Nationalist China Lobby—a group of conservative senators who champion the Nationalist regime on Taiwan.

9. *Open Secret*, p. 197ff.

10. J. B. Phillips, *Your God Is Too Small*, New York, Macmillan, 1954.

11. Arnold J. Toynbee, *Christianity Among the Religions of the World*, Scribner's Sons, New York, 1957.

Chapter 14

THE EMERGING SHAPE
OF THE CHURCH

I N the catechism of the Episcopal Book of Common Prayer, the
church is described with four adjectives: one, holy, catholic,
and apostolic.[1] They are interesting words that once had self-evident
meanings but today are, like everything else, caught up in a sea of
uncertainty. To seek continuity between the church of the past and the
church of the future, these words might well prove an exciting possible
guide.

"One" is defined as one body under one head.[2] That oneness clearly
does not exist today unless the church is interpreted broadly and
spiritually or unless one branch of the church claims to be the exclusive
church and dismisses all others as false disciples. That definition of
oneness also does not take cognizance of the wider human oneness to
which we are being called today, unless Christ is defined as a spiritual
presence which unites those who are not aware of that name.

"Holy" is defined in reference to the Holy Spirit who dwells in the
church, consecrates its members, and guides them to do God's work.[3]
History, however, reveals activity sponsored by the church that was
anything but holy—the Crusades, the Inquisition, the religious wars.
History also portrays the lives of many church members as not conse-
crated, and somehow, in retrospect, much of what we thought was
God's work turned out to be something much less indeed.

"Catholic" is defined as the proclamation of the whole faith to all
people until the end of time.[4] But our discussions thus far have pointed

to the conclusion that the whole faith has not only not been proclaimed, it has not been known. The idea that something called "the
catholic faith" was ever whole or fully developed is historically impossible. We have watched doctrine, interpretation, and theology come
and go. We have seen radically new insights force old doctrines to be
rethought. We have seen knowledge grow through the years in such
a way as to dismiss the possibility that the whole faith was ever present
or complete or known. Basically, Christianity is not universal. It is the
tribal religion of Western civilization and of those areas that have been
shaped and formed by Western power. What does the claim that Christians possess the whole faith mean in terms of the biblical promise that
the Holy Spirit will lead us into all truth? Progressive revelation and
evolving truth cannot exist side by side with a concept of "the whole
faith." One must wonder if the whole faith existed in those years when
the only Christian creed was the ecstatic proclamation, "Jesus is Lord."
If so, then later Christian claims for other creedal formulations have
been excessive.

"Apostolic" is defined as continuing in the teaching and fellowship
of the apostles and living out the apostolic role of "being sent to all
people to restore them to God and to each other in Christ through
prayer, worship, the proclamation of the Gospel, and the promotion
of justice, peace, and love."[5] But an analysis of the New Testament
reveals that even the identity of the twelve apostles was never agreed
on in the early church, and most of those who are named remain
faceless persons about whom absolutely nothing else is known. How
does one continue in apostolic teaching if apostolic identity cannot
even be established? When apostolic identity and teaching are known
as, for example, in the case of Peter and Paul, clearly there is no
unanimity between them. A mighty struggle, which determined how
Christianity would emerge from the womb of Judaism and escape the
limiting national concerns of its parent, marked the early years of the
Christian church. Apostles were on both sides of that struggle.

The oneness of the church, together with its holiness, its catholicity,
and its historic link to the apostles, may well be an expression of the
ideal, but it is hardly a description of what was real. It may reflect
God's purpose, but it does not describe our history. Far more than most
of us who love the church have consciously realized, we have been
shaped and formed time and again by the moving forces of history.
When that history presents us with a new consciousness that tran-

scends our tribal understandings of the past, we may be sure that the change will be massive, threatening, and traumatic.

The church may be the channel of divine grace, the body of Christ through which the eternal Gospel is experienced anew, but it is also and always a political, sociological, and historic institution that responds time after time to the changing patterns of human thought. If the church continues to live, it will continue to change; for it cannot escape the historic process.

My study of history reveals that the strongest force shaping the structure of the church has not been its Gospel so much as it has been the attitude of the world in which the church seeks to live out the Gospel.[6] Must we then abandon these church-defining words—one, holy, catholic, and apostolic—or can they be so drastically reinterpreted as to allow them to be descriptive of what must surely be the church of the future?

I am encouraged in my apologetic task in the twentieth century and in my call to the church to step boldly beyond the barriers of certainty, sexual stereotypes, and tribal identity by several notes in the New Testament that seem to imply a dynamic, progressive, historic revelation that will always mark Christianity.

There is clearly, in the Johannine corpus especially, a biblical sense of incompleteness about even the Gospels' understanding of the cosmic dimensions of God's truth. John portrays the Christ as saying, "If you continue in my word, you will know the truth, and the truth will set you free" (John 8:32). A future hope denies a present possession. Later the Johannine Christ says, "I have many things to say to you, but you cannot bear them now; but when the Spirit of Truth is come, he will guide you into all truth. . . . He will show you things to come" (John 16:12–13).

The early Christian apostles struggled against their provincial nationalism and won, enabling their Gospel to become a multinational and the apparently universal faith in the Western world. They could not have embraced a larger universalism, for they had no knowledge or experience of a world wider than the Western world. If they knew anything of racial distinctions, it was very little. When knowledge of racial distinctions did become universal, the explanation of racial origins was primitive and prejudiced, and it continued so into our century. Even class differences in Western feudal society hundreds of years later were thought to be divinely ordered, and the church clearly taught that revolution against class or racial status was evil. People were to do their best in "that state of life into which it shall please God to call me."[7]

But the new consciousness is forcing a new vision. Buckminster Fuller dismisses racial and class differences almost with the flick of his hand. For Fuller, and increasingly for our world, these ancient barriers are revealed to be neither substantive nor eternal. Race, Fuller asserts, is nothing but the human evolutionary adaptive capacity to the interaction of vitamin D and the sun. Vitamin D, we now know, functions in the conversion of calcium into bone structure. Human beings synthesize vitamin D through the action of the sun's ultraviolet rays on the skin. This biochemical function is a zoological counterpart of botanical photosynthesis of the sun's radiation into hydrocarbon molecules. Vitamin D, however, is a vitamin that needs to be regulated. It cannot be stored, and an excessive amount is detrimental. So those members of the human family living in tropical areas adapted to the intensity of the sun by increasing the filtering system of the body by producing larger amounts of melanin and carotin, the agents of skin pigmentation. As they migrated northward, those pigments gradually lessened. This alone, Fuller maintains, accounts for skin color, which is the primary basis of racial distinctiveness.[8]

Class differences, Fuller states, are the results of nothing more than the political and economic systems that guaranteed to the poor an inadequate diet that had the effect of dulling the brains of the powerless masses of peasant people.[9] Based on his scientific study, Fuller concludes, "There is neither race nor class differentiation of humans. All humans are of the same family."[10] All of the power structures, the myths, the suppositions, and the fears that assume that racial or class differences are of creation and therefore eternal will inevitably be swept aside.

Fuller further develops the thesis that human life originated in what are today the islands of the southern Pacific Ocean—Java, Indonesia, Australia—but which, he maintains, before the ice ages were connected to what is now called the Malayan Peninsula. From that origin human beings migrated in ships into the various river arteries of Asia, into the Middle East and Africa, across the Bering Straits to the Americas at the same time that they migrated into Europe. He demonstrates to his satisfaction that both the Portuguese and the Vikings were simply latter-day Phoenicians, the most efficient of the ancient seafarers.[11]

As the human family scattered to various regions and inbred over many generations, tribal differences and local languages were firmly established. This, Fuller argues, is the origin of today's nation states. They too are not eternal, and with the development of a growing world-consciousness and with human survival dependent upon an ever-deepening level of human cooperation, national boundaries and the myths, assumptions, and fears of a limited tribal mentality will also be swept aside. There are 150 different national groups in the world, Fuller asserts.[12] When these various groups realize that this planet is a tiny 8,000-mile-diameter spaceship hurtling through space at 60,000 miles per hour, spinning axially as it orbits,[13] the 150 national groups will realize that they cannot give 150 contradictory commands. Human unity and cooperation are essential for survival.

Racial differences, class differences, and national differences are doomed, as well as the religious interpretations that justified those human differences. That is the new truth of our day into which we have been led, and in the light of this new truth we must radically redefine almost all of our exclusive religious claims.

If the Christian church is to be marked with the adjective "one," it must discover that oneness in the entire human family gathered in worship of the one Creator God. Differences of race, class, nationality, and creed can no longer be viewed as substantive. Every religious symbol of both East and West must be broken open so that we can see it, not as wrong but as limited by our experience, our vision, our consciousness. In the moment of that recognition, a way must be found to move beyond our symbols. When life itself is forced into a new openness, the closed systems of a previous vision cannot remain intact. Inevitably there will be a cross-fertilization of our several versions of truth as the human dialogue is intensified at the level of the world.

If the Christian church is to claim the word "holy" as one of its descriptive adjectives, it will do so because it recognizes that the Holy Spirit dwells within all of the peoples of the world and that the Spirit's consecrating wholeness is manifested in all of the religious traditions of the world. When we enter deeply into knowledge of one another, we can see God's presence and God's work in the values of very different folk, in the love expressed through customs we once could not appreciate, in the sense of community that is created around thousands of different organizing principles. The holiness of God does not stop at the edge of Christianity or at the edge of Buddhism. All of us must walk beyond our systems into an ever-deepening sense of God's holiness that we share.

If the Christian church is to claim the word "catholic" as another of its descriptive adjectives, it must be a catholicism beyond the narrow definitions of today. It will have little to do with creeds, Bible, sacraments, or apostolic ministry. It will transcend popes, ecumenical councils, and worship traditions. Today the word "catholic" must really embrace all people, all races, all nationalities, all classes, all creeds, all worship patterns. None can be pronounced wrong. All must be seen as inadequate. A fullness must be sought that none of us has yet possessed. Catholic means universal in all time. It is not nearly so neat or so comfortable as once we thought.

The hardest note or definition of the church to rethink is the adjective "apostolic." How can we continue in the teaching and fellowship of the apostles and still embrace the universal world that is our constant new reality? Jesus called his disciples, I believe, into a universalism that they could not possibly have fully comprehended. Yet the power of this Christ was so real that barrier after barrier has fallen before him throughout history. In the glow of their faith the early Christians discovered that in Christ there is neither Jew nor Greek, bond nor free, male nor female (Galatians 3:28). When St. Luke has Peter say in the Book of Acts, "I now perceive that God is no respecter of persons but in every nation he that fears God and lives righteously is accepted" (Acts 10:34,35), a major revolution in consciousness was being achieved. It was so enormous a change that it seemed to them complete. We have since learned otherwise.

The revolution goes on. Dietrich Bonhoeffer urged us to see Christ beyond religion.[14] Our world is driving us to continue the apostolic experience of seeing barriers fall and human unity achieved. Christ's mission is to restore all people to God and to each other in him, says our catechism. That apostolic tradition will carry us beyond every line of human division, including the dividing lines of our creeds. For us to walk into human unity, carrying with us the inclusive values of our religious tradition and our cultural heritage but abandoning those exclusive qualities that served our security needs far more than they served God's truth, is to claim, I believe, an apostolic heritage, newly defined and newly appropriate to our day.

I am encouraged to move in this direction. My contact with and openness to the inner truth I have found in Judaism has led me to anticipate an even greater enrichment to my Christian life in the inevitably increasing interreligious dialogue that now beckons us all. My fears that I might lose my religious identity in this dialogue have proved unfounded. Judaism was for me a natural starting point, for we Christians share with our Jewish brothers and sisters so much that is similar, ancient, significant, and holy. Beyond Judaism, however, there is an even greater opportunity awaiting us.

When we Christians study our Christian heritage in the light of other faith systems, we will inevitably have to focus more on the questions that every religious system was developed to answer and the human anxieties that the religions of the world were destined to alleviate. Far less important will become the answers that each tradition in time developed.

For example, one universal human question rises from the realization that human life is filled with inequities and injustice. Our historic experience is that life is lived with scarcity and fairness is lacking in the distribution of inadequate resources to support life. All life was not created equal. There are vast discrepancies in genetic endowment, both physical and mental. There are vast discrepancies in the human environment that greatly exacerbate the genetic differences. A child possessing a genius-level intelligence who is abandoned on the streets of Bogota, Colombia, at age three or four to live by thievery, deception, and conniving is not likely to be able to develop his or her gifts. For every Leontyne Price or Gustavo Romero whose talent is discovered and developed, how many other potentially gifted persons live and remain unknown, their talent undiscovered?

There are inequities in the time and place of one's existence. Children born in Vietnam after World War II would never know peace and might well never live to adulthood. Children born in the drought-stricken sub-Sahara Desert may be so malnourished as to suffer permanent brain damage before they achieve twelve months of life. Black children born in America are the recipients of a prejudice forged in slavery and fed by the subliminal fears of the dominant white majority. Children in every land are born into the heritage of a particular national history with all of its shaping influences. Equality is an ideal to be hoped for, not a reality to be experienced. It is the stuff of dreams, not the fact of life. Its absence creates enormous questions, all of which begin with the word "why."

If we assert that God is the creator, then we must face the reality that

God is the creator of inequality. If God is not responsible for the inequities of this world, then God seems impotent, for the inequities abide more surely than God does. In the words of Archibald MacLeish in his popular play *J.B.*, "If God is God, he is not good. If God is good, he is not God."[15] These facts are observable by men and women the world over, and they cry out to be interpreted. The religious systems of the world all address themselves in some way to this problem of evil and inequity.

Christians, from the time of Luke's parable of Lazarus and Dives (Luke 20:16ff) have sought to explain life's inequities in stories about the afterlife. Heaven became a place of reward, and hell became a place of punishment. Hence the inequities of human experience could be redressed in life after death if they were not ameliorated before death. Judaism, which was never as enamored with life after death as was Christianity, tended to address this concern in two ways. The wicked only appear to prosper, the Psalms assert (Psalms 1, 37, 73). The mills of God grind slowly, but they grind exceedingly fine. Later in Jewish history, in the Book of Job (Chapter 42), the final conclusion is that the answer to this perplexing human issue must be left in the hands of the inscrutable God, for this God made the universe and this God alone understands the grand design.

In those religious systems of the East that believe in reincarnation, the problem of evil is addressed in terms of that idea. Why is there evil if God is good? Reward or punishment from a previous life is being visited in the inequities of this life, they argue, so one must bear pain nobly so that the next time one is born a similar fate can be escaped. Reincarnation, at its heart, is nothing less than an attempt to address the problem of evil.

In the secularized world one could argue that the communist system, at least in theory, and the political liberals who forge dreams of New Deals and Great Societies are both similarly seeking to speak to the problem of evil. God, to this group, may not be a relevant factor. Injustice, however, does exist, and it needs to be addressed concretely in order to have a just world. The social Gospel is a religious version of the same reality. Interestingly enough, the social Gospel did not emerge as a force in the church until the certainty of life after death began to fade.

Another secularized attempt to address the problem of evil comes from the political right. It argues that inequity is the norm that needs to be accepted. The strong were meant to rule the weak, the advantaged to rule the disadvantaged. So might makes right, and theories of the master race are justified.

In this quick survey of the ways human systems, both religious and nonreligious, address the problem of evil, a new way is seen to enter into the religious and secular consciousness of other people and other systems of thought. The task is not to argue about solutions but to understand the questions for which the various systems have organized to provide answers. Systems then cease to be either right or wrong, and they become insightful, illumining avenues of deeper and deeper understanding of human truth. Another step is taken away from particularity and toward universalism.

We look at the religious use of food, the development of dietary laws, religious meals, food symbols like bread and wine, and ask how they emerged, what they mean, why they endure. These are very different questions from "Am I right?" "Is my adversary wrong?"

We look at rites of passage—bar mitzvahs, confirmation, various puberty rituals—and inquire as to the understanding of life which they reveal. In that understanding there is an amazing agreement.

We look at the meaning of prayer, meditation, and worship in all religious systems and try to understand how and why they developed, as well as their truth and power. We find unique similarities in the holy life, the saint, the religious ideal in various traditions. Stripped from acculturation, a different standard of judging emerges.

We look at the human experiences of guilt and hope, mercy and forgiveness, yearning and fear that are so universal to our journey and try to comprehend how they are dealt with in each system and why. Empathy begins to emerge.

We look at individuality and community, personal needs and social needs, and the relationship between them. We examine various ethical systems. We inquire why it is that in the East the goal of the individual is to escape the self-centeredness of individuality, and in the West the goal seems to be the fulfillment of that individual self. We inquire as to what social needs were met in the development of those apparently diverse approaches to life. The deeper we go in analysis, the more they appear to be two sides of the same coin.

We look at the focal point of each religious tradition—the moment when eternity seems to invade time, when God becomes incarnate in history, the rending sense of the holy around which the whole religious system organizes and rotates—and we ask how it was that God was met in those people at those places, in those events, through that experience.

If this is one's approach, no part of his or her religious system becomes irrelevant or superstitious or nonsensical or unworthy of serious study. No secular revolt can be so thorough as to cause one to set aside a portion of one's religious tradition as irrational or impossible. Literalism and the claim of unchanging certainty will inevitably force one to choose between an increasingly impossible belief system and the abandonment of all belief systems. This questioning, searching journey beyond the system into the meaning at its heart, however, does not create such choices.

Truth is never found in words, but always beyond words. Truth is not found in doctrine or dogma, but always in the experience to which the doctrine or dogma points and which it seeks to interpret. There is a fluid, unending excitement to a religious journey that goes into the heart of the system in which one is privileged to be born. When that journey can be engaged simultaneously with another who explores the terrain of a different, but nonetheless holy, religious system in which that other was privileged to be born, then finally both pilgrims will meet and know the Holy of Holies. In that moment they will discover a new and deeper human and divine community that neither of them could possibly have known alone. So I anticipate with wonder the journey that I believe is inevitable beyond the boundaries of religious systems, beyond the boundaries of tribal identity.

Only one final stage remains, and it brings us startlingly near to a new, but very old, beginning. I return to Lesslie Newbigin for a moment to pick up a quotation early in the previous chapter: "Every person must be encouraged to go toward where the light shines for him or her. If one turns his or her back on the source where light is found, then the result can only be deeper darkness."

The legitimacy of the particularity of one's own revelation seems to me to lie in these words without any judgment being passed on the relativity or absoluteness of that revelation. One cannot enter the journey that I believe lies before us unless one enters that journey at his or her own natural point of entry. One will never appreciate the profundity of another's revelation if the profundity of one's own revelation is not fully engaged. Particularity is finally the only pathway beyond itself into the wonder of the God who is beyond every particular system.

Because I am a Christian, I must go to where the light shines for me. That is quite simply to the person of Jesus whom I call Christ, who is for me in some way I cannot fully apprehend or comprehend God of God, Light of Light, Very God of Very God, begotten not made, of one substance with the Father, conceived by the Holy Spirit, born of the Virign Mary, crucified under Pontius Pilate, resurrected from the dead, confirmed to be victorious over death by the experience of the church that was filled with the life-giving and Holy Spirit of God.

Jesus is for me the searing light that splits the darkness (John 8:12). He invites me to confront God as a heavenly Father who is prodigal in love, who cares for all creation. It was the whole world, says St. John, that God so loved (John 3:16). Christ is like salt in the earth, giving all things a new flavor (Matthew 5:13) or like leaven in the lump (Matthew 13:33). In him is found bread for the hungry soul (John 6:35), water for the thirsty one (John 4:10ff), rest for the weary (Matthew 11:28).

In the cross, which is the central event in Jesus' life, I find a new way to look at the problem of evil, for through the cross evil can be taken, transformed, and redeemed. Resurrection can flow out of crucifixion. In the Eucharist, which celebrates sacramentally this life, death, and resurrection, I find a new meaning for food. Since I become what I eat, I symbolically take into my life the life of my Lord, his body, his blood. In the water of baptism I find the symbolic cleansing that speaks to the guilt of human life. In the rites of passage I find my identity as the child of God renewed at every transitional stage of life. In the activity of prayer I find my life touched, sustained, opened, redeemed by that holy presence that my prayer life seeks—a presence that lifts me out of myself into community and binds me to that presence in a holy, life-giving relationship so intensely personal that only personal words can for me be appropriately employed when I speak of it. The deeper I go into prayer, the more powerful I find the identity between those who travel the route of self-denial to reach the heights of religious ecstasy and those who travel the way of self-fulfillment to reach the same heights, for both finally escape human limitations and rest in the holiness of God.

My human search for fulfillment, healing, wholeness, individuality, acceptance, and forgiveness leads me to use symbols like the kingdom of God, the presence of which, I discover, is like possessing a pearl of great price or like the experience the lost sheep had upon being found. I embrace the pain of inequity and injustice and discover that I cannot help but be passionately committed to those concrete actions that will alleviate human suffering and deprivation, doing so not because my vision of a future life is so faded but because my vision of God is so intense.

The symbols of my tradition, the content of my revelation, are now invested with new meaning. Beyond the literalism that once repelled me, beyond the certainty that once seduced me, there is the reality of the mystery of the holy that calls me to this journey. To that call I will respond.

I will walk past the barrier of theological certainty into the freedom and anxiety of relative truth. I will walk past the sexual stereotypes of the past into a new consciousness of sexual understanding, beyond moralism but not beyond responsibility, beyond rigid rules that are no longer in harmony with the biological reality of God's creation but not beyond relationships that impart a loving, essential humanity one to another. I will walk past the barrier of a tribal mentality, a nationalistic religious tradition, into a new consciousness of humanity, a new awareness of truth, a new sense of God that is beyond every human theological system. Empowered by that vision, I will, with renewed confidence, pick up those symbols of my own heritage, now freed to be real for me in powerful ways. I will claim them anew, using them to lead me step by step as I journey toward the light of God, as I see that light without ever needing to belittle, indeed sometimes even being guided by the light that shines differently in someone else.

That is, for me, the only doorway into a religious future. Before us swirl the winds of change. When we enter that whirlwind, cross the frightening barriers of transition, and embrace the anxieties of uncertainty, we will discover a hope, an integrity, a truth that we can never deny.

The journey into truth for me is finally the journey into God. It is a journey that will never end so long as we are finite and the Holy God is infinite; but it is a journey that I and others like me can never again avoid.

Amen.

---

1. *Book of Common Prayer*, 1979, p. 854. The terms are taken from the Nicene Creed.
2. Ibid.

3. Ibid.

4. Ibid.

5. Ibid.

6. This point of view I documented in an article published in *The Christian Century*, January 3–10, 1979, entitled "The Emerging Church."

7. *Book of Common Prayer*, 1979, p. 289.

8. Buckminster Fuller, *The Critical Path*, New York, St. Martin's, 1981.

9. Ibid., p. 10–11.

10. Ibid., p. 11.

11. Ibid., p. 73.

12. Ibid., p. 217.

13. Ibid., p. 55.

14. Dietrich Bonhoeffer, *Letters and Papers from Prison*, ed. Eberhard Bethge, trans. Reginald Fuller, New York, Macmillan, 1962, p. 161.

15. Archibald MacLeish, *J.B.*, Boston, Houghton Mifflin, 1958.

Bibliography

Adler, Alfred. *Cooperation Between the Sexes: Writings on Women, Love, Marriage, Sexuality, and Its Disorders*. Garden City, N.Y.: Anchor Books, Doubleday.

Bainton, Roland H. *Erasmus of Christendom*. New York: Charles Scribner's Sons, 1969.

_____.*Here I Stand*. Nashville: Abingdon, Cokebury, 1950.

Bettleheim, Bruno. *Symbolic Wounds, Puberty Rites, and the Envious Male*. New York: Collier, 1962.

Bonhoeffer, Dietrich. *Letters and Papers from Prison*, edited by Eberhard Bethge, translated by Reginald Fuller. New York: Macmillan, 1962.

Boswell, John. *Christianity, Social Tradition, and Homosexuality*. Chicago: University of Chicago Press, 1980.

Bowers, Margaretta. *Conflicts of the Clergy*. New York, Thomas Nelson, 1963.

Brooten, B. *Women Priests*. New York: L. and A. Swidler, 1977.

Brown, Raymond. *The Gospel According to John* (2 vols.). New York: Doubleday, 1966-1970.

_____.*The Virginal Conception and Bodily Resurrection of Jesus*, Ramsey, N.J.: Paulist Press, 1973.

Burton, Robert. *The Mating Game*. New York: Crown, 1976.

Bylinsky, Gene. *Mood Control*. New York: Charles Scribner's Sons, 1978.

Capra, Fritjof. *The Tao of Physics*. Berkeley, Cal.: Shambhala, 1975.

Clark, Anne. *Beasts and Bawdy*. New York: Taplinger, 1976.

Churchill, Winston S. *History of World War II* (6 vols.). New York and London: Harper, 1948.

Davies, W. D. *Paul and Rabbinic Judaism*. London: SPCK, 1948.

de Chardin, Teilhard. *How I Believe*. New York: Harper & Row, 1969.

_____.*The Phenomenon of Man*. New York: Harper, 1959.

de Corneille, Roland. *Christians and Jews*. New York: Harper & Row, 1976.

Delaney, Janice, Emily Toth, and Mary Jane Lupton. *The Curse: A Cultural History of Menstruation*. New York: Dutton, 1976.

Ditts, James E. *When People Say No: Conflict and the Call to Ministry*. San Francisco: Harper & Row, 1979.

Douglas, Mary. *Purity and Danger: An Analysis of the Concepts of Purity and Taboo*. London: 1966.

Eisenhower, Dwight D. *Crusade in Europe*. Garden City, N.Y.: Doubleday, 1948.

Ford, Clellen S., ed. *Crosscultural Approaches*. New Haven, Conn.: HRAF Press, 1967.

Freud, Sigmund. *Three Contributions to the Theory of Sex*. New York: Dutton, 1962.

_____.*Totem and Taboo*. New York: Vintage Press, 1946.

Friday, Nancy. *My Mother, Myself*. New York: Delacorte, 1977.

Fuller, R. Buckminster. *The Critical Path*. New York: St. Martin's, 1981.

Fuller, Reginald. *The Formation of the Resurrection Narratives*. New York: Macmillan, 1981.

Gambrill, James H. *The Bridge of the Cross*. Cincinnati: Forward Movement, 1982.

Gibbon, Edward. *The Decline and Fall of the Roman Empire*, edited by Dean Milman et al. London: 1898.

Harris, Thomas. *I'm OK, You're OK*. New York: Harper & Row, 1969.

Hays, H.R. *The Dangerous Sex*. New York: Pocket Books, 1976.

Hick, John. *Death and Eternal Life*. San Francisco: Harper & Row, 1976.

_____.*God and the Universe of Faith*. London: Macmillan, and New York: St. Martin's, 1973.

Hirsch, S. Carl. *He and She*. Philadelphia and New York: Lippincott, 1975.

Horney, Karen. *Feminine Psychology*. New York: Norton, 1967.

James, William. *The Varieties of Religious Experience* (Gifford Lectures, 1901–02). New York: Mentor Books, 1958.

Kinsey, Alfred C. et al. *Sexual Behavior in the Human Female*. Philadelphia: Saunders, 1948.

_____.*Sexual Behavior in the Human Male*. Philadelphia: Saunders, 1948.

Koenig, John. *Jews and Christians in Dialogue*. Philadelphia: Westminster, 1979.

Kolbenschlag, Madonna. *Kiss Sleeping Beauty Good-bye*. Garden City, N.Y.: Doubleday, 1979.

Küng, Hans. *Does God Exist?* Garden City, N.Y.: Doubleday, 1980.

_____.*Infallible? An Inquiry*. Garden City, N.Y.: Dobuleday, 1971.

_____.*On Being a Christian*. Garden City, N.Y.: Doubleday, 1976.

_____.*Signposts for the Future*. Garden City, N.Y.: Doubleday, 1978.

Latourette, Kenneth Scott. *The History of the Christian Church* (7 vols.). New York and London: Harper, 1941.

Liddell-Hart, B. H. *History of World War II* (2 vols.). New York: Putnam, 1971.

Luther, Martin. *Three Treatises*. Philadelphia: Muhlenburg Press, 1943.

McAdoo, H. R., and Alan C. Clark. *The Anglican-Roman Catholic International Consultation Report*. Cincinnati: Forward Movement, 1982.

MacLeish, Archibald. *J.B.* Boston: Houghton Mifflin, 1958.

Marshall, S. L. A. *The Crimsoned Prairie*. New York: Charles Scribner's Sons, 1972.

Michener, James. *Hawaii*. New York: Random House, 1959.

Moore, G. F. *Judaism*. Cambridge: Harvard University Press, 1927.

Moorehead, Alan. *The Fatal Impact*. New York: Harper & Row, 1966.

Into the Whirlwind

_____.*March on Tunis.* New York: Harper & Row, 1967.

Newbigin, J. E. Lesslie. *The Open Secret.* Grand Rapids, Mich.: Eerdman's, 1980.

Packard, Vance. *The Status Seekers.* New York: McKay, 1959.

Pagels, Elaine. *The Gnostic Gospels.* New York: Random House, 1979.

Parrinder, Geoffrey. *Sex in the World's Religions.* New York: Oxford University Press, 1980.

Phillips, J. B. *Your God Is Too Small.* New York: Macmillan, 1954.

Robinson, John A. T. *The Human Face of God.* Philadelphia, Westminster, 1973.

Rommel, Erwin. *The Rommel Papers,* edited by B. H. Liddell-Hart and Manfred Rommel. New York: Harcourt, Brace, 1953.

Salisbury, Harrison. *The 900 Days: The Siege of Leningrad.* New York: Harper & Row, 1969.

Sandmel, Samuel. *The Genius of Paul.* New York: Farrar, Straus & Cudahy, 1958.

Schoenfeld, Hugh. *The Passover Plot.* New York: Bernard Geis, 1966, (Bantam Books, 1977).

_____.*Those Incredible Christians.* New York: Bernard Geis, 1968.

Scholem, Gershom G. *Major Trends in Jewish Mysticism.* New York: Schocken Books, 1961.

Smith, Hedrick. *The Russians.* New York: Quadrangle, 1976.

Spong, John S. *The Easter Moment.* New York: Seabury, 1980.

_____.*This Hebrew Lord.* New York: Seabury, 1974.

_____.*The Living Commandments.* New York: Seabury, 1977.

Spong, John S., and Jack D. Spiro. *Dialogue: In Search of Jewish-Christian Understanding.* New York: Seabury, 1975.

Stone, Irving. *The Passions of the Mind: A Biography of Sigmund Freud.* Garden City, N.Y.: Doubleday, 1971.

Toynbee, Arnold Joseph. *Christianity Among the Religions of the World.* New York: Charles Scribner's Sons, 1957.

Warner, Marina. *Alone of All Her Sex.* New York: Alfred A. Knopf, 1976.

Weidiger, Paula. *Menstruation and Menopause.* New York: Alfred A. Knopf, 1976.

Wemple, Suzannah Fonay. *Women in Frankish Society, 500–900.* Philadelphia: University of Pennsylvania Press, 1982.

Yungblut, John. *Rediscovering Prayer.* New York: Seabury, 1973.

_____.*Sex and the Human Psyche.* Pendle Hill Pamphlet #203.

INDEX

Index